EVANSTON
WYOMING

Also available by Dennis J Ottley

Remembering (Korea: 1950-1953)

IZZARD PUBLISHING COMPANY
PO Box 522251
Salt Lake City, Utah 84152
www.izzardink.com

LIBRARY OF CONGRESS CONTROL NUMBER: 2018960342

Designed by Alissa Rose Theodor
Cover Design by Andrea Ho
Cover Photograph by Shelly & Deann Horne of Creative Ink Images
Cover Images: Robert Castillo/Shutterstock.com ivangal/Shutterstock.com
monofaction/Shutterstock.com

First Edition January 28, 2019

Contact the author at djottleybooks@gmail.com

Hardback ISBN: 978-1-64228-013-5
Softback ISBN: 978-1-64228-019-7
eBook ISBN: 978-1-64228-020-3

1967 to 1995

EVANSTON

WYOMING

VOLUME THREE

CITY OF
OPPORTUNITY
EQUALITY · FRIENDSHIP
EVANSTON WYO.

BOOM-BUST-POLITICS

"IN THE EYES OF A MAYOR"

DENNIS J OTTLEY

IZZARD INK
PUBLISHING

PART THREE

"A NEW ADMINISTRATION"

"A people that values its privileges above its principles soon loses both."

—BY DWIGHT D. EISENHOWER

CHAPTER 17

1983....It was now January, 1983 and I was getting ready to prepare my final State of the City Address for my term as the former mayor. I was also going to open the first city council meeting of the year on January 6th to take care of the minutes, the outstanding bills and other reports left over from the previous administration's last meeting.

In opening the meeting I asked City Clerk Don Welling to lead us in the Pledge of Allegiance to Our Flag, and then to take roll call of the council to make sure we had a quorum of the previous administration. Those present were me, Councilmembers David Bills, Ronald Davis, Roy Fruits, and Arnie Morgan. Councilman Russell "Bub" Albrecht and outgoing Councilwoman Jerry Wall were absent, and had been excused.

Therefore, with the city clerk declaring a quorum I asked for motions to approve the minutes of the previous meeting, to pay the outstanding bills, and minutes and reports from the various boards and commissions. I then gave my annual address, the State of the City, as follows:

"Four years ago when I first took the reins as Mayor of the City of Evanston....after spending 12 years as a member of the City Council....I felt like I knew pretty much of what I was getting into. Maybe I didn't know, but I felt like I did.

However, the only thing we really were looking at was a lot of problems and hoping to find solutions to those problems. These past four years Evanston has probably witnessed their fastest growth ever.

At first our primary concerns were probably directed at water, sewer, housing and crime more so than anything else.

I don't believe anyone knew to what extent of impact this new Overthrust Belt discovery was going to cause or for how long.

The oil and gas industry themselves weren't saying much. They were helping us some, especially in our police and fire problems. But the only help we were really receiving from anyone, at that time, was the Wyoming State Farm Loan Board in Cheyenne.

Impact is very difficult to deal with. It stretches your ability to manage to the limits. Sometimes you are stretched past your limits. It forces you to deal with crisis and challenge. If you get behind you spend time, not in acting, but in re-acting.

However, with the hard work….with the constant planning and with the co-operation of many….Evanston has been able to maintain its stature and now has the makings of becoming one of the finest communities in the country.

I have found out that to deal with rapid growth you can't solve your problems by staying home. You must work closely with the county, the state, and industry as well as many state and federal agencies. You must go to Cheyenne….you must also go to Denver….and in some cases you may even have to go to Washington, D.C. and other places to get the job done.

My goals were to bring Evanston through this crisis of impact….to meet all needs….and to make this city the community that we all want and hope for…. And still remain prosperous and progressive. This has been accomplished, not only by me alone, but with the assistance of many.

Our accomplishments have included such things as:

WATER:
- *Increased three (3) times the capacity,*
- *Upgraded filtration plant and distribution lines,*
- *Installed many other lines plus watermeters,*
- *Purchased additional water rights,*
- *Plus additional planning is in the works.*

SEWER:
- *Upgraded old sewer plant enough to keep the city in good operative condition,*
- *Completed plans for a new $10 million plus sewer plant,*
- *Selected location right-of-ways, etc. are close to being obtained,*
- *Plus we have already received a $7.9 million grant from the E.P.A.*

POLICE:
- Received a tremendous amount of equipment through grants and other means,
- Held the major crime rate down the past one and a half years to almost 20%,
- Plus we have obtained a 100% grant for the new Public Safety Building.

EMPLOYMENT & BENEFITS:
- Through the 1% optional sales tax we have been able to upgrade our salaries and benefits to the point where well deserved, and maintain our officers.

FIRE:
- Obtained additional equipment through financial assistance of the oil and gas industry and the County of Uinta Commissioners,
- Obtained funds out of budget for a new fire hall,
- Plus, through participation with the County, we are now initiating a new emergency evacuation plan.

TRAFFIC (Streets, etc.):
- We have obtained a good relationship with the Wyoming Highway Department, and they have agreed to assist us with our streets and roads where possible,
- Plus with the new optional sales tax we have been able to keep up with road maintenance.

PARKS & RECREATION:
- Obtained properties through subdivisions for additional parks (neighborhood parks), upgrades and lights for our baseball facilities,
- Obtained the land and funding, plus broke ground for a recreation center with an indoor swimming pool and other activities for all ages.

HUMAN SERVICES:
- Obtained a professional day care center,
- Obtained land and funding for a human service center with the County,
- Plus we are assisting in the funding of many public agencies.

ELDERLY CITIZENS:
• *We have obtained the funding and broke ground for senior housing, and also for low-income folks.*

AIRPORT:
• *The City of Evanston and Uinta County have obtained the land and location for a new airport, which is presently under construction.*

PLANNING:
• *We have also continued to complete the City of Evanston Master Plan with the assistance of the Evanston Planning and Zoning Commission,*
• *Plus we have also started on a Comprehensive Land Use Plan.*

Plus in other recreation, historic and revitalization areas, we have started the revitalization of the downtown area in order to save it as the "Heart of the City," and started some improvements on the east end, plus we have supported the new Bear River State Park.

All of this has been accomplished through the efforts of those who are very dedicated to this community: Allen Kennedy, Wayne Shepherd, Don Welling, Linnea Overy, Dennis Poppinga, Jon Lunsford, Dennis Harvey, Steve Snyder and Dennis Lancaster, plus all those employees under them. I would especially like to thank my secretary, Sharon Constantine, for all her help and advice.

And I wish to thank all of them for their assistance and cooperation.

Plus I want to thank all the members of the Planning and Zoning Commission, the Airport management, the Recreation and Parks Board, the Beautification Committee and all those on the Joint Powers Boards.

I also wish to thank all those members of the Evanston City Council who have worked hard and spent a lot of their time assisting me in getting all the projects and programs underway, and supporting me in my efforts in trying to keep up with the growth and making our community a great place to live.

The Overthrust Industrial Association deserves a great amount of gratitude for helping us through the mitigation plan that now is almost complete, and for the technical assistance and financing they have provided the City of

Evanston. *Without them we would have been in a lot more trouble than we were already faced with.*

Plus I wish to mention the Uinta County Commissioners; John Fanos, Dan South and Clark Anderson, who have all been so supportive to us in trying to keep up with the growth.

And a big thanks to the state of Wyoming, especially Governor Herschler, Secretary of State Thyra Thompson, plus all members of the Wyoming State Farm Loan Board and the Wyoming State Highway Department. They have all been extremely helpful in helping Evanston resolve their problems.

Through the association of all these people mentioned we have proven that local and state governments along with industry can work very well together in maintaining a better world.

But most of all I want to thank my wife Sandy. For thirty-two-and-a-half years we have been married, sixteen of those years I have served the people of Evanston as a member of the City Council. All those years she has stuck behind me, plus she has put up with a lot of crap, especially during this past election year. For what Sandy has gone through and put up with, she has to be one hell of a gal. For twelve years as a council member and four years as your mayor she has stuck by me.

I realize that there is still some old business on the agenda that probably should have been completed before the end of the year of 1982, but under the circumstances we could not get to them. The only unfinished business that I am concerned with and would like to mention is the following:

(1) Ordinance 2-134, concerning the rezoning of the Hamblin Park; I know that this is probably going to die because of the 3/4 vote ruling, but even if it does get passed, it is still up to the Council where the new Public Works City Shop is located. I would like to point out that there is large support in the measure, but there is also a lot of opposition. So I say to you, give this ordinance a lot of thought before acting on it.

(2) I would hope that the new administration will honor the previous council's commitment to the hospital board concerning the reimbursement to them for their building permit fees in the amount of $31,000 plus, and

(3) I hope the new administration can continue to assist on finding a solution to be sure that VHF television can continue, because there are still a number of rural folks that depend on it.

The future looks good for Evanston, the pattern has been laid… the plans have been drawn… all the new administration needs is to keep the momentum moving and follow those plans. If you do this, Evanston will be a great community.

It has been a great four years. The people of Evanston should be proud. We have come a long way to a better community. I know I am proud, very proud, even after going through one of the most unethical and underhanded campaigns and elections in the history of Evanston. This past campaign that the City of Evanston went through should never, ever happen again, anytime in the future.

These last several months or so I have been accused or it has been insinuated, that I have committed every crime in the book short of murder such as: conflicts of interest, bribery and payoffs, pro-industry, stealing, mismanagement of government, passing on Industrial Revenue Bonds where I received payoffs if approved, favoritism through planning and zoning, "pork barrel" politics, plus other corruptions.

Not one time, except in the defense of myself, did I ever say a thing against another candidate, including my opponents, not even once! Oh, I could have, if I would have slowed down long enough to dig it up. I could have found plenty, and it would have been the truth. There hasn't been a one of you that has lived a perfect life.

I only hope that the City of Evanston will never be put in the position of having to witness such a mud-slinging, underhanded election again. The people of Evanston deserve better than that….much better.

Maybe I haven't run a perfect government the past four years, but I never told anyone that I was perfect. My campaign promises four years ago were only that I would do my best, and that I would uphold the Oath of Office. Regardless of all the innuendos, all the insinuations, all of the half-truths and in some cases downright lies that I have been accused of through this past campaign. But, since the election, I can still walk down the street in this town with my head high. I don't have to prove my honesty to anyone. I don't have to be told, even though I have been told many, many times over, that we had done a terrific job in running the City… I knew we did.

You don't run a city for the benefit of a few… you run a city for the benefit of all.

You don't run it for a handful of constituents. If you do that then you had better go to each one of your constituents and ask each and every one of them their opinion on each issue that comes up. But in all fairness, make certain that they are aware of all aspects of the issue.

I believe the people elect you with a lot of trust. They hope that you will have the integrity, the loyalty, the dedication, and the leadership ability and the guts to make the right decisions of what's best for everyone.

If you are not honest and up front with everything, you are not really representing your constituents fairly… you are not honoring your Oath of Office. In all actuality you are cheating those people who put their trust in you at the polls.

You only keep the respect of other council members and city staff by being honest with them. You don't run a good government with a lot of BS and using sneaky and underhanded methods.

If you have a problem you meet it head on, whether it is one of your colleagues, one of your employees or just a citizen off the street. You must treat the problem with honesty and with high regards, just as you would want to be treated yourself.

Be constructive, don't be malicious and spiteful. If you don't agree, be flexible, give input, but be constructive. Don't knock it unless you understand all aspects of the issue or unless you come up with a better solution.

Remember, you are looking out for the best interest of all your citizens, not just a few.

I am only trying to give you a word of advice…good constructive advice. I only hope it sinks in.

You must look towards the future, not the past… that's history… learn from its mistakes, but look ahead, look towards the future for the benefit of the young people. Give them a community that they can survive in, a City that will be prosperous and remain progressive for the future so that they won't have to gather up their families and leave for greener pastures.

In 1966 I decided to join the local political world and run for the City Council seat of Ward 1. I had been involved in civic programs of all types previous to this and had proven myself as a local leader. Some of these programs I created myself, some of them I merely carried on.

In January of 1967 I took my first Oath of Office… 4 times since then I have taken that same Oath….the last time as your Mayor.

I have always had a lot of respect for that Oath and have lived up to it to the best of my ability. I only hope that you who are about to swear by that same Oath will listen very close and get the meaning; also I hope that those members who have taken it before will also listen once again. This Oath has a purpose.

I only hope, sincerely hope, that this past election, and even what has happened since the election, isn't an indication of the type of management the City of Evanston has to look forward to. I hope that you, Mr. Martin, realize that however you run the business of this City not only reflects on you alone, but also reflects on all members of the Council and also your staff... and in some cases may even reflect on the citizens of the community.

I hope and pray that this next administration manages the affairs of the City with a much higher standard of ethics and morals than had been demonstrated, not only during the previous election, but even since the election.

Gentlemen, GOD help us if you don't!!!

In the minutes of January 6, 1983 it was stated that: *Mayor Ottley gave an excellent report on the activities and progress of his tenure of office (Mayor) the past 4 years. When Mayor Ottley concluded, he received a standing ovation.*

After I gave my speech I did receive a standing ovation by everyone (except Councilman David Bills and his wife Claudia), which really made me feel good, and then Councilman Roy Fruits honored me with a wall clock/plaque engraved with my name and the 12 years I had served as a member of the Evanston City Council and the 4 years as mayor. Inscribed on the clock was *"In Appreciation for Dedication and Service to the Citizens of Evanston, Wyoming."* It was a gift from the city council and the staff. I thanked them for the wonderful gift and told them that I really appreciated it.

Administrative Assistant Steve Snyder followed with a presentation to my wife, Sandy, with a silver medallion inscribed *"Super Lady,"* and believe, me she was. All of the city staff thought an awful lot of her. They probably thought more of her than they did of me, because she was a great First Lady and was very active with the staff and in the community. She was probably just as active or more so than most of the council members. I was glad to have her at my side.

She also got a standing ovation (except from Mr. Bills and his wife).

I always liked to take Sandy with me when I went to different meetings and conferences that concerned the City of Evanston, because she was a great ambassador for the city, and people really liked her. She was an excellent communicator.

After my comments and after the presentation I turned to City Clerk Welling and told him to proceed with the swearing-in ceremony. He called District Judge John Troughton to administer the Oath of Office to the newly elected officials: Mayor-elect Eugene Martin, and Councilmembers-elect Lance Voss, Richard Sather, and Ronald Davis.

After the ceremony was over I handed the gavel to Mayor Martin and told him good luck, then Sandy and I, with our four sons, left the chambers, thanking everyone as we left.

Mayor Martin then made his appointments, such as Don Welling, City Clerk; Linnea Overy, Treasurer; Steve Snyder, Administrative Assistant; Dennis Harvey, Chief of Police; Wayne Shepherd, City Engineer; Dennis Poppinga, Recreation Director; and Mark Harris, City Attorney. The only change was the city attorney appointment, but Councilman Arnie Morgan made a motion to confirm all of the appointments with the exception of Mark Harris as City Attorney, seconded by Sather, with all voting in favor.

UINTA COUNTY HERALD   Friday, January 7, 1983   Page 5

Ottley blasts Martin as gavel changes hands

by David Fierro
of the Herald staff

Sparks flew in the Evanston City Council chambers last night when former mayor Dennis Ottley aimed a few parting shots at Mayor Eugene Martin.

Ottley, after thanking a number of people he had worked with during his four-year term, reprimanded Martin and other Council members for what he termed "the most unethical campaign this city has ever seen."

"I've been accused of everything except murder. People talk of conflicts of interest. Let me tell you, we all have conflicts of interest," said an obviously emotional Ottley.

"I hope this past election, and the time since the election, does not reflect how the city will be managed. I hope that you, Mr. Martin, will run the city with a higher moral regard than shown during the campaign. Gentlemen, God help us if you don't," said Ottley.

"I hope the city of Evanston will never have to witness a mud-slinging campaign like this again. Regardless of the half-truths, insinuations and downright lies that have been told, I can still walk through this town with my head held high," he added.

Ottley further defended campaign charges of "pork barrel politics" during his administration. "'This was the time the OIA and State Farm Loan Board came through and I'll be damned if I was going to refuse those programs because it happened to be an election year," he said.

Ottley also defended his support of industrial revenue bonds by telling the audience that "no one on the City Council ever voted against an industrial revenue bond and I supported them because I wanted to see the growth," he said.

Following swearing in ceremonies performed by Third District Court Judge John Troughton, the new City Council went to work.

One of the first items of business considered was the controversial zone change proposed for the Hamblin Park area.

The council tabled the ordinance on third and final reading and scheduled a workshop at 7 p.m. January 17 to discuss the issue.

Martin declared a conflict of interest on the Hamblin Park issue due to property ownership and did not participate in the vote.

The tabling action was recommended by City Attorney Mark Harris, whose appointment was contested by City Councilmen Arnie Morgan and Lance Voss only minutes earlier.

Morgan made a motion to discuss the appointment of Harris in executive session but Mayor Martin declined. Morgan then announced he would discuss the matter in open public meeting.

"I appeal to your better sense of judgement to take this matter into executive session. If you won't, I'll discuss it here in public," Morgan told the Council.

Morgan then addressed Harris and said, "I understand you plan to appoint Bob Morton as City Prosecutor," said Morgan. "If that is the case I oppose Mr. Harris' appointment as City Attorney."

Councilman Voss then added his opposition. "After consulting with my constituents I feel that Mr. Harris is not knowledgable enough for the position and for this reason I oppose the appointment," said Voss.

Harris' appointment was passed on 3-2 vote with Councilmen Bills, Davis and Sather casting favorable votes.

However, a motion to confirm the appointment of Harris as City Attorney was made by Councilman Bills, seconded by Sather, with 3 yes votes and 2 no votes. The motion passed by a majority. The two dissenting votes were Councilmen Arnie Morgan and Lance Voss.

The next issue of the *Uinta County Herald*, dated January 7th, came out with an article titled, OTTLEY BLASTS MARTIN AS GAVEL CHANGES HANDS, by David Fierro. The article said, *Sparks flew in the Evanston City Council chambers last night when former mayor Dennis Ottley aimed a few parting shots at Mayor Eugene Martin.*

Ottley, after thanking a number of people he had worked with during his four-year term, reprimanded Martin and Council members for what he termed "the most unethical campaign this city has ever seen."

"I've been accused of everything short of murder. People talk of conflicts of interest. Let me tell you, we all have conflicts of interest," said an obviously emotional Ottley.

The article went on about my outgoing comments and it may have made me look like a poor loser. But I'll tell you that I have never been a poor loser on anything that was fair and square. However, this past election was nothing but a campaign full of rotten lies and underhanded comments and other tactics by the competition. To me there is no one lower than a person who intentionally lies with the thought of actually hurting someone (election, politics or not), and I'm not one to sit back and let it happen without having my say back to them. So they can call me a poor loser if they want, but there is no one that will say it to my face. I don't mind a little bullshit, but I hate someone telling untrue stories about anyone unless they have proof of what's going on. I just hope the future elections run as smoothly as they had in the past prior to 1982.

There were also Letters to the Editor in the *Uinta County Herald* indicating their disgusted feelings about Councilman David Bills's actions during my final comments. They accused him of opening his mail, shuffling his papers, playing with his pen, drinking his Diet Coke, yawning, writing notes, and trying to get other members to talk to him during my speech.

One of the *Letters to the Editor* came from a group of young high school students that had attended the meeting for educational purposes, accompanied by a few teachers. In the letter they also indicated their disappointment of Mr. Bills's behavior. He was also a high school teacher. But as far as I was concerned Bills was just showing his mentality.

Amazed

Dear Editor;

I attended my first city council meeting on January 6th and I was amazed at the rudeness of Councilman David Bills. During Mr. Ottley's farewell speech, Mr. Bills was opening mail, shuffling papers, playing with his pen and drinking his diet coke. Is it asking too much for an elected official to pay attention? I'm sure Mr. Bills students cannot behave this way, so why does a member of the council? Sure I am partial to Mr. Ottley, but I was not the only one that left the council meeting wondering where are thy manners Mr. Bills.?

Tammy L. Ottley

Disappointed

Dear Mr. Baldwin:

On January 7, 1983 we, some of the students of Evanston High School, attended the city council meeting, which included former Mayor Dennis Ottley's final comments and the swearing in ceremony of Mayor Eugene Martin and the new council members.

We were impressed with the consideration and attention given to Mr. Ottley by Mayor Martin, the audience and most of the members of the council.

However, we were very disappointed in the behavior Councilman David Bills showed.

He read mail, yawned, drank pop, wrote notes, and tried to get other members of the council to talk to him while Mr. Ottley and Mr. Roy Fruits were making their final comments.

At one point he even slumped down in his chair and it seemed to us "nodded off" like we teenagers are always being accused of.

Students of EHS
R. Dean Milbrandt
Randy Matteson
Ray Hoey
Note: This letter was edited.

Uinta County Herald, January 12, 1983, Letters to The Editor.

I also received dozens of letters and cards from folks around town telling me how sorry they were that I lost the election. This made Sandy and I feel a little better about losing. It made us feel that all we had satisfied some of the folks and that we accomplished something worthwhile by being so active in the community that we loved, including my 16 years in city government. Our work was not "all for nothing," knowing that a lot of the local citizens did appreciate our involvement.

During the January meeting the mayor and council decided to reorganize the City Government. They decided that the mayor would no longer assign members of the council to the various city departments as had been done in the past. But council members would still be assigned as liaison to the various boards and commissions.

The mayor's assignments of council members to different department had been a policy of the mayor for many, many years, and the purpose of it was to make the council member feel more like they were a part of the process of managing the city's activities and projects, and to have the opportunity to understand more of what was going on, and to get to know the employees more. Each member of the council was required to give their report on their particular assigned department. However, I guess every Mayor has their own way and beliefs on how to do things.

The Overthrust Industrial Association and the Denver Research Group held a nice program in Denver that included dinner a few weeks after the first of the year. The program was set up to honor Sandy and me for our involvement in Evanston City Government and in the O.I.A.

In attendance was a large group of people representing the City of Evanston, Uinta County and the state of Wyoming, including Governor Herschler. There were also a number of officials from the oil and gas industry at the event, including board members of the O.I.A. and employees of the Denver Research Group.

Following dinner, a few speakers spoke honoring Sandy and me, and then they presented to me a beautiful plaque from the Overthrust Industrial Association that had inscribed on it the following:

> *"The measure of a man is not in what*
> *he achieves for himself*
> *but in what he accomplishes for others."*
>
> THE OVERTHRUST
> INDUSTRIAL ASSOCIATION
>
> *Presents this award to*
>
> **DENNIS OTTLEY**
>
> *With sincere thanks for outstanding service*
> *to Evanston, Wyoming, its people and industry,*
> *during a difficult time of rapid energy*
> *development, 1980-1982.*

Not long after the first of the year, Larry and Julie Lehman, Don and Sharon Constantine, and Don and Jo Roesler rented a limousine, at their expense, with two bench seats in the back facing each other, owned and driven by Larry Defa. They took Sandy and me to Salt Lake City to have a nice dinner at a really nice café (I don't recall the name), and then took us to see the stage show at the Capital Theatre of "The Best Little Whorehouse In Texas." It was a great show and Sandy and I really enjoyed the entire evening.

Larry Lehman and the others all helped me in my campaign and gave us the trip to S.L.C. to show their appreciation for our service to the community thinking it would make us feel better about losing. We did appreciate what they did for us and they were all very good friends, but it was hard getting over the outcome of the election, though eventually we did.

Under my administration, the city had started working on the project to improve and increase the city's water system by increasing the size of the filtration plant and obtaining more water rights, and looking for a location for a reservoir to hold city water, to get away from the water wells. Some of the wells were becoming contaminated and some were petering out.

During Mayor Martin's first meeting the water project came up for discussion, and City Engineer Wayne Shepherd reported the possibility of purchasing some water shares from the J. R. Broadbent Ranch with the idea of building a reservoir on LaChapelle Creek, which runs through the Broadbent property.

Also, Councilman Sather made a motion for the pre-engineering and land acquisition for the extension of Washington Avenue to be started, seconded by Bills, with all voting in favor.

The extension was another project that the previous administration had started, because after the North School was built the school buses had to use Highway 89 to get to the school and drop off the kids from a busy highway. Therefore, the school district had approached my administration to see about extending Washington Avenue so it would continue to go from County Road through to the new Highway 89 so the buses could use Washington to get the kids to school safely.

During the previous administration we approached the Wyoming State Highway Department for their help on construction of the extension and they indicated they would help in obtaining the right-of-way and the construction of the extension. I always had a good relationship with Leno Menghini, Superintendent of the State Highway Department. He never refused my administration anything we requested. But neither of the projects (the extension of Washington Avenue, nor the water reservoir) got completed until after the next administration took over.

The *Uinta County Herald* of March 9th came out with an article titled, RUTH RODRIGUEZ JOINS CITY FORCE AS ASSISTANT TO MAYOR AND COUNCIL. I thought they already had an Administrative Assistant in Steve Snyder, but I guess O.I.A. thought they needed more help because the mayor and most of the council were ignorant of the city's ongoing projects. Besides that, the O.I.A. was paying her salary, and they still had Ron Straka, also paid by O.I.A., to assist with the planning of the downtown area.

The March 9th article went on to report: *Management consultant Ruth Rodriguez has temporarily joined the Evanston city administration to provide technical assistance on such subjects as the city budget and finances, the city's capital improvement programs and other management issues.*

The article went on: *Rodriguez says her first priority will be the city budget which must be ready for public hearings by March 15th. "It takes quite a bit to put a budget together," she noted. After the budget is in preliminary form it will go to public hearings. "It's going to be a pretty intense effort in seeking public input, for the hearings," she said.*

The article went on to explain her qualifications and past experience. She had apparently dealt with boom areas before, and she had been a county manager and planner for Park County, Colorado, and a "circuit rider city manager" for four small towns in Colorado.

Her credentials appeared to be very good, but she was way off in stating that the city had to prepare the budget by March 15th to have the time for a public hearing. I think she was probably going by Colorado laws. But I'm sure she was well qualified and would try very hard in serving Evanston.

During late February they held the Second Annual Agri-Business Banquet and Sandy and I were invited to be there because I was to receive an award. But Sandy told them, *I will not go to something when the only reason they are honoring him is because they are just trying to soothe their own conscience for what happened to my husband during the election when he got beat because of all the lies and other bullshit said about him. I'm sure as hell not going to watch him get an award that is probably only given to him because he lost the election.*

I didn't particularly want to go either, but I thought I should because of those who worked hard to try to get me re-elected, and because of the Overthrust Industrial Association's concern for me.

An article by Tori Adams printed in the March 2nd issue of the *Uinta County Herald* read, *To a standing ovation, former Evanston Mayor Dennis Ottley was presented with the Chamber of Commerce's Business Person of the Year for 1982 award at last Thursday night's Second Annual Agri-business Banquet.*

The article went on to read: *Ottley has been active in city government for the last 12 years and community activities for over 20 years. He owns Uinta Realty, Inc. in Evanston and Lyman, and owns the Lockeroom Etc. with two of his sons and is a partner in two other businesses.*

I had opened up a real estate agency in Lyman brokered and managed by my son Tib. But neither locations of Uinta Realty, Evanston nor Lyman, were doing much. I already had to close Lockeroom Etc. because of the lack of business. Therefore, I couldn't believe how the Chamber of Commerce could even consider me unless it was because of what Sandy said. Anyway, I did appreciate the honor and accepted it, but I wasn't feeling all that great about receiving it.

The *Casper Star-Tribune* of March 7, 1983 came out with an article titled, EVANSTON STILL BUSTLING, ALTHOUGH BOOM BLOOM WILTS. The article went on: *The bloom is off the boom, but Evanston is still bustling.*

Traffic still moves at a snail's crawl downtown, and all kinds of construction is evident everywhere.

But it's also much easier to find housing, some merchants report a big drop in sales and, instead of an abundance of jobs, there is some unemployment.

Like the rest of the country, the recession has caught up with Evanston. At the same time, construction has ended on two massive gas processing plants, which, together, employed about 3,000 workers.

The article went on talking about retail sales dropping 30 to 40 percent. Motels no longer required reservations for rooms, and those now coming to Evanston could find a wide range of housing available. Apparently, as one developer stated, *"Supply has clearly caught up with the demand side."*

Meanwhile, construction continued on new schools, the addition to the Uinta County Courthouse and Library, the City of Evanston's Recreation Center, the Human Service Center, and a new overpass, new sewer treatment plant, enlargement of the water treatment plant, a new police department facility, a new fire hall, a new shopping center, and new banks.

Although the peak of the boom seemed to have come and gone, and we were now on the downhill side, some good things were still happening. Amoco Production Company was nearing the completion of their new office building on the corner of Overthrust Road and Cheyenne Drive, and at the time Evanston was expecting an influx of Amoco management personnel and their families, who would be moving to Evanston to man the new three-story regional headquarters.

Although there were not as many employees moving to Evanston to work at the office building as Amoco indicated, there were quite a few. Some of the local folks that had lost their jobs in other areas of the industry made up the slack. But the Amoco headquarters being located in Evanston certainly helped.

Because of the economic slowdown, mostly caused by the drop in oil and gas exploration and the drilling rigs pulling out, Evanston was actually going through a mild, but very evident, decline in population.

Star-Tribune, Casper, Wyo.

Monday, March 7, 1983

Evanston still bustling, although boom bloom wilts

By PAUL KRZA
Star-Tribune staff writer

EVANSTON — The bloom is off the boom, but Evanston is still bustling.

Traffic still moves at a snail's crawl downtown, and all kinds of construction is evident everywhere.

But it's also much easier to find housing, some merchants report a big drop in sales and, instead of an abundance of jobs, there is some unemployment.

Like the rest of the country, the recession has caught up with Evanston. At the same time, construction has ended on two massive gas processing plants, which, together, employed about 3,000 workers.

Like other boomtowns, Evanston has begun the transition from temporary to more permanent status. Needed facilities and services, like restaurants and food stores, are now in place, alleviating long lines and crowded conditions.

On one hand, Evanston Mayor Gene Martin said his survey of downtown businesses revealed that some stores report that sales are off 30 to 40 percent over last year. But, he said, "just the other night we approved a 153-lot subdivision and 130 lots have already been sold."

The skid in worldwide oil prices has Evanston residents a little worried since the former railroad town has become dependent on the oil and gas industry.

But Martin said he's still "confident," and despite some drop in revenue from sales tax, "we're not in dire shape, I don't believe."

WHAT appears to be hardest hit by the change in economy is the city's recently-developed motel industry. A year ago, reservations were a necessity. Now, an estimated 30 to 40 percent of the 1,369 motel rooms are vacant, according to Beth Carlson of the Chamber of Commerce.

The motel situation appears to be a result of workers no longer using them as places to live and because of less oil company management traffic into the city, she said.

Those now coming to Evanston can find a wide range of housing available, and even dropping rents, real estate agent Mike Pexton said.

"Supply has clearly caught up with the demand side," Pexton said.

In one type of type of housing, condominums and townhouses, the market is even "glutted," he said. The reason, Pexton said, is a combination of overpricing and a desire by people to live in single-family dwellings.

Many of the townhouses sit vacant, or, city planner Bruce Wright said, are being rented.

Last year, Wright's predecessor created a minor stir when he suggested that Evanston was "overbuilt." County planner Dennis Farley said that is the case now, but Wright shyed away from that view.

Martin said he's a firm believer in free enterprise, and "if a guy wants to build 1,000 units, let him."

But Farley said some of the vacant areas are "white elephants," which "can't be swept under the rug."

BECAUSE of the economic slowdown, Uinta County is actually "going through a mild decline in population," Farley said.

During the top boom years, there was much talk that the county might soon grow to 40,000, but more recent estimates put the population this year at about 21,500.

For at least the rest of this year, indications appear to point toward continued stability.

Chevron spokesman Jerry Barlow said the company is now "down to drilling one or two holes," and has no major construction planned of the gas plant magnitude.

School officials are bracing less for construction workers, who generally don't move to the area with children.

Instead, they are bracing for an expected influx of Amoco management personnel and their families, who will soon be in Evanston to man the new three-story regional headquarters, which is nearing completion.

Meanwhile, construction continues on new schools, a city recreation facility and a human services building, a new overpass and housing areas. A new shopping center will open soon, and two banks are talking about building six- and seven-story structures.

star/WYOMING

Paul Krza

Amoco's new regional headquarters is one sign that Evanston's not dead

Also, when the sweetening plants of Amoco and Chevron were completed, the man-camps were vacated and torn down, causing workers to leaving the county and resulting in a large drop in business, because these workers, when off work, would come to town and do a lot of business in the bars and various stores.

The *Uinta County Herald* issue of April 8, 1983 came out with an article titled, SUBDIVISION MORATORIUM SUGGESTION DRAWS ATTENTION OF DEVELOPERS. The article stated, *On March 30, City Attorney Mark Harris asked the City Council to consider a six-month moratorium on subdivisions and two days later, sketch plans for three new residential subdivisions were submitted to the city's Planning Department.*

The article continued: *The sketch plans submitted call for an additional 90 units being built in the Evanston area, units some proponents of a moratorium don't want to see built at the present time. City Engineer Wayne Shepherd said Thursday that his office has compiled the number of housing units planned and approved in the city but a decision on what action to take is up to the City Council.*

Shepherd said that his office has planned for a community of 25,000 residents if the population grows to that level. "We have to stay ahead of the growth and are constantly looking five and ten years down the road," he said.

The Southwest Wyoming Home Builders Association (SWHBA) responded to Harris's statements Thursday afternoon, issuing a joint statement from the SWHBA Board of Directors.

The article went on to quote the statement of the board: *"Currently SWHBA members are selling in excess of 80 homes per month. Prices have fallen from the peak demand to their current realistic value because of competition. We not only feel that there is not a surplus of single family units, but in fact, there may well be a shortage, with the exception of townhouses and condominiums. The development community has not created the alleged surplus Mr. Harris refers to."*

The SWHBA statement continued: *"The remarks of Mr. Harris appear to be politically oriented. The SWHBA would like to know what future political aspirations Mr. Harris has. We want to know if Mr. Harris is being paid by the taxpayers to do a function of the City Planner, specifically gathering demographics. We would like to see a job description for Mr. Harris."*

"...The SWHBA has always supported sound government and private planning for growth. To date, the city of Evanston has done an outstanding job in accommodating the growth and providing for the future of its citizens. We feel that a moratorium will not provide for the needs of the home buyer nor benefit the community," the SWHBA Board of Directors wrote.

In an earlier issue of the *Uinta County Herald*, Mayor Gene Martin had said that he disagreed with the concept of a moratorium.

"I still work on the principal of free enterprise," said Martin. "They'd have a real fight on their hands with me if they wanted to have a moratorium. I would fight them tooth and toenail on that sucker," Martin added.

An article in the April, 1983 issue titled EVANSTON, WYO-MING; A ROCKY MOUNTAIN BOOM TOWN, Evanston's 1982-1983 City Budget, reported: *Where the money comes from:*

1) *State Loan Account (from Wyoming severance tax)........30%;*
2) *User fees........16%;*
3) *Overthrust Industrial Association grants........15%;*
4) *U.S. Government (primarily from E.P.A.)........14%;*
5) *City sales tax........11%;*
6) *Mineral Impact Funds (from Wyoming royalties)........9%; and*
7) *Uinta County........5%.*

The article quoted Mayor Gene Martin as saying, *"The city's bud-get remains with a small surplus, despite a decrease of 30 percent in sales taxes. We're going to see a little tough time, but nothing we can't work our way out of."*

The *Uinta County Herald* issue of April 22nd came out with the headline, SALES TAX SHOWS CITY'S FINANCIAL BOOM MAY HAVE PEAKED, by David Fierro. He said, *Monthly sales tax revenues, a major economic indicator for the city of Evanston, have stagnated and could decrease, revealing that the city's meteoric financial boom may have peaked out.*

The article quoted Budget Officer Ruth Rodriguez as saying, *"It's not a depressing piece of news, but it is a sobering piece of news. It tells us that we have to continue doing what we are doing."*

Rodriguez was referring to the city's recent efforts to pare expenditures, which have cut the city's current operating budget from an anticipated $6.5 million to $5.6 million for fiscal year 1982-1983, the article continued.

Rodriguez said that at one point in the last few weeks city officials were thinking there might be a zero fund balance for the fiscal year 1984-1985. "That would be critical because that means that on July 1, 1984, when the city had to meet a payroll, it would have to borrow because there wouldn't be any funds in the savings account. That's a pretty eye-opening thought for the city to face. We should try and prevent that at all costs," she said.

The article continued, *Roderiguez said that the budget process will heat up in May when the city's department heads will be making presentations to the City Council and the Mayor's Budget Committee. Public hearings on the budget are scheduled for mid-June.*

Groundbreaking ceremony for the city's first 12 units of the Senior Citizens Housing Project in the Haw Patch Subdivision was scheduled for May 18, 1983, according to a report from the *Uinta County Herald.* Evanston Housing Authority (EHA) Director Julie Lehman stated that she was planning for a September occupancy date.

That spring of 1983 was a very wet year, with heavy rains and flooding. Folks were threatened by flooding all the way from the Sulphur Creek Reservoir to the Bear River through Evanston, Almy and what now is Bear River, Wyoming. The U.S. ArmyCorps of Engineers, the Uinta County Sheriff's Department, and the Evanston Voluntary Fire Department were furnishing sandbags and issuing warnings to people to start preparing for possible flooding because the Reservoir was starting to flood over and bridges were being washed out.

Homes in the Grass Valley area were preparing for the overabundance of water from the heavy rains, and businesses along the south side of Bear River Drive were very concerned because the ponds in the Bear Project were overflowing. North Evanston east of 2nd Avenue and the North Mobile Home Park were getting heavily flooded, and sandbags were being filled and put in place as people tried to protect their homes from flooding.

The communities of Almy, Bear River and all those who lived along the river were receiving heavy flows of water and were doing whatever was possible to protect their property. Sandbags were used and dikes were created to try to prevent the water from entering the properties and causing damage to homes. During that spring there was heavy rainfall like I had never seen before. However, I have seen the Bear River overflow in the past at times, causing some homes to be concerned, especially those in the North Evanston area, but nothing like the spring of 1983.

A news article in the July 13, 1983 issue of *The Evanston Post* headlined, SPECIAL COUNCIL MEETING LACKS QUORUM, by Kathy Broussard. The article read, *Mayor Eugene Martin bypassed normal procedures Friday night and awarded a contract to clean up the sewer sludge ponds in North Evanston.*

The article continued, *Martin sat all alone as he opened the special City Council meeting at 5:10 pm on July 8. The meeting was called to review and accept a bid for cleaning the sludge pit that has plagued North Evanston residents for several weeks.*

With all the council members absent, Martin asked City Clerk Don Welling if the meeting had been properly advertised, to which Welling replied that it had. The next step by the Mayor was to instruct City Attorney Mark Harris to notify the police department to "contact the members of the City Council and bring them here under his jurisdiction."

The meeting was recessed for 45 minutes while waiting for the council members to be gathered, the article added.

Administrative Sergeant Forrest Bright returned alone at 6:00 pm and gave his report to the Mayor. He stated that Russ Albrecht was not at home; that Arnie Morgan was off on Friday and also not at home; that Rick Sather was in Salt Lake City and Ronald Davis had a death in the family and could not attend.

The article continued: *Of the two remaining members, Lance Voss was also not present when Bright arrived at his home. He was contacted at a construction site where he was working and said that he would be there soon. The last member, David Bills, had already notified the council that he would not be able to attend but later phoned to say he would be right over.*

Even with the presence of Voss and Bills, the article continued, *the meeting still lacked the necessary three members needed to make a quorum. The Mayor stated that he would not make a practice of it, but because he felt the sludge problem was very crucial and required immediate attention, he bypassed normal council procedure. Martin accepted the lowest bid, submitted by the Double T Roustabout Company for $63,628, and instructed them to begin the cleanup on Monday, July 11.*

The accepted bid will be legally finalized at the regular City Council meeting on July 13 when hopefully enough, if not all, members will be present.

The article concluding: *Double T is reported to have begun the work as scheduled. The sludge is being gathered by vacuum trucks and put into sealed containers. It is then transported to a state-approved disposal site north of Evanston.*

We had never lacked a quorum or been in a situation like that, either during my term as mayor or during my 12 years as a member of the City Council. I felt for Mayor Martin, and I'm not sure what I would have done if I had been in his shoes. I'm sure it was a tough decision for him, but I couldn't blame him for taking the action he took—but I do believe he brought this on from lack of good leadership.

I read a statement once that went like this, *"Participation in community affairs not only affords outlets for creative interests, it plays important roles in bettering local conditions, in molding the character of the community, and in contributing warmth to its personality. While thus engaged the doer acquires a growing sense of belonging. The resultant recognition and increasing respect from others brings added stature as a solid citizen."*

The author of the statement is unknown; whoever made it wasn't listed. But I have got to admire the person who wrote it because it had a lot of truth to it, and it's only too bad those members of Mayor Martin's city council hadn't read it before they decided not to attend a very important meeting.

When you run for any government office, you take an Oath of Office that you should honor at all costs, and that means attending your designated meetings, unless you have a very legitimate excuse not to attend. You owe it to your constituents and all other citizens you represent.

All the planning that my administration had put together and worked on seemed to be going very well, including the location of the new Evanston Post Office. Apparently the U.S. Postal Department had finally agreed to stay in the downtown area, because an agreement signed by Mayor Martin and a packet prepared to build the new facility on Block 13 of the Original Town of Evanston had all been presented and agreed upon.

Block 13 was the block where the Old Town Hall was located, but it was agreed that the Old Town Hall would be preserved for historic purposes. Later, for some reason or other, the city council changed the location to Block 6 of the Town of Evanston.

To be honest, I was hoping that they would go ahead and build on Block 13 because I was part owner of some rental units located on that block, and I needed to get rid of some property because my real estate agency, Uinta Realty, Inc. was having a tough time keeping up with the large payments I was trying to make on the mortgages I took out to pay off Lockeroom Etc. debts. However, I don't know why the change was made unless it was because a good share of Block 6 was owned by the city, and one of the city council members, Rick Sather, owned a large lot on Block 6 with rental units, retail and residential.

However, whatever the reason was, I was glad to see the post office stay in downtown Evanston, and either location would have been a good choice.

Both Amoco and Chevron sour gas plants were in full operation and all man-camps were now gone. At this time a number of folks were starting to leave Evanston because of drilling rigs being taken down and the oil well workers were starting to leave.

Although the production part of the oil and gas industry was going great, those workers in the drilling and exploration part of the industry, and all the employees that had been living in the man-camps, were leaving. There were more folks starting to leave Evanston than were coming in.

An article in an early issue of 1983 of *USA TODAY* headlined: WYO. BOOM TOWN GOES BUST BECAUSE OF DROP IN OIL PRICES. The article read, *Evanston was a retirement community of 4,600 when the oil business took off in 1976, prompted by the Arab embargo. "From then on, the population expanded so rapidly it was absolutely unbeliev-able," said Mayor Eugene B. Martin.*

The article continued: *At the peak of the oil boom a few years ago 5,000 workers were drilling wells and servicing pumps. Now, virtually all that's available are 600 jobs opening up this week for drilling two gas wells. A total of 4,000 people applied.*

Thirty businesses have closed in the past month.

Beth Carlson, Executive Director of the Chamber of Commerce, says the city is trying to pick up the pieces by promoting tourism, the article continued.

"Things are pretty bad here right now," said Carlson. *"We just have to find a way to get people to spend some time here."*

A good share of families that worked for the oil and gas industry was not only leaving Evanston, they were walking away from their homes, sometimes leaving them in pretty bad shape, to be foreclosed on by the various mortgage holders.

The main reason they were just walking away from their homes was because there weren't many folks moving into Evanston wanting to pay the high values that owners needed to sell. Values dropped because appraisals were not coming in high enough. The folks leaving Evanston were finding themselves underwater as far as their mortgages were concerned. At the time they purchased their home, the mortgage companies were requiring low or no down payments, and they were charging very high interest rates of 18 to 22%, leaving no equity for the homeowner.

This made it tough for the real estate industry for a while because when a mortgagee foreclosed on a property it took them several months, sometimes as much as a year or more, to get the property ready for the market and get it listed for sale.

Most of these foreclosures had been purchased through FHA loans and were not assumable without credit qualifications. There were only a few homeowners that had assumable loans without buyers having to qualify. They stopped that type of loan pretty early, because they were getting too many foreclosures by allowing buyers to just take over a home owner's mortgage without having to qualify. At this time selling real estate, agencies were required to do their own closings. Title companies only furnished the title search and insurance. Uinta Realty, Inc. got stuck with two sizeable returned checks while closing on two different oil-affiliated companies that had left Evanston, listing their property with our agency. One check was returned for "insufficient funds," the other was returned on "stopped payment." It was almost impossible even to try to collect on these checks, because once these folks left Evanston there wasn't much use even trying to find them. This hurt Uinta Realty, Inc. financially, and we were already hurting because of the slowdown and the market situation.

We generally demanded certified funds when closing property sales, but I got to know the owners of these two companies and they appeared to be people I could trust, but apparently they were just like a lot of companies that were leaving Evanston…going broke.

There was a lot of construction going on in Evanston at this time. A number of city and county facilities were under construction, and the new sewer treatment plant, which was expected to be completed by fall of 1984, two new schools, and a number of new businesses were being built. Also in the next few years there would be lot of highway construction including the new overpass (Ottley's Folly), the new interchange at Wyoming State Highway 150 and improvements on the east end of Evanston's Bear River Drive.

All this construction was helping to keep up the economy by creating jobs and by increasing retail sales. Otherwise, the way the oil and gas industry was changing, things could be a lot worse.

The *Uinta County Herald* issue of August 5th had an article written by Greg Livovich titled, MARTIN SAYS HIGHER TAXES ARE TO BE EXPECTED HERE. The article went on: *Evanston Mayor Gene Martin said Wednesday that city residents can expect slightly higher property taxes as a result of a recent move by the city to tighten up its fiscal policies.*

According to the first-term mayor, the city council has not only elected to assess the maximum 8 mill general levy allowable by Wyoming statute, but also dusted off and put to use a long-ignored provision allowing a special levy to retire bond debts.

The article continued: *City Consultant Ruth Rodriguez said debt service on the single "general obligation" and two "revenue" bonds has been paid by water and sewer service fees, despite a stipulation in the original bond proposal that property tax funds be allocated for that purpose. The city council, intent on creating "self-supporting" city services functioning with funds generated by the individual departments themselves, voted the special levy to cut off the drain of service fees being used to pay off bond debts rather than as operating capital for the departments. She added that not utilizing the special levy had been an "oversight" of previous city administrations.*

I have got to agree with her on that, but I'm not so sure we would have used it or not even if we had been aware of it. It's hard to say because I was never in favor of raising taxes of any type. Services was a different subject: You had to keep up with inflation.

Another article came out in the *Uinta County Herald* of August 19th with the headline: RODRIGUEZ TELLS CITY: "I WORK FOR YOU," also by Greg Livovich. *Ruth Rodriguez has become the center of a behind-the-scenes City Hall controversy generated by her efforts to remake a city government she describes as "in transition from Good Old Boys to a professional staff,"* the article's first paragraph read.

Some city officials grumble privately that Rodriguez has been heavy-handed in implementing changes within the city, the article continued. *She's sometimes accused – off the record – of contradicting Mayor Gene Martin's day-to-day directions to employees.*

Wednesday she said the accusation "is more a misconception than any-thing else." She added, "I don't do anything the mayor doesn't know about and he didn't tell me was okay."

The article continued: *Rodriguez came here as part of a technical assis-tance package offered by the Overthrust Industrial Association, made up pri-marily of energy giants Amoco Production Company and Chevron USA. Her interim position, funded by the O.I.A., still raises some local eyebrows eight months after she began the task she refers to as "bringing Evanston into the 20th century."* The article ended with, *Rodriguez stated that the "council didn't like all the things they heard from me but I presented my ideas in a professional manner. The O.I.A. has always understood that I would work at the pleasure of the mayor and council. That's where my loyalty and working relationships are and I can honestly say I kept an arm's length in any nego-tiation on mitigation and relationships between the city and O.I.A. It comes down to professional ethics and this is my profession...this is my life's work."*

I actually thought that Ruth Rodriguez was trying hard to do a good job, but I believe she was acting more like a city manager or administrator than just an advisor. She only had one month left on her contract with O.I.A.

I have never felt good about the city manager or the city admin-istrator type of government. I always thought that was what folks elected a mayor for, to run the government. Mayor Martin already had an Administrative Assistant to the Mayor, Steve Snyder.

That same issue of the *Uinta County Herald* had another article titled, MAYOR DEFENDS HIRING ADMINISTRATORS, again by Livovich. The article stated that Mayor Martin was indicating that he wanted the City of Evanston to hire a City Administrator, after Rodriguez leaves, plus a Personnel-Finance Director to oversee City Treasurer Linnea Overy and the budget.

This idea sure didn't say much for Martin as Mayor. He was looking to have more management than workers, but then, he's the mayor. He's got to know that this type of management costs a lot of money.

They had already spent a lot of money on a study concerning the police department that hadn't changed a thing. The big issue was whether or not to keep Chief Dennis Harvey on as chief or to appoint someone else, but nothing happened. As far as I was concerned, Harvey was doing a good job as chief and didn't deserve to be replaced, and he wasn't. Nothing was changed in the department to any degree.

The city council had put out applications for a city administrator to take the place of Ruth Rodriguez. Rodriguez had been hired by O.I.A. to assist the City of Evanston the past several months through the process of implementing their mitigation plans, but her contract with O.I.A. was coming to an end.

After going through dozens of applications applying for the position of City Administrator, the city council ended up with John F. Hendrickson, apparently a well-qualified and experienced person who had been the city administration of Soda Springs, Idaho for two-and-a-half years, as well as being city administrator for Cedar City and Payson, Utah.

The *Uinta County Herald* of August 26, 1983 reported: *The Evanston city government will take on a new "experience" approach to the coordinating of city affairs effective September 12th with the hiring of John F. Hendrickson as the new City Administrator. News of the decision to hire Hendrickson was made public during Wednesday's City Council meeting.*

So now the City of Evanston has a full-time administrator paid by the city, Steve Snyder, Administrative Assistant, and a City Clerk, both paid by the city. And now they would be looking to hire a Personnel-Finance Director to oversee City Treasurer, Linnea Overy and act as Budget Officer.

My question is: How many high-paid top managers does a mayor of a small city need to run the office? It seems, in my opinion, ridiculous. What is there left for the Mayor to do?

Evanston Hires New City Employees

The recent reorganization of the city government has brought two new faces to the Evanston area. They include City Administrator John Hendrickson and Finance Director Lee Galeotos.

John Hendrickson

"I'm really looking forward to working in Evanston," stated new City Administrator John Hendrickson. "Evanston is a dynamic and growing city and I'm glad to be a part of it," he added.

Mr. Hendrickson has an extensive career in city administration. Prior to his present role as City Administrator, he held a similar position in Soda Springs, Idaho. He also served as City Manager of Cedar City, Utah; worked as City Administrator of Payson, Utah and was Administrative Assistant to the Mayor of Mapleton, Utah.

Mr. Hendrickson graduated with a Bachelor of Arts degree in Political Science from Brigham Young University in 1973. He received a Master of Public Administration from the Graduate School of Management at BYU in 1975.

As City Administrator, Mr. Hendrickson is responsible for the organization and coordination of all city services and activities. In addition, he acts as a liaison between the Mayor and City Council and citizens.

Mr. Hendrickson is responsible for ensuring that Evanston is running smoothly and effectively and is responsive to the needs of its citizens. In this effort, he plans to formalize the policies of the city government and its departments, as well as establish a long-range planning program to ensure organized development in Evanston.

Mr. Hendrickson also hopes to develop a budgetary process which will guarantee a stable financial future for Evanston. "The citizens need to know that the city is financially able to meet the increased demands in services now and in the future," he stated.

Lee Galeotos

The new Director of Finance, Lee Galeotos, brings a strong background in state and national administrative leadership to his new position in the city government. Prior to moving to Evanston, he was the Director of Human Services for the Western Governors Policy Office in Denver for three and one-half years and Deputy Controller for the State of Iowa for three years.

Evanston City Administrator John Hendrickson

Evanston Finance Director Lee Galeotos

From 1972-1976, Mr. Galeotos was Director for Executive Management and Fiscal Affairs for the National Governors Association in Washington, D.C. Prior to 1972, he held the positions of Wyoming State Budget Officer, Director of Social Services in Wyoming and Director of Research and Statistics for the Wyoming Labor Department.

Mr. Galeotos received his Bachelor of Science Degree in Economics from the University of Wyoming in 1959 and a Master of Arts in Economics from the University in 1961.

As Director of Finance, Mr. Galeotos is responsible for the city's financial matters as well as its personnel. In this role, he hopes to set up a new budgeting process as well as update the city administrative policies.

Commenting on the budget, Mr. Galeotos stated, "I'd like to look at a more comprehensive budget process which will allow the major administrators, council and department heads to organize expenditures and insure that adequate budget controls are in effect."

As Personnel Director, Mr. Galeotos wants to strengthen the city's new central management system, noting that good management and procedures are basic to the operation of a city government. "People have the right to know that their city is operating as efficiently as it can with the resources available," he concluded.

NOTE:

The Overthrust Industrial Association Evanston telephone line (307) 789-2759 currently is not in service. Local residents wishing to contact the OIA may call collect—(303) 333-5474.

Overthrust News, Overthrust Industrial Association, Issue No. 8, January 1984.

The *Casper Star-Tribune* dated August 27th had an article titled, MAYOR BUYS GIFT WITH CITY MONEY by Mary Kramer. The article went on to read: *A city purchase order filled out by Evanston Mayor Eugene B. Martin lists $27.04 for earrings for his secretary.*

The earrings were purchased at Sather's Jewelry for Sharon Constantine, executive secretary for Martin. She is also the secretary for the Overthrust Industrial Association and the city council.

Martin said the earrings were an acknowledgment of exceptional effort. "I feel it as justified," he said. "She's done a whale of a job."

The article went on, *No city council members contacted by the* Star-Tribune *were aware of the purchase, and there had been no discussion during council meetings regarding the expenditure.*

Councilman Ronald Davis felt that the council should have been advised of the purchase, which should have been listed on its own individual purchase order.

He said when city employees excel at their work, tokens of appreciation from the city should be decided upon by the council. The earring purchase was on a purchase order that included several listings for travel reimbursement for the mayor, the article continued.

The fact that the purchase was buried in with the reimbursement is what bothers Davis, and Councilman David Bills.

Councilman Lance Voss was also concerned about the manner that the bill was presented. However, he doubted it was done intentionally.

He said perhaps one of the secretaries or the treasurer had lumped the bill with Martin's travel receipts before turning them over to purchasing agent Michael Lake.

The order was signed by Lake, with administrative assistant Ruth Rodriguez initialing her approval, the article concluded.

The set of earrings was purchased from Sather's Jewelry, which is owned by Councilman Richard Sather, but the article had no mention of any comment or explanation from him.

However, the *Uinta County Herald* dated August 31st came out with the headline: MAYOR PAYS CITY BACK, 'ACCEPTS THEIR CRITICISM'.

Mayor pays city back,
'accepts their criticism'

The city treasury was $27.04 fatter Monday when Mayor Gene Martin handed over a personal check for the amount of a pair of earrings he purchased last month for his executive secretary.

The mayor said he originally paid a clerk at Sather's Jewelry for the pearl earrings. He then submitted the bill, along with receipts for other personal expenses, to a city hall employee who listed the $27.04 on a city purchase order for the mayor's monthly travel expenses. The P.O., totalling $354.41, was apparently initialed by city management consultant Ruth Rodriguez and was included, non-itemized, in the August payments list approved by the city council.

Martin, in a Monday press conference, noted the criticism he's received for the potentially illegal purchase. "I'll admit it was a slipshod way of doing things," he said. "They made an example out of me and I'll accept their criticism."

Martin pointed out that the city has never drafted a policy concerning employee's gifts and he compared his presentation to executive secretary Sharon Constantine to a special breakfast purchased at city expense for employees who worked all night to pump water from the flooded Union Pacific underpass during heavy rainfall two weeks ago.

"That's the way I thought the city could say thank you for a job well done," Martin said. "I like to thank people when they do something right."

He cited Constantine's efforts in planning a Boulder, Colorado, trip last summer for citizens here interested in seeing that city's downtown mall. Martin added that her work on last summer's Renewal Ball was "beyond what I felt was the call of duty as an executive secretary for the city of Evanston."

While the mayor's gift fell outside the realm of city policy and ordinance, Uinta County Attorney Scott Smith said Monday the gift "potentially would be a misdemeanor misappropriation of public funds." Smith added that "it's more likely a lack of discretion on the mayor's part than a criminal matter that merits any consideration in the judicial system." He noted that the mayor's speedy action in repaying the city "would probably weigh very heavily in any decision" concerning possible criminal charges.

City Treasurer Linnea Overy said the mayor's travel expenses are routinely "lumped together" by clerks in her office. She added that if the city had a purchase account with Sather's Jewelry, the earrings would likely have been listed as a line item when purchase orders were submitted for council approval.

Mayor Martin, who noted that the flap over the gift has prompted an executive order that administrators make no more similar purchases with city funds, added that "I'm sorry it happened this way. From now on, I'll say 'thanks' to Sharon or anyone else but it won't be with a purchase order from the city but with my own money."

Gift earings
Councilmen comment

The responses of city council members asked to comment on Mayor Gene Martin's use of city funds for a secretary's gift were primarily sympathetic to the mayor.

The following are responses from five council members polled Tuesday. Councilman Arnie Morgan, an employee of an oil field service company was on location and unavailable for comment.

Russ Albrecht: "Learning the hard way."

"The main thing is the council wasn't informed. The mayor wouldn't do anything to deliberately shortchange the city. He shouldn't have to give Councilman Davis a check to return to the city. What the mayor should have done was ask the council for permission to grant a gift to Sharon for her services. He's a new mayor and sometimes you have to learn things the hard way.

David Bills: "It's the principle."

"It's a little, tiny item — 27 bucks. But it's the principal. He should have discussed it with the council first or it should have been included as a line item for the good Lord and everybody to see. I'm sure the mayor was trying to do a good thing. It's a small item blown out of proportion. We have no policy on this and we need one."

Ronald Davis: "I wouldn't have questioned it."

"It's just something that happened and we just didn't think it was going to cause a problem. I wouldn't have questioned it if I'd known about it.."

Rick Sather: "Mickey Mouse situation."

"If you had to discuss every item like this, the city council sessions would be 22 hours long. The mayor should be able to react immediately. If something's done well by an employee rather than take it to the council and talk it through. The gift was bought in my store and I am always the first person who's yelling 'conflict of interest.' I wrote a memo to the city saying I wouldn't allow any purchases between Sathers and the city. This just passed me because it was bought with a personal check from Gene Martin and there was no mention of the city. This is just a Mickey Mouse situation blown up by an overzealous press."

Lance Voss: "Through council first."

"Sharon deserved the gift, but it should have come through the council first. As far as it being on a P.O. with other items instead of listed separately, it's probably more a mistake of the staff than of the mayor himself."

Uinta County Herald, August 31, 1983.

The article started out: *The city treasury was $27.05 fatter Monday when Mayor Gene Martin handed over a personal check for the amount of a pair of earrings he purchased last month for his executive secretary.*

The mayor said he originally paid a clerk at Sather's Jewelry for the pearl earrings. He then submitted the bill, along with receipts for other personal expenses, to a city hall employee who listed the $27.04 on a city purchase order for the mayor's monthly travel expenses. The P.O., totaling $354.41, was apparently initialed by city management consultant Ruth Rodriguez and was included, non-itemized, in the August payments list approved by the city council.

That same issue of the *Herald* came out with *Councilman Comment,* asking each member of the city council to comment on the purchase of earrings for Mayor Martin's executive secretary, but there didn't seem to be much said.

In the same issue of the *Herald* were articles titled: REVISIONS PREDICTED FOR CAR POOL PLAN; PLANS FOR HIRING ASSISTANT POLICE CHIEF SIDETRACKED: and CITIZENS OBJECT TO THE CLOSING OF EVANSTON'S OUTDOOR SWIMMIMG POOL.

All of these articles brought criticism from various groups, but the reason to close the outdoor swimming pool was because the new Recreation Center was almost finished and it would have a swimming pool that would meet all Olympic requirements. There were also quite a number of people upset at the mayor's plan demanding that all employees would be required to return their vehicle to the motor pool at the end of their shift. This new policy would include the fire chief, the police chief, and all other employees who needed their vehicles on an emergency basis.

This first year of Mayor Gene Martin's administration took it up on itself to make many changes in city politics, politics that had been set up by previous administrations with a lot of thought and consideration, and was working very well. Why they would do this I can't say. But I know the mayor and council were getting an awful lot of flak because of it.

I'm sure a few changes were in order, but not the as many as they made. There are always changes to be made when really needed, but why change things that are working?

The City of Evanston's improvements to the water treatment plant were almost finished, and the Recreation Center and Human Service Center were also coming to a completion.

Wyoming's Secretary of State Thyra Thompson headed the list of state dignitaries attending the dedication ceremonies at the grand opening of the Human Service Resources Center. Calling the project the first in the nation that she knew of that administers all human services in one building, she told the capacity crowd at the Human Service Center, *I don't know any other city in the state that has done what you have done; you are going to be a model for the state.*

The new Evanston High School was well on its way and the mayor and city council kept their commitment to reimburse the school district for the large cost of a building permit.

In September the City of Evanston hired another top employee, Lee Galeotos as their new Finance and Personnel Director to help update the city administration and set up a new budgeting process.

The September 28th issue of the *Uinta County Herald* stated that, *Aware of the growth Evanston has undergone during the last five years, Galeotos expressed the belief that, "Evanston handled the impact problems well… relatively speaking. I feel the mayor and council are far-sighted in planning ahead," he commented.*

According to the *Uinta County Herald* of October 21st, the City of Evanston secured $850,000 from the Wyoming Farm Loan Board for funding the $8.5 million construction on an interchange at Wyoming State Highway 150 S and Interstate 80.

Administrative Assistant Steve Snyder said the grant represents one-tenth of the total amount, but based on the fact that there were about 100 requests for funds from the F.L.B. at the last meeting, Snyder said he believed the City of Evanston fared very well.

The project is to be called the Diamond Interchange and construction will begin in the spring of 1984 and is slated to take approximately 10 months for completion.

Administrator John Hendrickson announced that the City of Evanston was proposing to raise the rates of water and sewer services.

This did not go over very well with the public, but Hendrickson announced that it was necessary to raise rates to keep up with the costs involved with the new sewer plant and the addition to the water treatment plant.

But later in the month, Hendrickson announced that the study of current and proposed fees for city water and sewer was been concluded, and it was presented to the public that there would be a flat fee of $2.00 per month for water rates, plus 95 cents per 1,000 gallons of water used. Also, the new sewer rate would be $3.60 per 1,000 gallons, based on how much water is used. Sewer rates have always been based on the amount of water used, but the previous user fee for water was a $2.00 flat fee per quarter.

Many of the citizens, new and old, complained at this rate increase, saying that it was way overboard, and requested that the city council take a better look at the situation, but the increase was acted upon and passed as proposed and stated by Hendrickson.

In the November 23rd issue of the *Uinta County Herald* was an article titled, SALES TAX DROP MAY CHANGE BUDGET. The article read: *A re-examination of the budget figures for fiscal year 1983-1984 may be in the offing if sales tax trends within the city do not take a dramatic up-turn.*

Reflecting on a 28 percent decrease in the first quarter of the fiscal year for sales tax revenue to the city, City Administrator John Hendrickson said that "any time your revenues are down 28 percent that's got to concern you."

He added, however, that "My feeling is, we probably are going to have to look at cuts or slow-downs. I don't feel we want to put a burden on people unfairly, but costs of water and sewer are going to have to be borne by those departments," he said in regard to one of the largest current drains on the general fund, the article continued.

The same issue of the *Herald* announced that the City of Evanston hired a new police lieutenant. The article stated, *Police Chief Dennis Harvey said that Evanston, taking a cue from Rock Springs and other cities of similar population, decided to scrap plans to hire an assistant police chief and elected instead to fill a new "Administrative Lieutenant" slot on the city's police force.*

Harvey announced that Larry Levens, a 39-year-old veteran of the Ana-heim, CA Police Department will assume the same rank as two lieutenants currently supervising the patrol and detective divisions of the city's 30-man police force, he added.

Also in November, the *Herald* ran an article stating, *Evanston Housing Authority Director Julie Lehman went on record on Wednesday evening before the Evanston City Council to advise them of the "potential" for creating "an excessive amount of low to moderate rental housing" in the city with the construction of both private and city supported projects.*

Lehman told the council that the Evanston Housing Authority (EHA) was starting on its low-cost projects two years behind schedule. "In the meantime," she said, "these private developments have come on board." She stressed the financial responsibility for the EHA projects falls on the city and its tax-payers should the city be unable to fill the units presently planned for construction, the article continued.

❦

The City of Evanston selected the site of the Sulphur Creek Reservoir to enlarge its water storage capacity if a level II feasibility study gained legislative approval to allow for funding of a level III design stage project needed to prepare for construction.

Under consideration since 1981 when the state legislature authorized the Upper Bear River Program, the feasibility study received $400,000 last year in 1982 from the legislature to have the engineering firm of Forsgren and Perkins under take the study. Officer Manager Brian Honey of Forsgren and Perkins said the study was running on schedule and would be ready to submit to the Wyoming Water Development Commission by December 20, 1983 for review.

Sulphur Creek Reservoir presently was for the use of the ranchers for irrigation purposes, but with the City of Evanston getting involved the reservoir would be triple the size it is at the present, giving the city ownership of 2/3s of the reservoir. This would give Evanston a capacity of water badly needed, and would give them the opportunity to get rid of the water wells located in various sites within the city.

In 1983, in spite of the apparently big drop in revenue, the City of Evanston had permitted approximately 235 building permits to be issued, even though there was every indication that the big "Oil Boom" was on the downhill side, and city revenues had been dropping for several months.

The year ended with the issue of legalizing fireworks so that certain areas within the boundaries of the city could be annexed coming up in December, and a large opposition to the issuance of Industrial Development Revenue Bonds for the construction of the proposed "Pines of Yellow Creek" apartments.

Mayor Gene Martin asked the developers of the "Pines" whether they were aware that the motel and hotel business was down in Evanston, leaving 427 vacancies in the city.

However, during the next year both issues, the legalization of fireworks for sale and use in the city limits, and the Industrial Revenue Bonds, were approved by the city council. But the legalization of the use of fireworks was limited to just certain days, and during certain holidays.

CHAPTER 18

1984....1984 appeared to be starting out with quite a number of concerns. First, Mayor Martin's administration hired two high-paid outsiders, Mr. John Hendrickson as Evanston City Administrator from Soda Springs, Idaho, and Mr. Lee Galeotos as Evanston's Director of Administrative Services to help run the city. Why they needed this kind of personnel to run the city was beyond me. They already had a City Treasurer, a City Clerk, a Budget Officer and an Administrative Assistant to the Mayor that helped me run my administration in a good manner.

In January of 1983 the City of Evanston was running well and we had handed over the reins to Mayor Martin's administration in a good working condition. The budget was well balanced with a sizeable carryover, the departments were working well together and communicating with each other, and the department heads were reporting to their appointed council members as their liaison to the mayor and full council. And now after one year, Martin's administration had to reach out and hire additional high-paid employees to get them out of trouble.

In the Letters to the Editor column of the *Uinta County Herald* dated January 11, 1984 was a letter written by Lewis D. Powers. The letter was titled *"Committeeized" Administration,* and read:

> *Dear Editor,*
>
> *In one of your front page articles, it states that Mayor Gene Martin began to "professionalize" his administration upon being elected. "Professionalize" is the incorrect word. I believe that what Mayor Martin is doing is to "committeeize" and "consultize" his administration.*

Evanston city government has become a fruitful ground for consultants, particularly those in the field of administration and urban renewal architecture.

There are probably more committees appointed so that the mayor can avoid decision-making than any other place in Wyoming. The "Messiahs" have rolled into town to save us all.

Too bad Mayor Martin doesn't believe in the old adage: "The buck stops here." In his case, the "buck" is spent on a consultant and the final responsibility rests with a committee.

Sincerely,
Lewis D. Powers

However, in the *Uinta County Herald* of January 13, 1984, Councilman Rick Sather published a Letter to the Editor rebutting Mr. Powers' letter. Sather's letter stated: *When I came into office there was no coordination between departments. The city had never had a staff meeting involving all the departments and in talking to the department heads, they did not understand administration. Individual department heads were doing a tremendous job within their own departments but had no coordination with the other departments.*

He continued in his letter to say many other things that were not true when he came into office. Mr. Powers's letter was right on. The truth is that after a year of the Martin administration the city had become all screwed up. The new administration didn't understand the word "administration"; that's why they had to bring in all the high-paid outside help, which in the long run only made things worse, which the future will show.

On top of all the additional help the city was bringing in, they still had the Overthrust Industrial Association's Ron Straka helping with the downtown improvement district, and I might say he was doing a terrific job.

However, in all fairness, I would commend Mayor Martin and his administration for keeping all projects going that were started in my term as mayor, as well as those started in previous administrations, such as the airport and the new sewer plant. I know they made a few changes, but nothing that was significant, and I praise them for that.

The January 25th issue of the *Herald* stated in an article that Mayor Martin was not going to re-appoint Georgia Harvey to the Evanston Planning and Zoning Commission, who at present was the Chairperson of the Board. The article read: *"Conflict of Interest" is the official word from Mayor Gene Martin concerning his decision to replace Planning and Zoning Chairperson Georgia Harvey effective the first of March. She is the wife of Police Chief Dennis Harvey.*

Maybe he was right, but I failed to see a conflict just because her husband happens to be the chief of police. What has that got to do with the Planning and Zoning Commission? But then, that's the way his administration did business.

The January 20th issue of the *Herald* reported that revenue shortfalls were threatening the city's budget for the first five months of the fiscal year, but had begun reversing themselves with a two percent increase in revenues recorded in December 1983.

The article stated that *Evanston's Director of Administrative Services Lee Galeotos said the increase, along with more austere spending practices, has reduced the city's projected $1.4 million deficit, based on November 1983 figures, to a new $920,963 level in the city's latest fiscal year.*

The *Herald* went on to indicate that the deficit in revenues was still projected because of the drop in the economy since the oil and gas boom apparently came to an end.

Ron Straka, a design consultant, was brought to Evanston in 1982, contracted and paid for by the Overthrust Industrial Association, to assist the City in their downtown planning and designing. In the February 1, 1984 issue of the *Uinta County Herald,* an article stated that STRAKA THREATENS TO LEAVE TOWN.

The article went on: *Noting that he thinks a city council "vote of confidence" is in order for his unfinished Evanston downtown plan, design consultant Ron Straka says that despite assurances of sufficient funding to continue his work, he may leave Evanston permanently to fulfill "other commitments."*

Apparently his contract with O.I.A. had expired and if he was expected to finish the plan, it would be up to the city council to extend funding for it. Now, Straka had been brought into Evanston and paid for by the O.I.A. in the late part of 1982, which gave him over a year to do the job. Why it would take that long to complete the planning program that had already been started by the previous administration and the Urban Renewal Agency was beyond me, unless it was because he couldn't get enough support and confidence from the mayor and his new council. And that would not surprise me one bit the way Martin was running the city.

The article of February 1st went on to say, *Straka says a host of other projects requested by the city officials has delayed completion of the study. Thursday evening he presented at a city council work session proposals for completing the project at city expense.*

Mayor Gene Martin and the two councilmen present [apparently four members of the council were absent], *along with Urban Renewal Board members, agreed to recommend Straka's 50 day – $25,000 proposal which will be presented to the full council for vote Feb. 8. The proposal was the most extensive and costly of three alternatives offered by the Boulder, Colorado urban designer.*

The article continued: *Straka said that other commitments place him in a "state of limbo" because the council will not be able to vote on his proposal for two weeks. He said that "you're not sure how enthusiastic they [council members] are... I think what urban renewal needs is a vote of confidence from the council." He added, "If they are going to make urban renewal work in the '80s, they have to make it a strong agency. The issue that has to come out is, 'Where is city council in terms of the agency?' "*

He also lashed out at unnamed city officials for alleged failure to follow up commitments to the Urban Renewal Board.

"We were promised a lot of things that we didn't get," Straka said. Among those, he said, was hiring an acting director of the Urban Renewal Board who would have provided 75 percent of his—and staff's—time to the completion of the downtown plan. "The reason we've stopped is council hasn't transferred funds and there is no way to guarantee they will," he said.

The article stated: *Mayor Martin said between now and the next council meeting he planned on getting together with members of the council to apprise them of his position. "The big thing I'm after is a completed plan. That's number one."* In that same issue of the Herald, there was an article titled: GALEOTOS WARNS OF DEFICIT.

The article started with: *Facing a possible unbudgeted $25,000 expenditure to finish Evanston's downtown plan, officials at Thursday's city council work session were told by Director of Administrative Services Lee Galeotos that the city government is going to have to "pay the piper" to balance its budget.*

Galeotos told Mayor Gene Martin and councilmen David Bills and Rick Sather that decision-makers should consider every option for saving money, in light of the city's current deficit spending course. "Someday we are going to have to pay the piper," Galeotos said. Cities are prohibited by state law to end the fiscal year (July 1984) with budget deficits.

However, the article continued: *The three elected officials agreed, not without reservations, to recommend consultant Ron Straka's $25,000 proposal to finish the downtown plan in 50 days. The council will vote on the proposal Feb. 8.*

On February 3rd, the *Uinta County Herald* ran an article titled, COUNCILMEN HAVE RESERVATIONS — UNCERTAIN ABOUT COMMITTING $25,000. The article went on: *Some city council members have expressed some reservations over committing the City of Evanston to spending an additional $25,000 for completing the city's downtown plan.*

The article continued: *"I think he's holding us hostage. Either we come up with $25,000 or you won't have a plan," Councilman Rick Sather said. He added, "It's really hard for me to make these comments. I've been fighting for urban renewal for the last 10 to 12 years and to criticize something I've been so much involved with bothers me."*

Of course, Rick Sather is a downtown merchant and has a right to be concerned with trying to save the downtown area. I didn't blame him a bit for that, because I always felt that downtown Evanston was the "Heart of the City," and it should be improved and preserved the best way possible.

The article of February 3rd continued: *If Straka were not able to finish the plan, Sather said, "I think we've got the staff at the city who can take it and run with it. I think we can pick up the pieces and try to make it work" without Straka finishing the plan for the city.*

Should this take place, the responsibility for completing the downtown plan would fall on the shoulders of the Community Development Director Bruce Wright and his staff. Commenting on the possibility of being requested to complete the plan, Wright said, "My only comment is—if council elects us to take it over, we'll arrange our priorities." He noted, "The ideas were in written form before I came here. The framework for the downtown plan and Front St. district plan are already adopted as part of the Comprehensive Plan. They were adopted a while ago. The reason we asked Ron (Straka) to finish the details is because of staff priorities," the article continued.

There seemed to be a question concerning the method that the City of Evanston officials were using to hire the new administrative positions. In the *Uinta County Herald* of February 17, 1984 there was an article titled, CITY HIRING: INCONSISTANT BUT LEGAL – COUNTY ATTORNEY PROVIDES OPINION.

The article went on: *Uinta County Attorney Scott Smith said Wednesday that he found "inconsistency" in the way the city has appointed its administrators but has discovered nothing illegal about recent city hiring practices.*

Smith, responding to an Evanston League of Women Voters request for an opinion on city appointments, noted that "the city has a great deal of discretion in making appointments."

The article continued: *League members pointed to last year's appointments of City Administrator John Hendrickson and Director of Administrative Services Lee Galeotos as possibly departing from established precedents.*

Hendrickson was appointed by city council resolution and unlike other more traditional city positions, for the city administrator a job description is not included in the Evanston City Code which itself was adopted by city ordinance.

The Code contains descriptions for several administrative positions including city treasurer, clerk and engineer. Other administrative posts, created since Gene Martin became Evanston Mayor in January 1983, are noted in the revised code but job descriptions for those positions are apparently not part of the document.

The article concluded: *Smith added that "appointments are the function of the council. The form is secondary." According to the county attorney, "The bottom line is there is no precedent set but it (appointment by resolution or other means) is inconsistent with previous city appointments. Because of the inconsistency, it leads to confusion.*"

In the fiscal year of 1983-1984, all the shortfalls, the drop in revenues and increase in change orders were causing many problems for the city in trying to complete the projects that had been committed to. However, spending big bucks for additional administrative personnel isn't really needed and isn't helping the matter, especially when you already have good people employed that can do just as good a job, if not better, because they were in a position where they know the city and its problems better than outsiders.

And there were problems, such as the *Uinta County Herald's* report concerning the Personnel Manual and the schedule of wages when it was brought up for review. According to the news article the council had agreed to spend $10,000 on another study to another consulting firm to update the manual.

Spending this kind of money was ridiculous. The present employee manual had only been completed a few years ago. Before that there never was an employee manual even available. Why contract with an expensive firm when, with a little common sense, the council with the extra ordinary high-paid staff could amend the manual where needed?

The new proposed Personnel Manual apparently was adopted by the mayor and city council, causing some employees to get a drop in pay while others got an increase. Because of this there were a number of employees very disgruntled with the new plan, according to the newspaper, and there was also confusion among some of the council members.

Sometimes the old adage, *"If it's not broken, why fix it?"* is something to think about. In February the issue of keeping the U.S. Post Office in the downtown area came up again and was getting closer to being a reality. Although there had been an official offer to the U.S. Postal Department of 5 acres of free ground if they would consider building the new post office in the Yellow Creek Center area, according to the *Uinta County Herald* issue of February 22nd it was pretty much decided that the new office would be kept in the downtown area as had been the plan all along.

When Administrative Assistant Steve Snyder and I went to San Francisco during the last part of 1982 to talk to the U.S. Postal Service about keeping the post office in the downtown area, they told us that they would do everything they could to do so.

Block 13 of the Original Town of Evanston had been Evanston first choice, because It appeared to be the most blighted area in downtown, because a number of the buildings were rental units that were in bad condition. Some were even vacant and were real eyesores. Block 13 is also the block where the Old Town Hall is located. The plan was to clear the entire block except for the town hall, which would help to keep some history on the block and preserve the Old Town Hall.

The second choice to locate the P.O. was Block 6 of the Original Town of Evanston, but it was more expensive because there were many homeowners and businesses that would have to be bought out or relocated, which would be much more expensive than Block 13.

However, when the City's Public Works moved it left quite a large parcel of property vacant that was already owned by the city, as well as the alley way. But in my and my administration's opinion, either location would have been sufficient.

At this time, in 1984, Mayor Gene Martin and his administration were having a lot of opposition, but also a lot of folks in favor, of keeping the P.O. downtown. Those in opposition were mostly against it because of the free-land offer that had been made by the developers and investors of the Yellow Creek Shopping Center and area. And it was quite obvious that they were offering the free property for selfish reasons, but you couldn't blame them for that and it was a sweet deal.

Nonetheless, that was also the same reason why some of the city officials wanted it kept in the downtown area: because some of them had businesses downtown and also owned property on one of the chosen blocks. But in the end the City Council and the Postal Department decided that the post office would remain downtown. In my "horse manure opinion" (as Dennis Boal would say) I believe it was a good decision for the entire City of Evanston.

But, as I was accused of having so many "conflicts of interest" during my mayoral term, this administration is no different. So be it!

In March the Public Safety Building was completed, and now we had a new police station to be proud of. After final inspection it was said that the building was structured with "quality materials," with electronic doors and surveillance cameras throughout the building for security purposes, and bulletproof glass, one inch thick, between the waiting room and receptionist-surveillance monitoring area.

On March 21st the *Uinta County Herald* ran an article titled, CITY STILL WAITS FOR AMOCO-O.I.A. ASSISTANCE: The article went on to read: *Overthrust Industrial Association (O.I.A.) President David Wight said there is still information that needs to be collected "relative to projects and income" of the City of Evanston before officials here will receive a final mitigation offer from the consortium of oil producing and service companies.*

The article continued: *Wight said he expected an offer to be forthcoming in the next two to three weeks. City Administrator John Hendrickson said "approximately $900,000" in requests were presented Feb. 16th in Denver. Included in the city's "wish list" were funds for city parks, storm water and sewer systems and a computer management system.*

Hendrickson said that "my indications at this time are that we certainly will get what we asked for on the water projects and storm water projects... On the other things, I'm not sure."

Wight said the O.I.A. could be looking to enter into a "caretaker role" once it has addressed these issues. According to Wight, "The only requests in front of the O.I.A. of significance are from the city." He said the O.I.A. has concluded most of its participation in county projects.

The article concluded: *The caretaker role Wight spoke of will include keeping the information arm of the O.I.A. intact for several more months as well as continuing to monitor projects partially funded by the O.I.A..*

Other problems concerned the new personnel study that the city was adopting. According to the March 24th issue of the *Herald*, the city council voted during their March 14th meeting to amend the resolution outlining the method of implementing the study.

The resolution as amended would give 17 employees pay cuts, while 61 employees would get a raise, and the remaining 50 employees' pay would remain at their present rate of pay, according to City Administrator John Hendrickson, the Herald read.

Some employees said their concerns included a prevailing sense that their value to the city had been reduced to nothing more than a monetary consideration, void of any regard for their loyalty or dedication.

City Operations Supervisor Allen Kennedy acknowledged the general attitude of employees. "We've got a lot of unhappy guys...in every department. Other employees said they have seen a work slow-down as a result of ill feelings."

Underlying all of the sentiment is the employees' belief that they were not given any time to evaluate or comment on the study. City Engineer Marion Malnar said, "After the Employee Plan came from the consultants it was passed without input by employees or staff."

Apparently, City Administrator John Hendrickson was also talking about a 10% cut in city personnel. The Herald continued: Public Works Director Wayne Shepherd this was a "big concern" of his, noting that he doubted the residents in the city could be given the same level of service as a result of this decision.

Hendrickson said, "I guarantee you that if I feel strongly that by cutting that number of employees we'll damage service to residents, I'll let that be known," the Herald concluded.

It seemed to me that the best way the city could adjust their budget to fix a deficit would be to start at the top. At this time Mayor Martin's administration was very top-heavy, so if they were to lay off someone they should start with the city administrator himself, because they still had Steve Snyder as Administrative Assistant to the Mayor. Why do they need an administrator over him? He did a good job for me when I was mayor.

Later, in the Uinta County Herald issue of April 13th an article by Greg Livovich stated: The third incarnation of the City of Evanston Personnel Wage and Salary Schedule passed the city council by a narrow 3-2 margin...and drew fire from one councilman who said the continuing controversy over the plan is damaging employee morale.

David Bills, who along with Russ "Bub" Albrecht voted against the resolution, which is a compromise of recommendations by a consultant who *analyzed city wages, said after Wednesday's meeting that "my feeling is there has been a mistake. It doesn't seem to be working."*

Bills also noted that pay cuts given some employees may have an adverse effect on productivity. "We've hammered some of our people and hurt morale," he said. *"We are a service agency and if morale is down and it affects productivity, then the citizens suffer,"* the article concluded.

The *Uinta County Herald* issue of April 27th headlined: MAYOR USES VETO POWER. The article went on: *Gene Martin tried his mayoral veto power on for size at Wednesday's Evanston City Council session – and with some help from a 4-3 sustaining vote from the council – managed to override an amended raise for a handful of city employees whose wages were recently slashed following the city's controversial personnel study.*

The *Herald* went on to report that Councilman Arnie Morgan sponsored an amendment that would have lowered the pay cut maximum to $1,200 annually per employee in place of the $3,000 maximum that was presently the amount stated in the resolution at this time. Apparently there was no maximum pay cut in the original resolution and one employee would have lost $300 per month ($3,600 per year). Morgan's amendment would set a maximum so that pay cuts wouldn't be more than $1,200 annually, or $100.00 per month.

But according to the article, Councilman Ron Davis, who originally supported the amendment, joined the mayor's camp to support the veto and voted to go along with Mayor Martin, Councilmen Voss, and Sather, while Albrecht, Bills and Morgan failed in the attempt to override the veto. The vote was 3-3, without the mayor voting, a tie vote, causing the attempt to override the veto to fail.

The *Herald* went on: *Mayor Martin said* [concerning Morgan's amendment] *that "if we're going to have this brought up it should be brought out during a work session." Before the council meeting Martin remarked about the poor attendance at work sessions, noting that councilmen Sather and Bills were the only two members of the six-man council to maintain a regular attendance at the sessions.*

During the next council meeting of May 9th a letter of resignation from Councilman Arnie Morgan was read. He was not present, but his resignation was accepted.

During this meeting the fourth and latest attempt to amend the resolution to alter employee salaries, proposed by Councilman Lance Voss, passed the council with a vote of 4-2 with Mayor Gene Martin and Councilman Rick Sather being the two dissenting votes.

The mayor also tried to veto Voss's amendment which limited pay cuts to a maximum of $1,800 annually, but this time the mayor's veto was overridden by a 4-1 vote with Sather, who said he was concerned about overspending, offering Martin's only support. The mayor, by law, cannot vote on his own veto.

Councilman Russ Albrecht, who had supported every measure to lighten the employees' pay cuts, questioned Sather's commitment to limiting spending when he has voted consistently to support the city's expensive effort to keep the U.S. Post office in downtown Evanston. The *Uinta County Herald* of May 16th read, *Sather, who owns downtown property and excused himself from the discussion and vote on the city's plan to provide $800,000 for a downtown improvement district, told Albrecht to "vote your conscience" concerning employee salaries. Albrecht responded, "You don't have to vote, sucker* [concerning Sather's conflict]. *You go out there in the hallway."*

This resolution to accept the proposed personnel study, the maximum of $1,800 per annual pay cut, finally passed as amended after all the dissension. The *Herald* reported: *Mayor Martin, explaining why he chose to try and veto the measure, said that "we went over this personnel study until I'm sick of it."*

The following information was taken from the *Uinta County Herald* issue dated April 18, 1984:

On April 15, 1984, 35 year old Linnea Miller Overy Cheatham was found dead at her home in Evanston. Her widowed mother, Edith Miller, said that although she did not at the time suspect foul play, she requested that Evanston mortician and Uinta County Coroner John Crandall arrange an autopsy of the victim because of the suddenness of her daughter's death. Mrs. Miller said her daughter had a history of heart trouble and had previously undergone open heart surgery.

An autopsy conducted that afternoon revealed the victim died of suffocation after receiving a "blunt force" to the rear cranium, which resulted in a massive blood clot and bleeding within the brain. It was also discovered that more than 100 bruises were counted on the victim's body and an affidavit filed in Uinta County Court noted "large severe bruising about the hands" of the victim.

Her 53-year-old husband Lentz Cheatham was later charged with second degree homicide in Uinta County Court. Prosecutors said Cheatham admitted to knocking Linnea down and leaving her lying several hours in the hallway of the couple's home.

According to the court affidavit, Linnea went with her husband Lentz Saturday evening to a fraternal organization banquet at a local restaurant. Witnesses said the couple were seen later that evening at two different private bars and were arguing noticeably during their stay at one of the clubs. This was a shocking thing for Evanston. Both were well known and well respected. Linnea was City Treasurer at the time of her death. I had appointed her as City Treasurer in 1981 during my time as Mayor. At that time she was the widow of Sheriff Larry Overy, who had passed away. She also worked for me as secretary at the Wyoming Railway Car Company (now known as Union Tank Car Company) until I resigned.

I knew Linnea and her family very well and was pretty shook up and surprised when I had heard what had happened. I was also well acquainted with Lentz. At first I couldn't believe what I was hearing and what I read in the newspaper; it just didn't seem possible.

Lentz Cheatham came to Evanston in the mid-1970s as a truck driver for the Time-D.C. Trucking Company with his family, but had later divorced his previous wife and started courting Linnea and then married her.

Lentz admitted to beating her up and the courts found him guilty and sent him to the Wyoming State Penitentiary for many years. I don't recall the exact amount of time he got sentenced to, but I do know he ended up in prison. Conviction of second degree homicide carried a 20 year to life sentence.

However, in the June 20th issue of the *Herald* it read: CHARGES AGAINST CHEATHAM REDUCED.

The article went on to read: *Charges against Lentz Cheatham, accused last month of murdering his wife, Linnea Overy Cheatham, were reduced Monday from second degree homicide to involuntary manslaughter.*

The issue of the *Herald* indicated that the involuntary manslaughter would carry a much lesser charge of one to twenty years.

It was a terrible tragedy and a shocking thing to happen. It ruined the lives of two people. Linnea a good person who was well liked and respected, and Lentz, who always seemed to be very likeable, but surprisingly turned out to be a different person that no one suspected.

On May 9th, 1984, Mayor Martin and the Evanston City Council adopted Resolution 84-55, titled:

RESOLUTION NO. 84-55
NOTICE TO ALL PERSONS LIABLE TO AS-
SESSMENTS FOR IMPROVEMENTS
OF MAIN, 12TH, CENTER AND 11TH
STREETS (BLOCK 13) AND ACQUISITION
AND SITE CLEARING OF BLOCK 13, AND
PARKING LOT CONSTRUCTION NEAR
11TH STREET AND CENTER STREET AND
9TH STREET AND CENTER STREET
IN EVANSTON, WYOMING. THE GOVERN-
ING BODY OF THE CITY OF
EVANSTON, IN UINTA COUNTY, STATE OF
WYOMING, ON THE 9TH OF MAY,
1984, PASSED THE FOLLOWING RESOLUTION
OF INTENTION.

The resolution was passed. Block 13 had been acceptable to the U.S. Postal Department. However, three months later, on August 23rd, 1984, Mayor Martin and the Evanston City Council adopted an amendment to Resolution 84-55 that was titled the follows:

RESOLUTION NO. 84-98
A RESOLUTION AMENDING RESOLUTIONS
NO. 84-55 AND 84-85;
CORRECTING AND CHANGING THE DIS-
TRICT BOUNDARIES AND PROPERTY TO BE
ASSESSED IN THE PROPOSED DOWNTOWN IM-
PROVEMENT DISTRICT.

Resolution 84-98 amending Resolution 84-55 enabled the City of Evanston to select Block 6 for the site for the new post office. This didn't bother me that much because I felt that either block would have been sufficient, but what bothered me was the fact that all the owners of Block 13 had already made arrangements to move, only to be disappointed when the news came to them about the change of locations.

I can understand why the owners got upset, but what made me more concerned was that there was one hell of a "conflict of interest" – one of the owners of property in Block 6, Rick Sather, was a member of the city council. He owned a rental building that had a business in front and several residential rental units in back, and in addition, Mayor Martin owned property downtown that was located in the improvement district.

I can't blame Sather and Martin too much for this, because I know they both abstained from any discussion or voting by leaving the room, but I did the same thing and Mr. Sather and Mayor Martin accused me, during the campaign, of conflict of interest. They also accused me of using the mayor's office for personal gain. I was getting rich by being the mayor. What were they doing?

This didn't bother me all that much, but then they told the public that some owners in Block 13 were holding out for too much money and that Block 6 would be a lot less. I don't think they were telling the entire truth. Anyway, that is what I was told by several people owning property on Block 13, and I had good reason to believe them.

I was told that city officials didn't even try to negotiate with the two owners that had asked for more than the appraised price.

The city just dropped Block 13 and told the public that Block 6 was less money, but the fact was that there were about four or five businesses on Block 6 that would have had to be bought out and that sure as hell wouldn't have been very cheap. But, it was true that there was a sizeable piece of property that was owned by the city, plus the alleyway.

However, the post office would remain in the downtown area which was what most folks wanted. The City of Evanston was successful in getting the Postal Department to keep the post office in the downtown area. I was very much in favor of that.

But the Downtown Improvement District, which included the new post office and parking lots backed by the city, drew mixed reviews from affected business owners located in the district, and caused a lot of dissension from those that would be assessed for the $800,000 bonding of the district.

According to the *Uinta County Herald* in May, *The council voted 3-0 to endorse the plan and continue a public hearing process regarding the proposed improvement.* Apparently the vote was made without a quorum according to the *Herald's* announcement – only 3 votes when it takes 4 council members, including the mayor, to make a quorum. Something was wrong!!

In the latter part of May 1984, the Overthrust Industrial Association (O.I.A.) announced that they were starting to phase out their activities, proclaiming that their impact mitigation goals in Evanston had been accomplished. At the May 23rd City Council meeting O.I.A. President Owen Murphy of Chevron U.S.A. awarded the City of Evanston an additional $250,000 and announced that they'd be "phasing down" activities here.

Most of the projects O.I.A. was involved in were either completed or close to it; the Recreation Center, the Human Service Center, the Public Safety Building, the new fire hall, and other projects that O.I.A. had put funds into.

Thank God we had formed the O.I.A., because without it we would never have had the Evanston Recreation Center or some of the other facilities that we now have. Since it was built the Evanston Recreation Center has been very popular with a lot of folks.

When Amoco Production Company announced that they would be willing to give up their maintenance shop located on Allegiance Circle at a reasonable price to the City of Evanston to be used for the Evanston Public Works building, it was a good thing. Because, now the city didn't have to worry about building their public works facility in the Hamblin Park area.

After the resignation of Arnie Morgan from the city council, Mayor Martin, in a late meeting in May, appointed Dale Davenport in place of Morgan as councilman representing Ward 2. Davenport would replace Morgan for the remaining time left in his term, which I believe would be through December 31, 1984. If Davenport wanted to try for another term as a member of the city council, he would then have to file for election before the filing deadline, which would probably be sometime in July of 1984.

Davenport, with a unanimous vote from the council to confirm the mayor's appointment, was president of Rocky Mountain Engineering and Surveying Company. Although the company did slightly less than $40,000 of business with the city the previous year, Davenport said that his company would continue to bid on projects when the City of Evanston called for bids for the purpose of engineering and surveying, regardless of his position on the city council. But he also stated that he would abstain from voting on any project that his company may bid on.

It seemed that the "boom" days were definitely over, and we were now in a "bust" period. On the downhill side of one of the largest boom periods in the history of Wyoming.

People were leaving. Their jobs were finished. They came with the oil boom and paid high prices for their homes with very high interest rates. When they left, they didn't list their homes with any agency, because values had dropped and there was no use trying to sell their homes. Most of them had left their property, causing the mortgage holders, mostly guaranteed by the Federal Housing Authority (FHA) to foreclose through the U.S. Department of Housing and Urban Development (HUD).

Very few people that were leaving Evanston were listing their homes for sale, which hurt the real estate business in the area, including all real estate agencies. Uinta Realty was already hurting because of my term as Mayor.

At that time real estate agencies were doing their own closing. I, as broker, closed two outgoing oil service company sales that were moving out because of the boom being over. When I closed on their properties I made a terrible mistake and accepted their personal and business checks at closing. After these people that owned the companies already left the country, the checks that I had taken at closing were returned from their banks, one for insufficient funds and one for "stop payment," the accounts were eventual just closed. These checks were both written on out-of-state banks. Trying to collect on them was useless; I didn't even know where the people were now located.

I had gotten to know both of the owners of these companies pretty well, and thought they were good people that could be trusted, but boy, was I ever wrong. Both checks were for substantial amounts and really hurt U.R.I. financially. I had taken total responsibility and made sure the buyers of the properties were taken care of.

Folks were leaving Evanston and a number of them were just leaving their homes to the mortgage holders, because it would have been tough for them to try selling their home without having to pay out of pocket. House values had been dropping because the boom was over and we were now in a bust situation. The economy was declining and not many people were coming to Evanston, but those who were coming in were buying reasonable priced homes or building their own homes.

Later on folks started to buy the foreclosures, but when a bank or lender forecloses on a property it takes years before the property comes on the market. Most of the foreclosures were by HUD, some of them were by the Veterans Administration (VA) and some were by banks and other loan agencies.

When people left their homes and they were under foreclosure, some of the homes were left dirty and damaged, some in very bad condition. Therefore, before the mortgage holder would put the property on the market they would have the unit cleaned and repaired where needed.

Most houses needed cleaning before going on the market, so Sandy and my daughter-in-law, Tammy (Tib's wife), started up a cleaning business to help our families financially, because the real estate business wasn't doing very well.

They cleaned a lot of houses for a few years until Tib and Tammy decided to leave Evanston for work elsewhere. Then Peggy Harvey, taking the place of Tammy, joined Sandy cleaning houses for the next few years.

In the meantime I was working hard trying to make a living at the real estate agency, U.R.I., but things weren't looking too good. I had to replace my son Tib, who was running the Lyman office. Broker Gary Hollis took over from Tib.

In July 1984 the Greater Evanston Development Corp. started up again. I was still President and I still had my Board of Directors. During the busy "boom" times we kind of went into a recess because there didn't seem to be a need for the development company at that time, but there was now that the boom was over.

Bill Frisby, who came to Evanston with his brother Bob to work during the oil and gas boom, approached me about a new program that the United States Congress had passed that the G.E.D.C. could get certified for. He said the new program was referred to as the SBA-504 program under the Small Business Investment Act and that our development company was qualified to get its certification.

Previously we had been qualified for the SBA-502 program through the Small Business Administration (S.B.A.), and had used it quite frequently in the 1970s until the oil and gas boom hit the area. Frisby had become aware of the 504 program, which we hadn't been notified about yet. When he mentioned it to me, he said that Evanston's development company could qualify for the new 504 loan program. It appeared to be a better program than the 502, and the S.B.A. would be the participating federal agency to entice new businesses and industry to come to Evanston and Western Wyoming, which was the territory that the G.E.D.C. was qualified to serve.

Frisby asked me if he could meet with the board, and said that he had a proposition for us if we were interested in getting active again. The development company had a large balance of over $70,000 in the First National Bank (now known as the First Bank) that had been sitting there drawing interest, because we hadn't done anything to encourage business or industry the past four or five years.

If there ever was a time that we needed a program like the 502 or the 504 it was now, because a lot of businesses were hurting at the present, and a lot of folks were leaving. Evanston's economy was worse now than it was when the railroad pulled their engine crew's dispatch office out of town and closed their roundhouse and railroad repair shops, because our city limits had expanded to four times the size that it had been, and our population had tripled.

Frisby met with the G.E.D.C. board and explained the new program to us and told us that we needed to become a certified development company. The board members (luckily we had a quorum) were quite impressed with Frisby and were ready to listen to his proposition.

Frisby's proposition was that if G.E.D.C. could send him to a S.B.A. seminar to get certified for the 504 program, and then hire him as director of the company at a fair salary for at least a year, he would work really hard to get more commercial and industrial companies to come to Evanston and western Wyoming to improve the economy.

The board hashed his proposition over after he left and decided that, as we had the money, we would take him up on his deal, and hoped he would do a good job. We figured if he got the 504 program working in Evanston at all, it was worth a try. That was what the G.E.D.C. was for and we had the finances to try his plan for a couple of years, and more if he was successful: every time he got a loan through for a new company to come to western Wyoming, G.E.D.C. got a fee which was based on the amount of the loan, to be used for operating purposes.

So the Greater Evanston Development Company went into a contract with Bill Frisby, hoping to improve our economy as well as that of the four other counties that our certification would cover.

On July 26, 1984 the development company received our certification for the Small Business Administration 504 program authorizing us to serve Uinta, Sweetwater, Sublette, Lincoln and Teton counties. Frisby would retain his office in Evanston, but would be working all of the five counties in western Wyoming. The rest of the state of Wyoming was served by the Frontier Certified Development Company in Casper, Wyoming.

We were now considered the Greater Evanston Development Company, dba Western Wyoming Certified Development Company. This was a good move for Evanston and western Wyoming for the next four or five years, but after a while we ran out of money and had to break our contract with Frisby. During the time Frisby was director he brought several businesses to Evanston and a few to Jackson, Wyoming, but not enough to keep us going much longer. After running out of funds we let Frisby go, and dissolved the development corporation and had no other dealings with the S.B.A.

During Frisby's contract he was able to bring in the Fireside Lanes, a bowling alley, through the 504 program, plus the Sun Ridge Deli and Gas Center, located on Yellow Creek Road across from Smith's Food and Drug.

He also got a 504 loan to get Smith's Auto Body Shop going, now known as T Bar S Body Shop, and the Revelli Auto Repair Shop on Bear River Drive, now occupied by Plain's Tire Company, and several other businesses that helped employment in Evanston.

I don't feel that hiring Frisby for the four to five years he was here was a total loss. He did get a few new companies that helped the employment situation and upgraded the economy quite a bit over the years. I just felt bad that we had to let him go because of a lack of funds, but the economy looked much better than it had been before hiring him.

Among many problems the city was having, were the muss and fuss within the city administration over the new personnel manual, with the employees' positions being reshuffled; all the pros and cons concerning the post office; council members' heavy absenteeism at meetings; and the dissatisfaction and lack of interest of some of the city officials. As a result, the city was starting to lose some of their top employees.

In early September of that year, Wayne Shepherd, who had been hired by my administration as the city engineer in 1982, was switched from city engineer to public works director back to what they called "staff engineer." He became so disgusted with the way things were being run he decided to quit. In his letter he stated that he was resigning because of his lack of "optimism" and other reasons. His letter of resignation, read by Mayor Martin, was accepted by the council.

The September 5th issue of the *Uinta County Herald* printed an article titled, HENDRICKSON OUSTER BLOCKED DURING SPECIAL COUNCIL MEETING. The article written by Greg Livovich went on: *A surprise effort to display city council support for firing City Administrator John Hendrickson backfired Friday after two angry councilmen tried to force adjournment of a special council session before a vote on the measure could be taken.*

Ward III Councilman David Bill's "non-binding" resolution recommending that Hendrickson be terminated as city administrator was tabled at the request of Mayor Gene Martin until the Sept. 12 regular council meeting.

The *Herald's* article continued: *A motion to table until Sept. 12 was passed 4-2 with the support of Davis, Bills, Martin and Sather while Voss and Davenport cast negative votes.*

During the meeting there was more discussion, not so much about terminating Hendrickson, but about the way Councilman Bills presented his resolution without any prior discussion or notification to the rest of the council members. This made the council members very irate, causing a very "hard-nosed" discussion during that same meeting.

Hendrickson remained as the city administrator for the remainder of the year, hoping to get re-appointed in 1985. There were many hard feelings within the council concerning keeping Hendrickson on board, and there was a very good chance that he would not get re-appointed the coming year.

My personal feelings had been all along that I didn't feel that there was a need for all the "top" city hall employees that Martin had hired, or an out-of-town public works director. After all, they still had Steve Snyder and Allen Kennedy, two employees who knew more about what the city needed and where the city was going than anyone else.

Evanston was considered a Strong mayor/council type government, and there was no need to change it. It is my opinion that the mayor/council system is the best type of government for a small city. That makes the mayor the top administrator and that should be "where the buck stops," because the mayor is elected by the people, and he or she should be the one that has to answer directly to the people.

On Saturday, September 29th the new $3.9 million Evanston Recreation Center was officially opened and dedicated. Both Mayor Martin and I attended and spoke at the ceremony. I was very pleased to hear some of the remarks made by the city dignitaries, and I was quite surprise with the number of Evanston citizens that attended the dedication. I was very glad to see how pleased those in attendance were, especially after all the hell I went through concerning the center during the last election.

The Recreation Center was a big asset for the community and one of the busiest public facilities in Evanston. I was very pleased with it and I really appreciated the way Parks and Recreation Director Dennis Poppinga operated it. His staff, under his supervision, put together some great programs that included folks of all ages over the years.

1984 was another election year and three members of the city council would be up for re-election. Those council members were David Bills, Dale Davenport and Russell "Bub" Albrecht. Apparently, Davenport and Albrecht had announced that they would not be running for re-election this election year.

This was also a Presidential election year, and President Ronald Reagan would be running for another term. He had been a good president and had brought the country out of the terrible recession that the country was in when he took office.

In the meantime the city council was meeting regularly and having a lot of disagreement over issues. Because of the new census estimate, Evanston became qualified for several additional liquor licenses, causing a tremendous amount of controversy over where these licenses should go.

The Evanston Post, October 4, 1984 Section 1 Page 8

the
inquiring
post

The Question:

"what do you think of evanston's new recreation facility?"

"how do you feel about the rate structure?"

sarah lee	jackie dean	debbie ludwick	gary brown
"Now that it is finally finished, it appears to be well planned to facilitate a lot of people's needs. I do wish they had a lane for lap swim. As far as the rates, I think they had to do what they had to do, and it is a lot more than we had before."	"I think it's really neat, but I do think the rates are too high. It's about time Evanston had something like this. After I run tomorrow morning on the indoor track maybe I'll feel better about the rates."	"I think It's wonderful, a very nice facility; there are so many different activities available. I'm looking forward to using all of them and working out a full program. I don't think the rates are bad, in a few areas a little high-priced."	"The facility is just unbelievable. I'm skeptical about the rates, but I haven't used the center yet. I think the City should be very proud. One thing I'm concerned about is the upkeep and that it stay this nice."
evanston	evanston	evanston	evanston

. . . Evanston Community Recreation

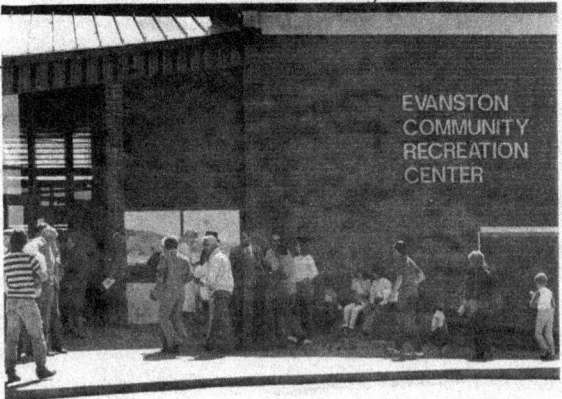

EVANSTON
COMMUNITY
RECREATION
CENTER

". . . we'd like to encourage you to use the facility and improve your quality of life." Dennis Poppinga, Parks & Recreation Director. Post photo by Michael Matts.

Residents head inside to tour the center. **Post** photo by Michael Matts.

Center Is Open To The Public.

The Evanston Post, October 4, 1984 Section 1 Page 9

Fantastic, Beautiful Facility Dedicated

The swimming pool area provides the feeling of being outdoors with the warmth of being indoors. **Post** photo by Michael Matts.

" . . . hope the people realize just how lucky they are. Facility is on par with any . . ."

Dennis Poppinga

By Michael Matts

"We encourage the community to take advantage of their new facility and improve their quality of life," stated Parks and Recreation Director Dennis Poppinga.

"It has been five years from the idea until this opening ceremony. Now that it is open, the ultimate goal is to use the facility to its fullest potential."

Poppinga's remarks were heard during the dedication of the Evanston Community Recreation Center, Saturday, September 29. The center began as an idea in 1979, recommended independently by both the Parks and Recreation Department and the OIA Impact Studies.

Financing for the project was a unique arrangement. "As far as we know, nothing like this has ever been done in the state," stated Steve Snyder, Director of Economic Development and Programs for the City of Evanston. The city applied to the Farm Loan Board for grants and loans on five projects. The five were: the sewer treatment plant, the public works building, the public safety building, the library, and the recreation center.

The Farm Loan Board could not justify funding recreation facilities, and thus a financial package was worked out, where the board would fund the other four projects more heavily, and the city would pick up the majority of the tab on the recreation center.

A final $4.25 million figure for construction, architect fees and equipment was given to the **Post** by Snyder. The city's portion of the bill was $2.2 million. $1.5 million was granted by the OIA and Uinta County contributed $550,000 over two fiscal years.

Most residents that have toured the facility have been overwhelmed by the beauty and quality. "I hope the people realize just how lucky they are. This facility is on par or better than most facilities, public or private, in a large metropolitan area," stated Poppinga.

A staff of eight full-time (four custodians) and 21 part-time employees will be operating the center, at this time.

Operating costs have been estimated between $650,000 and $750,000 per year, and necessitate a rate schedule for use of the facility.

"We spent eight months arriving at our fee schedule. We looked at public and private rates in a five-state area surrounding Wyoming. We realized we didn't have the tax base, for example, that Casper has, to subsidize the operation," Poppinga explained. "The final rate schedule was approved by the city council," he added.

Public confusion over the rates has been common and caused a few problems. "We want the public to call us or come to the front desk at the center. Our staff will gladly explain the rate schedule. The staff can also help people figure out which plan is the best for them," Poppinga said.

Racquetball rates appear to be the most misunderstood in the early going. Many people have thought that they must pay $6 per person for the court, plus $2 per hour for the court. However, if you pay $6, or $3 per person to play racquetball, there are no additional fees and you are free to use the facility after or before playing racquetball.

"Our fee schedule looks complex, at first, but it is built

on a base of one person visiting twice a week at $2 per visit. As you use the facility more, either on a punch pass or a monthly pass, it becomes more economical; the cost per visit decreases," Poppinga explained.

Dedication ceremonies on Saturday included the laying of the cornerstone by the Grand Lodge AF & AM of Wyoming, and the following items were placed in the vault:

List of Grand Officers of AF & AM of Wyoming
List of those who took part in the cornerstone laying
Register of members attending
Copy of the minutes of the laying of the cornerstone
Copy of the **Evanston Post** and the **Uinta County Herald**
A 1984 coin
Program for the dedication of the Recreation Center
Schedule of events put on by the Parks and Recreation Board
List of members of the Parks and Recreation Board
List of members of the Evanston City Council
List of Parks and Recreation Staff
List of members of Youth Athletic Board

Also, in re-issuing liquor licenses there was a big protest once again from the neighbors of Whirl Inn and the Boom Town. The city council also issued the first liquor license to a grocery store, a convenience store located south on Wyoming State Highway 150 called Gas & Grits (at present it is The Last Chance). Although I had been against issuing liquor licenses to grocery stores, I knew that sooner or later, it was bound to happen that licenses would eventually be issued to stores selling groceries.

There were also quite a number of folks opposed to the new zoning ordinance. One reason was that they hadn't included any regulations concerning signage in the city. Some members of the commission and the city council thought that it was very important to regulate signage and it should be in the new ordinance, but it was overlooked.However, it will come later.

Overall, folks were just concerned with some of the various regulations within the ordinance, but there is no way you can satisfy everyone. Let the new ordinance get passed and as regulations come up in the future that don't appear to be working is the time when the commission and city council should make their decision on whether or not to amend the ordinance. Chances are there will be very few changes in the ordinance unless there becomes a big economical or political change in the city.

Folks were also very much concerned about the new optional sales tax that would be on the ballot in the November election, and there was still a lot of contention concerning the positions of some employees.

A few years ago the citizens of Uinta County voted for the optional 1% sales tax that was allowed by state law, and it has to be voted on during a general election to have it continue. This is one of those election years that it will have to be voted on again. If the vote is defeated then the cities and counties will no longer receive that funding. This would put an enormous financial burden on the entities in which they would have a very serious budget problem to contend with. The entire 1% optional tax comes back to the local entities 100% to be used as needed in their budget.

Also at this time, the mayor and city council were in the process of determining a substantial change in the system of government which would affect the present number of employees. This was a big concern of some of the employees, but nothing ever become of it, and for the time being, everything stayed "status quo." But it did concern the employees.

However, the City of Evanston did get some good news that would help the economy. It was announced by Lair Petroleum, Inc. that they planned to construct a gasoline refinery 10 miles east of Evanston, just a mile or so west of the Eagle Rock Ski Area on the old U.S. Highway 30 S route. They called it the Golden Eagle Refining Company and it would create dozens of new jobs for Evanston, which were very much needed since we had gone into a bust period from the oil boom.

The November election was over and President Reagan was re-elected by a landslide. City council members elected were Tom Hutchinson of Ward III, beating Bills out; Julie Lehman of Ward II, taking Davenport's seat who did not run again; and Clarence Vranish of Ward I, taking Albrecht's seat who also did not run again. The three new city council members would be sworn in during the first meeting in January of 1985, joining the three carry-over council members, Ronald Davis of Ward III, Lance Voss of Ward II, and Richard Sather of Ward I.

CHAPTER 19

1985....We are now going into Gene Martin's third year as Mayor. During his first meeting on January 9th of the new year he had City Clerk Don Welling swear in the three new city council members: Clarence Vranish representing Ward I, Julie Lehman representing Ward II, and Tom Hutchinson representing Ward III. These council members would now join the three holdover councilmen: Rick Sather of Ward l, Lance Voss of Ward II, and Ronald Davis of Ward III.

During the meeting Mayor Martin read a letter of resignation from Assistant Fire Chief Ken Bloomfield, who had served the Evanston Voluntary Fire Department for over 38 years. His resignation was accepted by the mayor and council with some regrets, but they did commend him for his long-term service as a member of the department, and wished him well.

According to the *Uinta County Herald* of January 11th, the three outgoing city council members, Albrecht, Davenport and Davis, gave short speeches and wished the new administration their best.

According to the article, Mayor Martin also made his top official appointments: *Marion Malnar was appointed City Engineer and Acting Director of Public Works until a full-time Director would be hired; Mark Harris was appointed as City Attorney; Lee Galeotos as Director of Finances; Steve Snyder as Director of Programs/Economic Development, and in addition Snyder would have responsibility for grants and public relations; Dennis Harvey as Police Chief; Larry Levens as Deputy Police Chief; Dennis Poppinga as Director of Parks and Recreation; Jon Lunsford as Fire Chief; Don Welling as Acting City Clerk; Bruce Wright as Director of Community Development; and Tom Mealey as City Judge.*

The article continued: *The preceding appointments were routine appointments of current city employees – but there was one surprise. City*

Administrator John Hendrickson was not reappointed to his position. Mayor Martin and the City Council issued a press release stating, "It is with regret that the Mayor and City Council announce today that the position of Evanston City Administrator will not be filled. After re-evaluating each department and in consideration of the personnel policy that is in the process of being finalized, it is the consensus of the Mayor and City Council that the position of City Administrator will not be filled now or in the foreseeable future.

"John Hendrickson has filled this position for the city since the establishment of that position, and has conducted himself in a professional and commendable manner. Since John's acceptance of this job, he has been saddled with even more responsibility and burdens by also assuming the duties of Acting Director of Public Works.

"Although John has served with the city during difficult and trying times, he will be leaving us in good standing, and in fact will be assisting the city in finalizing several projects he was actively involved with. The past and current administration wishes John and his family well," the press release continued.

The official news release went on to say that *"the position of City Clerk will be filled by Don Welling on an 'Acting' basis. Again, as a result of re-evaluation of departments, it is felt that the city can better use Don and his skills to fill other areas of need. Don has serviced the city well as City Clerk for the last 10 years and has seen tremendous growth and change in his position. Don is still highly valued for his unfailing trust and loyalty to the city.*

The article just went on to say that City Engineer Marion Malnar would fill the position of Director of Public Works on a temporary basis, and that the position had been left vacant for the last several months. They were at the present interviewing candidates for the position, and it was expected to be filled soon.

The *Herald's* Friday, January 11th issue also had an article titled, COUNCIL ALMOST FAILS TO MEET PAYROLL. It read: *Evanston City came close to not meeting its payroll today because the city council inadvertently neglected to appoint a city treasurer and assistant city treasurer during its regular meeting on Wednesday.*

The article continued: *The city was required to appoint new department heads for city offices during its meeting on Wednesday and Evanston complied with the law — except for an oversight concerning the office of city treasurer.*

The city was able to hold a special meeting because enough councilmen were located at the last minute to form a quorum (the minimum number necessary to hold a meeting is four council members).

Councilman Ronald Davis, President of the council presided at the meeting because Mayor Eugene Martin is in Cheyenne, the article added.

This was a special meeting called on Thursday afternoon. The four council members present took it on themselves to appoint Lee Galeotos as City Treasurer and Linda Templeton as Assistant City Treasurer so the city employees could receive their pay checks that day, thanks to the council's swift action. There was no other business brought up during the meeting making it very short.

In the January issue of the *Uinta County Herald,* an article ran with the title, CUTBACKS ARE MANDATED BY CITY TO BALANCE BUDGET, by Rebecca Chavez.

The article read: *A blanket reduction of 5 percent on all city departmental operations budget in addition to individual cutbacks on specific departments was approved by the Evanston City Council last week following public hearings on the proposed revisions Jan. 4 and Jan. 18.*

The article continued, *Director of Administrative Services Lee Galeotos* (either Galeotos had been appointed as Director of Administrative Services also or this was a mistake by the *Herald*) *noted that during the first half of fiscal 1984-85 the city expenditures exceeded revenues by $1,334,000 and until the recent cuts were approved the imbalance for the upcoming second half of the fiscal year was estimated to possibly hit $1.9 million. "Our revenues were considerably down," Galeotos said.*

It stands to reason, as people are leaving an area that had just gone through a pretty tough boom period, that a city would be thinking ahead so they wouldn't run into budgetary problems, but I can see where things could possibly creep up before the problem was noticed. Therefore, it would not be fair for me to criticize the present administration for getting into a financial problem. It could have happened with any administration, but I can honestly say that it never happened any time that I was a member of the council or during my time as mayor.

The city was having a lot of problems continuing the programs already in progress with the shortfall in revenues. They were also having some freeze-ups that winter in various residential areas. Some of these freeze-ups lasted as long as six hours. That also wasn't helping the budget problem any.

Obviously, the reason local revenue was down was because the state of Wyoming's income was also down. The city is, by law, only permitted to levy 8 mills of ad valorem taxes (property tax), which they get through the county, but the 3% sales tax and the additional local optional 1% sales tax were both down by approximately 25%. Also, the revenues the city was receiving from the state on the coal tax and severance tax from natural resources were down from previous years. The overall city revenues were down between 7 and 8 percent, and the future wasn't looking much better.

According to the February 13th *Uinta County Herald*, the high cost of housing in Evanston kept the community in the top three for the highest cost of living in the state, according to a January survey by the Wyoming Division of Research and Statistics. Jackson was reported as number one in the fourth quarter of 1984, and Gillette was ranked number two. The cost of living in Evanston was 11.83 percent higher than in Cheyenne.

However, the cost of living in Evanston had been dropping since 1984 and would continue to drop as folks moved out, leaving the community in a major "bust" period.

In late February, Mayor Martin and the Evanston City Council, acting on the recommendation of City Parks and Recreation Director Dennis Poppinga, voted to shut down Evanston's outdoor swimming pool, located on 6th Street next to the tennis courts. Since the new recreation center was now opened and it provided an official size swimming pool, the city no longer needed to keep the old outdoor pool operating.

It was kind of a shame that they had to close it, because many local kids learned to swim there, but since it was built in the 1930s (I believe it was built during depression times by the W.P.A. under President Franklin D. Roosevelt's administration), it now needed a lot of repairs and cleaning up.

It was a very busy place during the three months of summer, and everyone had to pay a fee to swim so it was self-sustaining to a point, but with the city already having a budgetary problem, there weren't enough funds in the budget for all the repairs and renovations that the pool would need for it to meet state safety specifications. I'm sure that was one of the reasons for Poppinga's recommendation.

The new Evanston/Uinta County Airport had been in use for a few months, but they were still doing a lot of work on it, such as building new hangars. The old airport, located north of Evanston in Almy, was officially shut down with approximately half of the land going back to the original owners, the Bear River Coal Company, and the remaining land on the north end of the runway being retained by the newly formed Evanston/Uinta County Airport Joint Powers Board, which now also oversaw the operations of the new airport.

In April of 1985, Evanston City Councilman Ronald Davis passed away. He had been re-elected as President of the Council in January for his third term as councilman. He had first been elected in 1974 and was sworn in during the first meeting in 1975, along with our former Mayor Dan South, and had been a member ever since, for over ten years. I believe Davis' main objective in running for city council seat was because he knew that the issue of supplementing the Evanston water system with fluoridation came up. He ran as an opponent very much against the fluoridation.

At that time there was a big push by a strong group of Evanston citizens in favor of supplementing the water system with fluoridation. But the opposition, with strong support from Councilman Ron Davis, caused the issue to be dropped, and it never came up again during his term as a member of the city council. Davis was one of the most out-spoken people to help defeat the issue.

During The Evanston City Council meeting of Wednesday, April 10, 1985 Councilman Tom Hutchinson nominated Craig Nelson of Ward III to replace Ron Davis on the city council. The nomination was accepted unanimously by the city council. Nelson would serve out Davis's term, which would end on January 1, 1986.

The Evanston Voluntary Fire Department moved into their new fire hall located on Front Street right next to the new Evanston Police Department building between 11th Street (Harrison Drive) and 12th Street.

Fire Chief Jon Lunsford said everything was operating normally (sort of). In referring to the transfer of moving from the old hall, said, *We're living out of boxes right now, and some of the lights have not been shipped and none of the furniture is in. But it's going to be great. It's going to be a mess for a little while, but we had gotten used to living in a garage-type environment.* He went on to indicate that *as soon as the building is completed it will be a great addition to the community.*

The new fire station was financed through a joint effort by the city, county and federal government. The state provided 50% of the funding, which was administered by the Wyoming Farm Loan Board from federal funds. The City of Evanston and Uinta County each provided another 25% of the funds necessary to complete the project.

On May 10th the *Uinta County Herald* issued an editorial by Carl Haupt titled, COUNCIL ABUSES POWER. The editorial started out: *It is commonly believed in this country that citizens enjoy the benefits of living in a democracy.*

The truth is that the United States of America isn't a true democracy – it is actually a republic. Citizens of this country don't vote on every issue that comes before the government. The people of this country have elected representatives to act in their name on matters of public interest.

The danger of a republic is that the elected officials don't always act in the public's best interest. Such has been the case with recent actions of the Evanston City Council.

The editorial went on: *In the past several weeks, the city council has, on two different issues, demonstrated that it intends to act as it desires despite the wishes of the people to the contrary. The first of these acts has been the city council's attempt to make an end-run around Wyoming state law regarding a requirement of three readings of ordinances before they become law. The obvious purpose of such a law is to allow time between readings for members of the public to support or object to each proposed ordinance. The letter of the law hasn't been broken by the city council but the spirit of the law is being subverted.*

The editorial continued: *On April 23, the City Council called a special meeting to vote on a single issue – the first reading of proposed Ordinance 85-12, which would authorize the issuance of bonds in the amount of $760,000 for Downtown Improvement Development. The second reading of this ordinance was held 24 hours later in the council's regularly scheduled meeting on April 24. And the third reading was held, and the ordinance passed into law, in the council's meeting on May 8.*

The editorial continued: *Yes, there was time for the public response between the second and third readings of this ordinance. And no, there was no time for public response between the first and second readings. The council chose, on the grounds of expediency, to eliminate that time for comments from the public. This action goes directly against the intent of the Wyoming state law concerning readings of proposed ordinances.*

The editorial continued: *The second of these acts was played out at Wednesday's council meeting. Residents of the Red Mountain subdivision are objecting to a liquor store which Painter & Co. wants to build at the intersection of Red Mountain Drive and Highway 89. Representatives from both groups were at the city council meeting – clearly with the intent to support their positions before the council. But in a maneuver which had obviously been discussed and planned prior to the meeting, the city council lumped three different issues into one vote and passed all three on a vote. No time was given for public discussion. Following the vote, Mayor Eugene Martin announced a recess. During the recess, opponents of Ordinance 85-13 were told they could have asked for the ordinance to come up for public discussion. They were not told this fact until after the ordinance had been voted on by the council. Once again the public was denied the chance to comment on a proposed law.*

It can be argued that the city council didn't deny opponents of Ordinance 85-13 the right to speak. It is true they could have asked for time to participate in a discussion. But it appears to be a deliberate move on the part of the city council to hold the vote before informing the people of their right.

Public officials are treading on thin ice when they resort to slick parliamentary procedures to gain their objectives. That tactic is just another version of the old cliché, "The end justifies the means."

Mr. Haupt concluded his editorial with: *The public has a right to know what their public officials are doing. The public also has the right to attend public meetings and express their approval or disapproval. Those are reasonable rights to expect in a Republic.*

Mr. Haupt was right, especially if the "special meetings" weren't advertised properly, or pre-announced and posted in a very conspicuous location. We always had to have special meetings because of all the business that was called for. However, we always announced when and where the meeting would take place, and we always posted notice, and if we had time we would publish it in the local newspapers. It's only fair to give the public adequate time to take notice of any issue that may come up in a meeting.

Also, any new ordinance that is passed should be published in the newspaper in full prior to the second reading. Sometimes that may be hard to do. There were times when, during my administration, we didn't follow through like we should have, but we always gave the public plenty of notice. I don't really think that what happened concerning Mr. Haupt's editorial was intentional by the mayor and council, but it did appear that the administration used very bad judgment.

The city recently hired Chuck MacIlvaine, another high-paid employee, to take over the position of Public Works Director, and relieve Lee Galeotos, who was holding the position temporarily after Hendrickson resigned, until they could hire a new director. Galeotos retained the position of Director of Finances, and he was also City Treasurer.

MacIlvaine, from Fremont County, had a lot of experience in public works and appeared to be well qualified. This position put him in charge of all departments of public works, except the engineering department. He would oversee Allen Kennedy (not sure of his position at the time), and all department heads of roads and storm sewers, water, sanitary sewer and all utility plants.

In May of 1985 the city council voted to end the one-way traffic in downtown Evanston on Center and Main Streets, and go back to the way it was prior to the heavy traffic caused by the boom. They decided that there would be angle-parking on both sides of Main and one side of Center, and the other side of Center would be parallel parking. This caused a little controversy, but it was time for the change.

As usual, the city administration had problems throughout the rest of the year. Their biggest problem was the budget. With revenues dropping it was difficult to maintain the roads and other infrastructure. The past winter they had severe freeze-ups in some water mains, causing unanticipated expenses.

Also, they had breakdowns in some of the city water wells, causing them to have to go to other sources for a while, such as a water well privately owned by the Carpenter Ranch located just outside the city limits on Yellow Creek Road, causing another unanticipated budget expense. Shortly after using the Carpenter well, a power surge twisted off the drive shaft on the motor of the well and also knocked out one of the city wells.

With more water problems, the city had to start rationing water from June until October, longer than usual, until they could get all the city water wells back in operation. The council put out notice that all houses must use the odd and even house number system for irrigating of yards and so on, and they also limited the hours for irrigation.

That summer the administration had a lot of public controversy over zoning, issuance of liquor licenses, and animal control. A local's dog had recently bitten a child in the face, causing severe damage. When taken to court, the judge determined the dog was not dangerous and refused to have the dog killed. A lot of folks, especially the child's parent, were extremely upset.

On top of all the other problems, the issue of fluoridation in the water system came up again. Fluoridation was a nationwide movement and finally reached Evanston again this summer of 1985. Fluoridation was defeated during the mid '70s during Mayor Dan South's administration, but now it came up again and it looked like the mayor and city council were once again going to be faced with it. The headlines in the *Uinta County Herald's* issue of July 10th read,

FLUORIDATION PROPOSAL WILL BE PRESENTED TO CITY COUNCIL TONIGHT.

The article went on: *An issue which has spawned countless emotional debates across the United States will come to Evanston today when the Evanston City Council will hear a request for fluoridation of the municipal water supply.*

Dr. Earl S. Condie and Miriam Johnson are expected to address the council during public participation advocating the beginning fluoridation of water in Evanston. It is not known if there will be any opponents to fluoridation present at the meeting, the article continued.

Before any action on the issue of fluoridation was taken, the Evanston City Council voted that they would call for a public hearing on the subject on August 21st at 6:30 p.m. The decision to hold a public hearing was made by the council after members agreed that more information was needed before a decision could be made. The public hearing would be well publicized, according to the council.

During the public hearing of August 21st two local dentists, Dr. Earl Condie and Dr. Randy Hancock, among others, spoke in favor of fluoridation, while some in attendance were against it.

The council did not take any action on the issue during the hearing, but at the conclusion of the hearing, Mayor Martin said that the Evanston City Council would render some kind of decision on the matter in the near future. He gave no indication which direction he or the members of the city council were leaning.

The resolution to add fluoridation in Evanston's water apparently never got put on the agenda or adopted, because there never has been fluoridation added to Evanston's water system, and probably never will, because the issue has come up twice in the past and has been denied both times.

The Youth Alternative Home Association (YAHA) was well under construction. The facility, which was being built across from the Human Service Complex on the 40-acre parcel that the City of Evanston purchased a few years ago. The city donated the building site to them by leasing the land to them for one dollar per year.

The facility would be designed like a large home with three bedrooms, a living room, conference room, kitchen, bathrooms and a full basement. It was designed to provide shelter and treatment for youths between the ages of 10 and 18 who had been abused or neglected or who were moderately troubled.

The YAHA home would be serving the Uinta and South Lincoln County region, according to Kevin Smith, Secretary of YAHA. He said the need for a youth home here has been around for a long time, and that young people in need of emergency facilities have currently been placed in the Uinta County Jail or the Wyoming State Hospital.

Also, Evanston was well on its way to developing a higher education program locally, with the Uinta County School District No. 1 forming a Board of Community Education Services (BOCES), with representatives of Western Wyoming College in Rock Springs, Wyoming.

The BOCES program had grown to the point that they now had their own building and had become a great educational asset to the City of Evanston and to Uinta County.

In September it was announced that the Union Pacific Railroad officially donated the train depot to the City of Evanston. The depot sits on part of the railroad right-of-way, and due to federal law, the U.P. cannot sell or donate any of the original right-of-way to any public or private concern. Therefore, the building would still be sitting on railroad property, which could probably be leased at a very low rate.

The *Uinta County Herald* issue of September 6th reported: *Wyoming's unemployment rate for July, at 6.2 percent, was about the same as the June rate of 6.1 percent…In Uinta County, the labor force in July dropped to 10,999 from 11,688 listed in June for a 5.9 percent decline. Unemployment in the county dropped slightly to 6.6 percent for July from 7.0 percent in June.*

The unemployment rate didn't look good, and that had a big downward effect on the economy. Although the gas plants were all going strong and we now had the Golden Eagle refinery, because of discontinuing the drilling and other oil and gas well services, a number of the industrial service companies were moving out and folks were leaving.

On September 27th, the *Uinta County Herald* ran an article written by Carl Haupt titled, CITY OF EVANSTON FACING SERIOUS WATER SHORTAGE. The article went on to indicate that if something wasn't done quickly about the water situation, Evanston could seriously have to restrict the use of water as early as next year.

Mayor Gene Martin stated: "If we have a real bad winter like last year there is a chance you (Evanston residents) won't water lawns. We had a shortage this year and every year it is going to get worse." The Mayor continued with, "We have got to find some way to finance Sulphur Creek."

The Sulphur Creek Reservoir had been chosen as the dam that the city wanted to enlarge to gain more water for the City of Evanston. The city was trying to locate funding to get the project underway. The plan was to enlarge the dam to triple the amount of water in the reservoir. The two-thirds increase would be for city use.

This was a very expensive project that would also have to include the new pipeline into the city, and a new intake and pipeline off of the Bear River where Evanston holds a significant amount of water rights.

The city was now in the process of meeting with the Wyoming State Water Commission, seeking their assistance in this matter. Apparently, the estimated cost of the planned water project would be $20 million, and the state of Wyoming had indicated that they would give the City of Evanston a grant in the amount of $15 million and the remaining $5 million would have to be repaid to the State Treasury by the City of Evanston on a 50-year loan at an interest rate of four percent. Four percent was a terrifically low interest rate at that time because home loans were still at about 8 to 10 percent.

The new sewer plant had been completed and was built in three parts to serve a population of over 25,000 people. It was now in operation and the dedication of the plant was scheduled for October 2th, when tours of the plant would be available to the public.

The year 1985 wasn't a very year for the council as far as public criticism was concerned. It appeared, through the Letters to the Editor, both in the *Uinta County Herald* and the *Evanston Post*, that there was a lot of public concern about the way the city was running meetings, including the "work sessions," how the budget was being used, the handling of the employees, the way "Pride Week" was handled, and the city hiring a Public Relations person, which probably was because of the budgetary problems they were having.

I had never ever witnessed so much controversy through the Letters to the Editor columns as this year. This was great for the newspapers, but almost every member of the council and the mayor wrote letters defending their actions during 1985. I felt that there had to be a better way to communicate with the public than through the letters in the paper, but that's just my opinion.

However, city officials did get some wonderful projects finished during 1985: the Recreation Center, the Human Service Center, the new sewer plant, the ownership of the railroad depot and purchasing the U.P.R.R. property between 9th and 10th Streets. I appreciate the fact that they followed through with all the projects that had been started by other administrations, and they got Block 6 cleared and ready for the new post office.

One of the last acts of the city council for the year was to reopen the budget process for the current fiscal year, because of shortfalls. Mayor Martin said the city will reopen the budget hearings "following the Christmas Holidays."

CHAPTER 20

1986....The year started off with a lot of disagreement and dissension, according to the *Uinta County Herald* and the *Evanston Post*, between not only the public, but also within the council. The Letters to the Editor column was kept pretty busy with letters going back and forth between some members of the city council and some of the citizens.

The dispute concerned such issues as positions of employees, whether to hire a public relations person (or communications person, as Councilman Rick Sather called it), budget shortfall, cost differences, conflicts of interest over changing the location of the post office, misuse of city credit cards, and many more questions and accusations.

Rick Sather ended one of his letters with: *P.S. If we don't need a communications person, why am I writing so many letters to the editor?* To me that was a good question. I thought to myself, *Just why in the hell do you write so many letters?* Why couldn't they, Sather and Voss, just go talk to the people or to each other? It would be much more personable and friendlier approach. Just a suggestion!

Anyway, after Marlene Falkman O'Rourke's Letter to the Editor titled, "Enough is enough," came out in the Herald of January 10th the letters slowed down.

One of the big issues that were being discussed in the city council's first meetings of the year concerned the Administrative Services Department. The January 10th edition of the *Herald* ran an article titled, CITY COUNCIL POSTPONES BREAKUP OF ADMINISTRATIVE SERVICES DEPARTMENT.

The article started out: *The Evanston City Council came close to a major dismantling of the Department of Administrative Services during council meeting Wednesday night.*

Near the conclusion of the meeting Councilwoman Julie Lehman proposed that the General Services Division be taken away from Administrative Services and placed under the control of the Public Works Department. Lee Galeotos is in charge of Administrative Services and the Public Works Department is headed by Chuck MacIlvaine, the article continued.

Following Lehman's proposal, Councilman Clarence Vranish made a motion that at midnight that night General Services be transferred to the Public Works Department, the article added.

My question to that was *What the hell do they mean by 'General Services'?* It seemed to me that all city offices would come under "General Services" except maybe the Judicial and Police Departments. You have administrative and you have public works. What other concerns would you have, other than your Boards and Commissions?

The *Herald's* January 10th issue continued: *"I feel we have to look at the organization of Administrative Services," said Councilman Rick Sather.* And he was right. It certainly did need looking into.

It seemed to me that Councilwoman Julie Lehman was the one council member who was trying to make sense. According to the article she said, *"Our bureaucracy is out of control,"* and she added, *"There have been problems with this in the past…Problems of who is in charge,"* talking about the General Service Division.

The article continued: *If General Services was transferred to the Department of Public Works, commented Lehman, "it would be one year of maybe Hell. But it would save 25 years of bureaucracy building."*

When the motion finally came to a vote it was defeated and General Services remained under the control of the Department of Administrative Services. But a second motion passed which committed the City Council to reach a decision on the matter by February 12, 1986. "We will return to the public to give our decisions based on organization" in Administrative Services, said Lehman, the *Herald's* article concluded.

On January 24th the *Uinta County Herald* published another article announcing that Lee Galeotos, Evanston's Director of Administrative Services, had submitted his letter of resignation to Mayor Gene Martin on January 21st to be effective the last week of February 1986. Mayor Martin read his letter to the city council during the meeting of January 22nd.

Galeotos also announced that evening that he had plans to run for the office of State Treasurer of Wyoming in the upcoming election this year. He told the council that he was appreciative of the courtesies and support they had extended him during his tenure with the city.

The January 24th issue of the *Herald* article stated, *Galeotos leaves his position with the City of Evanston at a time when the City Council has been studying the organization of the Department of Administrative Services. Two weeks ago there was a move during a City Council meeting* (Galeotos was not present during this move) *to take the Division of General Services away from the Department of Administrative Services.*

The article continued: *The City of Evanston is also on the verge of opening new public hearings on the current budget because of a shortfall in anticipated revenues. Galeotos will be leaving the City of Evanston about four months before the conclusion of the fiscal year of 1985-1986. The fiscal year runs until the end of June 1986.*

Budgetary problems continued to be one of the big items on the agenda of the city council meetings. During the same meeting of January 22nd, the question of how they were going to finance their required 25% portion of the cost of the Sulphur Creek Reservoir project came up. During the discussion, Mayor Gene Martin said, *My main concern is this budget problem.*

That night the Evanston City Council voted to retain the Dain-Bosworth Company of Casper, Wyoming as financial consultants for the Sulphur Creek Dam Project. After retaining the D-B Co., the most common expression of the City Council members was that too many questions concerning the financing were left unanswered.

"We have got to find a way to finance it and take it to the voters," said Mayor Martin. *"If we don't approve some way to finance it we are going to lose it,"* Martin said about the dam project.

No matter what financing scheme is adopted for the water project, the City Council says that in order for it to succeed it will have to have the support of the Wyoming Water Development Commission (WWDC). Councilman President Lance Voss said that through past experience the city has found out "The WWDC has a lot of muscle with the legislature." He was right; they did.

The City of Evanston had originally called for a public budget hearing on January 30th, but during their latest meeting they had changed it to February 7th. Prior to the public hearing, the city council met with the heads of the various departments to iron out a final budget before presenting it to the public at the upcoming hearing.

We have got to have a balanced budget, said Mayor Martin. *We cannot operate the city without a balanced budget.*

On February 5th a memo was sent to all Department Heads from the mayor and city council concerning the budget. The memo read:

The following is a culmination of the Mayor and City Council's efforts to identify budget constraints and formulate possible solutions to those constraints. The following is submitted to the Department Heads of the City for <u>discussion</u> and <u>review</u> prior to placement of the items in the budget resolution:

The Police Department of the City of Evanston is directed to immediately implement five (5) day shifts of eight-and-one-half (8½) hours per shift for all divisions in that Department.

All non-employees, as defined by the Fair Labor Standards Act, shall have their rate of pay stated on an hourly rate.

Effective immediately, all City Employees will have their gross rate of pay cut ten percent (10%).

In the Executive/Engineering Department of the City:

The Electrical Inspection Home Rule will be withdrawn, effective March 1, 1986. The City Engineer is hereby directed to delete a position of Building Inspector.

The City Engineer is hereby directed to change the position of Electrical Inspector to Electrical Maintenance, effective March 1, 1986, at a wage rate of $12.40 per hour, which shall not be subject to the ten percent (10%) cut hereinabove mentioned.

In the Department of Administrative Services:

The position of telephone and mail clerk shall be deleted.

The position of carpenter assistant shall be deleted.

In the Fire Department, the position of Equipment Technician shall be deleted.

In Parks and Recreation Department:

All Cemetery Positions shall be reorganized under the Parks Division.

The job title of Cemetery Section Supervisor shall be changed to Municipal Service Worker III at a wage rate of $10.96 per hour, which shall not be subject to the ten percent (10%) cut hereinabove mentioned.

In the Police Department:

The position of Community Relations Officer and Trainer Coordinator shall be combined at a salary of $26,473, which is <u>not</u> subject to the ten percent (10%) cut hereinabove mentioned.

Delete the position of Secretary II in administration.

Delete the position of Deputy Chief.

The Detective Division shall be reorganized to include the following positions:

1 Lieutenant

1 Evidence Technician

4 Detectives

The Patrol Division shall be reorganized to include the following positions:

1 Lieutenant

4 Sergeants

13 Patrolmen II

1 Parking Control Officer

1 Animal Control Officer

The Public Works Department shall make the following changes:

In Sanitation Division, delete one (1) Municipal Service Worker.

In the Water Division, delete two (2) Municipal Service Workers.

In the Street Division, delete two (2) Municipal Service Workers.

There shall be no new employees hired in the City for the remainder of the fiscal year.

The Department Heads shall be directed to prepare and effectuate layoff plans for their departments in which positions have been deleted. If an existing employee will be transferred to another position, that employee must qualify for the position in which transferred to.

Signed: *MWH* (Mark W. Harris, City Attorney)

That was the extent of that memo, which did not go over very well with the employees, understandably. However, it was pretty obvious that the city council had to do something to balance the budget mid-year, and after a considerable amount of time and a continuance of meetings of the city council and department heads they hoped, with their proposals, that they could finally come up with a way to balance the budget for the rest of the fiscal year.

All I could say about that was: *Good luck, I know it had to be tough, because I was in a similar situation and I knew what they were going through.* It's a shame when you have to spend so much time on something that you thought you had taken care of, but it happens, and I guess that is part of being a public servant. As stated in the *Uinta County Herald* of February 5th: *According to a report distributed Monday to city officials from City Finance Director Al Hays,* (Al Hays was hired to replace Lee Galeotos) *salaries and benefits make up the majority of the budgets of most of the city departments.*

The *Herald* also stated that there were a total of 17 top employees who earned more than $30,000 per year on base salary (a pretty fair wage at that time), and the number of employees exceeding this figure rose when overtime pay was taken into account.

It seemed to me, and many other citizens, that the city's employment had gotten top-heavy in the past few years. A Letter to the Editor from Denise Peterson, published by the *Herald* on February 7th stated that, *"Too many chiefs and not enough Indians should become the new motto for the City of Evanston."*

The city council held their public budget hearing on the evening of February 7th to come up with a balanced budget for the rest of fiscal year 1985-1986. An article in the *Uinta County Herald* of February 12th said, *the City Council Chambers were filled to overflowing with Evanston residents anxious to hear what decisions had been made by the Evanston City Council in regard to the budget deficit. "By law we are required to balance our budget," Councilman Clarence Vranish told the crowd.*

Although Evanston has taken large cuts in its budget, one councilman said the goal of a balanced budget had not been reached. "We still haven't come to a balanced budget. I just hope that in another three months we don't have to come back and do this again," the *Herald* continued.

"In my mind, we have to cut an additional $300,000," said Vranish.

During the hearing it was mentioned that the City of Evanston and its non-exempt employees reached an agreement to cut employee work hours 10 percent instead of cutting wages by the same amount.

According to the *Uinta County Herald* of February 7th, members of the Evanston Police Department had been so worried about job security that they asked an attorney to be present at the work session of the City Council on Tuesday night, February 4th. The attorney, Fred Wasilewski, representing the Western Alliance of Government Employees, ran into a difficult situation when he arrived. He was told by members of the city council that the City of Evanston did not recognize the union and would not accept his authority to negotiate on behalf of the members of the Police Department.

The article continued: *"They're scared," said Wasilewski. "There are a lot of scared people there."*

"We've heard rumblings here and there," said Wasilewski. "They are concerned about trying to maintain their jobs."

"There have been no layoffs ordered by this council," replied City Attorney Mark Harris.

Wasilewski was invited by the Council to attend the entire meeting since it was a public meeting, but he chose to leave following a brief discussion with the City Council.

Employees of the City of Evanston will retain full fringe benefits for the next 30 days despite the fact that non-exempt employees are now working only 36 hours per week.

During their regular meeting on February 12th, the city council amended Resolution 86-8 which read: *"Full-time permanent employees shall work a minimum of forty hours per week, or such other minimum hours as the Governing Body may from time to time designate by resolution or ordinance."*

The city council amended the resolution to not include sections that concerned sick leave and vacation leave for city employees. They would retain their benefits. The resolution as amended passed, but not before considerable discussion by the council, according to an article in the *Herald* February 14th.

The *Herald* read: *"I don't think we made these cuts deep enough in the first place...," said Councilman Clarence Vranish earlier in the meeting.*

"What we are doing is making a short term fix on a problem that is going to have to be addressed in another two or three weeks," said Vranish about the vote on employee benefits. "We're initiating a 36 hour work week and I'm against it," added Councilman Rick Sather.

Councilwoman Julie Lehman noted that she voted the way she did on the reduced work week for employees at the budget public hearing last Friday because "I was afraid of mob rule."

"I think it would be fiscally irresponsible to pass a resolution that would lower hours worked and lower wages but not benefits," said Council President Lance Voss.

Voss also said that the employees should have thought of all the consequences of their proposal cutting work hours before their plan was presented to the City Council at last week's public hearing on the budget.

After reading Voss's remark, I thought to myself, "Just who in the hell is running the city, the employees, or the mayor and council?"

The *Herald* continued: *The vote to provide full benefits even though employees are working fewer hours passed on a 4-2 vote with Voss and Sather voting against it.*

It's too bad the employees had to take such a big cut to get the budget balanced, because as far as I was concerned they were the most important part of running the city, the backbone of the city, and they should be taken care of fairly. To repeat the words of Francis W. Bettinson, a former employee, in his Letter to the Editor: *"These employees are the best asset this city has."*

But, after all was said and done, the council ended up drastically cutting expenses in response to the anticipated drop in city revenues. Until the new budget of fiscal year 1986-1987 was acted on, I was sure the city council will be keeping close tabs on their on-going expenditures to keep from spending beyond their revenues.

However, the concerns on how the budget cuts were made didn't stop there.

More Letters to the Editor came out in both local newspapers, the *Uinta County Herald* and the *Evanston Post*, from interested citizens and members of the city council. A questionnaire asking public opinion on what employee wages was sent out to all residents receiving a water bill, which most citizens laughed at and ignored. The biggest questions I heard around town about the questionnaire were: *"Why should I address this questionnaire when I have no idea what goes on and who does what? Isn't that what we elected the mayor and council for: to determine how the city must be operated?"* Some citizens returned the questionnaire blank, to show how ridiculous it was.

The budget wasn't the only item on the agenda that the city officials were having problems with. There was the dam project about to begin at Sulphur Creek Reservoir and the question of how they were going to pay for it.

During the city council meetings in February, the increase in fees and utility rates was on the agenda. An increase was discussed for water and other fees and rates, such as wastewater fees, animal control fees, cemetery fees, general utility charges, water connection and tapping fees, fire department fees, administrative services fees, planning and zoning fees, sanitation service fees and various other charges for city residents (this information was taken from the *Uinta County Herald* issue dated February 26, 1986).

The budget issue and dispute continued through March. A feud between Mayor Martin and Councilman Voss had started over who was to blame for overspending the budget. Letters between the Mayor and Voss were written concerning Voss's comments during a meeting, appearing to put the blame on Lee Galeotos, former director of financing. Letters to the Editor were written by some council members and by some citizens, disputing each other. A letter written by Carl Williams was titled, *"Childish and senseless spending of mayor and council."* Williams concluded his letter with, *"P.S. What a convenient way to hide results of the city questionnaires. Please Councilman Vranish, let the press publish the results by letting them examine the questionnaire. Councilmen (and women): Beware, it's not only the city employees watching your every move but also the public."*

The *Uinta County Herald* of March 14th ran an article written by Carl Haupt titled, VOSS DEFENDS STATEMENTS MADE IN LETTER. The article read, *Voss told the Uinta County Herald that some statements in the [earlier] article were read out of context by those objecting to the story. Following the meeting of the city council on Wednesday, Voss wrote a letter to Mayor Eugene B. Martin. "The only problems in the article are context problems. How many times did Lee [Galeotos] tell us not to worry about the budget? 'We will fix it all in January',"* wrote Voss. *"Did you know that the 'we' didn't include Lee? Yet you let him quote all his memos. What did he tell you? 'Don't worry.' That is what I took exception to. He wrote one thing to protect himself and told us another. Then, when things looked like they were going to get messy he skipped and Al (Hays) and I got to pinch hit for him. Do I get a thanks other than Tom (Hutchinson) tonight? No! I get cut to ribbons by the Mayor to make Lee look good. Do I get an opportunity to explain my feelings to the Mayor? No! That might not make Lee look so good."*

The news article went on concerning the conflicts and dissensions of Councilman Voss and others, but Galeotos was gone now and there was no point for the mayor and council to keep up the hard feelings. The mayor and council's job was now to get the budget straightened out, and run the city as it should be run, and they appeared to do just that.

But they still had an employee problem. According to another article in the *Uinta County Herald* published in March, there were still a number of municipal employees who were worried about how Wyoming's current shaky economy would affect their jobs.

The article stated that, *Out of a police force containing 28 people, 19 Evanston City policemen are currently looking for work on other police departments. The number rises to 20 when Patrol Lieutenant Forrest Bright is added. Bright is seeking election to the position of Uinta County Sheriff.*

"It's like a mass exodus," said Uinta County Attorney Scott Smith, who has been kept busy writing letters of recommendation for policemen.

The article continued: *"We have a fine Police Department," said Lance Voss, President of the Evanston City Council. "My belief is we have come to a number [of policemen] we can afford to allow for job security. I feel it is very unfortunate there are 19 police officers looking for work but, as my grandfather Leo Robert Voss, used to say, 'Loyalty is only tested in the bad times'."*

During the summer of 1985 the Wyoming Highway Department made massive improvements on Bear River Drive, from the underpass to the East Interchange, closing down Bear River Drive almost all of that summer. I don't know why it took so long for the highway department to get the job done, but it hurt a lot of businesses on the east end and put some of them out of business. My brother Bob owned and operated the Flying J Service Center on the west end and also had a truck tire shop located on Bear River Drive in the same building where Parnell's Glass and Body Works is now. Bob ended up closing that shop because of lack of business during that summer due to the construction.

The highway department widened Bear River Drive and they put in sidewalks, curbing and storm drains, making the road much better and safer not only for road traffic but also for pedestrians.

This year, 1986, the highway department announced in March that they would be closing down the east end interchange of Interstate 80 until August, according to a news article in the *Evanston Post* on March 27th headlined: EASTSIDE BUSINESSES GET COMPROMISE FROM HWY. DEPT.

The article went on: *The highway department's plans called for the eastbound off-ramp, and both the westbound and eastbound on-ramps to be shut down for most of the summer, during the heart of the tourist season… The department is re-designing the interchange on the east side to accommodate access to the travel information center and the new State Park, which is under construction south of the freeway.*

The article continued: *East Evanston businessmen were outraged by the department's plans. Last summer the road through town to the east interchange was completely rebuilt. "I didn't have enough customers last year, and I'm just barely making it. Now, if I don't have any this summer, I'm just going to barely make it," one business owner stated.*

The article added: *Don Larson of the WHD indicated that the (closed) signs on the Interstate would be covered when the interchange was open. "We will work with you," he stated. "There are going to be a few days, like today and tomorrow, when we're going to have to close it down. There will be a few days next week for dirt work and then it should be open pretty much until we start paving."*

It was too bad this had to happen two summers in a row because it did hurt the businesses on Bear River Drive. However, this summer wasn't anywhere near as bad as the summer of 1985, because in 1985 Bear River Drive was almost completely closed down for the entire summer.

In March, Kilburn Porter was presented the Rex Jones Memorial Award by the Evanston Chamber of Commerce. The award was well deserved: Kilburn was the key player in starting up the Eagle Rock Ski Area, and he was instrumental in starting the boat club at Sulphur Creek Reservoir and Little League Football, among many other recreational programs. He was also among the first members to serve on the Evanston Recreation Board, and was very supportive of the new Evanston Recreation Center.

The Rex Jones Memorial Award was named for Rex Jones because of his involvement and support in many recreation programs in the Evanston area. He was instrumental in helping Kilburn Porter start Eagle Rock and was a known ski advocate. Rex was killed several years ago while working for the Wyoming Highway Department. He was plowing snow west of Evanston on Interstate 80 when a bus hit his Wyoming state truck, killing him and others and injuring several people. It was a privilege to have his name attached to the award in his honor, and well deserved. His death was a big loss, not only to his family, but also to the City of Evanston and area.

In March of that year a public hearing was held concerning the possibility of forming a Recreation District with Uinta County School District No. 1. There seemed to be a lot of support from all the citizens in the school district, including the Evanston City Council and Mayor Martin. The City of Evanston requested that the school district use their taxing authority to raise the property tax within the school district's jurisdiction to help fund existing and future parks and recreation services. During the hearing it was the consensus of those in attendance that the increase in property tax would be no more than one (1) mill. Apparently, Wyoming State Statute gives any governing body authority to establish a recreation district and levy up to one mill of additional property tax to fund it.

After the decision was made by the City and School District No. 1 to go with the recreation district, a nine-member volunteer board was jointly appointed by the School Board and City Council to manage the funding and the operation of the Parks and Recreation facilities. The board would operate separately from the city council and the school board, but all appointments to the recreation board would be made by the two public entities.

In my opinion, forming the recreation district was a great move for the community. It was a good way of funding the many parks, playgrounds and other recreation programs, including the recreation center within the school district, which also included the town of Bear River. Although the one mill levy took a big load off of the City of Evanston, the city still had to budget additional funds for the district. But it was a lot less than it had previously been.

On March 21st, the Wyoming State Supreme Court ruled in favor of a judgment presented by Uinta County, City of Evanston and the two towns of Lyman and Mountain View, as Plaintiffs, in the total amount of $3,201,511.82, representing construction impact funds for a natural gas processing plant constructed by Amoco Production Company and built within the County of Uinta.

The money would be divided up between the Plaintiffs, with Evanston receiving about $1.6 million. These funds would come from the Wyoming State Treasurer's office which, for whatever reason, had been held back from the county and towns, including Evanston, until the State Supreme Court ruled in favor of them.

Mayor Martin and city council members voted in favor of investing the majority of these funds in an interest-bearing bank account and committing them to be used towards the Sulphur Creek Reservoir Dam Project.

Mayor Eugene Martin said the unexpected funds from the Supreme Court judgment were "just like Pennies from Heaven." However, it would be several months before the city received them. On July 14th the Sulphur Creek Reservoir expansion would be brought up for a vote by the people of Evanston. The project had been approved by the Wyoming Water Development Commission (WWDC) with an estimated total cost of approximately $25,000,000, with the state of Wyoming providing 75 percent, 25 percent matching. The state legislature had allocated an $18,750,000 grant to the city for the project. They had also authorized a $6,250,000 loan to the City of Evanston at 4 percent interest, payable over 45 years to complete the cost of the loan.

It appeared to prove that Councilman Lance Voss was right in his statement about the "WWDC having a lot of muscle with the state legislature." Because, through the WWDC, the City of Evanston received a sweetheart deal from the state legislature to pay back their required 25 percent of the Sulphur Creek project.

Payments on the $6,250,000 loan would not be required to start until 5 years after construction of the reservoir is completed. This was a great deal for Evanston to get their water problems taken care of, and Mayor Martin's administration should be very proud of getting the state of Wyoming to approve such a compromise.

More good news came to the City of Evanston when The *Uinta County Herald's* issue of April 11th ran an article titled, CITY CLIMBS OUT OF RED. The article went on: *The City of Evanston is climbing out of the red ink according to a cashflow report prepared for the Evanston City Council by Council President Lance R. Voss.*

The article continued: *The report shows that as of March, 1986 the city had a deficit, Year to Date, of $397,572. This compares to a deficit of $2,028,203 in November of 1985.*

The report shows that during the last four months revenues have exceeded expenditures and the size of the deficit is decreasing.

The article concluded: *This report does not include the approximately $1.6 million the City expects to receive in settlement of a case which was decided in favor of Evanston a couple weeks ago by the Wyoming State Supreme Court.*

With that report, and during a council meeting in late April, the Evanston City Council voted to restore the 40-hour work week and abolish the ten percent wage reductions that had been in effect since the recent budget crunch in the city. The council members restored the hours and wages for employees for the balance of the fiscal year ending June 30, 1986. According to the *Uinta County Herald* of April 25th, the action would become effective April 27th, and the matter would be reconsidered when the new budget was formulated for the fiscal year of 1986-1987.

In May of 1986, Beverly Enterprises, an enterprise out of Minneapolis, Minnesota requested a zone change of property they were in the process of buying on Yellow Creek Road in order to build a 60-bed nursing home. After some discussion, the city council voted to allow the zone change, and in next several months the City of Evanston had a new nursing/rest home called the Rocky Mountain Care–Evanston. This was another service that Evanston was very much in need of.

It was election year for the State Officials: Governor, Secretary of State, State Treasurer, State Auditor and Secretary of Public Education; and the Mayor of Evanston and three (3) council members would be up for election.

After Governor Ed Herschler was elected for a third term, the Wyoming State Legislature passed a bill limiting a governor's seat to two 4-year terms; therefore Herschler could not run for the governorship again. Whether he wanted to or not, I couldn't say.

In a June edition of the *Uinta County Herald*, an article by Janet Kolb stated that Mayor Eugene Martin had announced that he would not be running again for a second term. He said in the article, *"I'm all burned out."*

The article continued: *The location of the new post office – now being built on a lot just across from City Hall – was "the hardest decision I had to make," said Martin. "I had in my mind one thing and the public perceived another. I do not think the public understood fully how much money the city put into the project. It all got lost in the shuffle when you looked at grant monies, downtown merchants who put up money and funds from the Post Office."*

Martin believes the biggest failure of his term in office might have been the very fact that the public "never really understood all the reasons why we [the Council] did certain things. Our communications from the city to the general public could have been better. I don't think we got out enough information to the public on general issues." But, in hindsight, Martin admits he is not sure of the answer to that problem, the *Herald* added.

The article continued: *Martin will indeed leave behind problems to the next mayor, something he says each mayor leaves to the next, "because of issues that continue from one administration to another." In his case, it will be the Sulphur Creek Reservoir project that the next mayor will have to continue working on. Martin is quick to point out that "one of the biggest things this mayor and council has done is put the time and effort into securing the money for this project." Martin is deeply concerned that, if the issue is voted down, there will be no alternative for the program. He stresses that "the project will not cost the taxpayer one dime" and that should Sulphur Creek be voted down, the answers to Evanston's water supply "will be a long time coming." The issue to be voted on by electors July 15, Martin explained, is whether the city will incur an indebtedness until state funds become available for the project. The election will force the public to "decide if it wants to secure a solid water course for the community." If the expansion money is not taken advantage of, Martin said, "The state will take the $77 million allocated back into its general fund and the money might never come again."*

Martin's announcement not to run for a second term drew a lot of interest to the office of mayor. Seven citizens filed for the office, including me.

I wasn't going to run for the office again because my agency, Uinta Realty, Inc. was not doing too well because of the current economy, and the numerous foreclosures were affecting property values so that folks leaving Evanston couldn't sell their homes, because most owners owed more than the property's current value.

Sandy and a friend, Peggy Harvey, had their house cleaning business going, cleaning up some pretty trashy houses that people had just left, scrubbing floors, and cleaning toilets. Most of the houses were foreclosures. Sandy was working hard to help me keep our real estate agency going, but U.R.I. had too much debt, making it almost impossible for me to run again.

But there were many local folks after me to run again. I had dozens of people talking to me about running. Former Councilman Russell "Bub" Albrecht said to me, *Denny, you are the only one that can go in there and clean up the mess that they [Martin's administration] have left the city in, and you have got to think about running again. You will not have any problem getting elected, I'm sure of that.*

I told Bub that I just couldn't afford to run, but then my two oldest sons, Rand and Dave, also got on me to run, and John Proffit of Uinta Engineering and Surveying told me that the Martin Administration would not give any business to local engineering and surveying firms, and that they had given everything on the Sulphur Creek project, including the pipelines, to a firm out of Denver, and that they gave the County Road improvement project to a firm out of Casper.

Well, this kind of pissed me off, but I still didn't feel that I could afford to run again, and Sandy was very much against it. She felt that we had sacrificed enough for the City of Evanston after 16 years of service. We got hurt financially, and were criticized so unfairly during my last election, causing me to lose the election in a very close race.

But more and more people were coming forward, offering contributions to my campaign and telling how much Evanston needed me in office. Elaine Blakeslee Michaelis, owner of Uinta Title and Insurance, Inc. called and asked me to come see her that she wanted to talk to me. She had been such a good friend that I couldn't very well refuse her so I told her that I would be there to talk.

When I got to her office she asked me what it would take to get me in a financial position to where I could run for mayor. I told her that it would take a substantial amount of money to get caught up with my Uinta Realty debts, and that unless the economy changed I couldn't put myself in the same position, so I told her I wasn't sure.

But she offered to sign a good-size loan with me to guarantee payment at the First National Bank. She offered to do this for me with no strings attached, only that I make every effort to make the payments. I told her that I had to talk to Sandy and that I would get back to her soon, because the deadline for filing for election was coming up fast.

During the city council meeting of June 25th the city council passed the budget for fiscal year 1986-1987 in the amount of $10,234,480, which was down from the previous year by approximately $4 million, the *Uinta County Herald* reported in their June 27th issue.

According to Albert Hays, City Treasurer, most of that $4 million was in grants that were used to build the fire station and sewer project. *There's not a lot of grant money left for the coming year,* he stated.

The *Herald* stated: *According to Hays, there is a total overall decrease for the city budget of 31 percent from last year.*

The article continued: *The general fund of this year's budget comes to $6,473,888. Making up the remainder of the budget is the water fund at $1,202,123; wastewater, $1,741,016; sanitation, $368,153; cemetery, $23,500; and shop fund at $425,800.*

Mayor Gene Martin said that he felt the budget was pretty close to what it should be.

Councilman Rick Sather cast the only negative vote to the budget approval, according to the *Herald.*

Valuation up in Valley, Down in Evanston

The year 1985 was very good for Bridger Valley, giving them a higher assessed valuation — but in Evanston, the slump in oil production brought the valuation downward. That decrease in oil production during 1985 became apparent with the total 1986 county valuation dropping over $100 million.

Valuation figures were released by County Assessor Lulu Decker this week — figures that reflect 1985. Valuation figures the amount of revenue available to fund cities and schools for the 1986-87 fiscal year. This year, Uinta County valuation declined to a drop of $837,868,266, a drop of $107,656,631 from the previous year.

And this year, if oil production continues to slump as it has — especially the past six months — Uinta County will face fiscal year 1987-88 with an even bigger decrease in valuation, according to Decker.

In 1985, Bridger Valley saw a bigger increase in oil production than in 1984, bringing its valuation higher and supplying more funding for its schools and cities. But Evanston's school district faced a cut of $1 million from its budget this year and the City of Evanston cut its budget $4.5 million this year, both a result of 1985 lower oil production.

It's a tightening of the belt for the west end of Uinta County with the City of Evanston valuation at $35,050,651, a decrease of $1,364,368, and in Uinta County School District No. One a valuation of $715,792,120, a decrease of $116,127,300.

Mountain View valuation was $2,293,860, an increase of $113,632, and School District No. Four saw an increase in its budget with a valuation of $45,195,451, an increase of $4,260,036.

And in Lyman, valuation increased by $186,208 to a total $3,146,128 with District Six valuation at $36,390,056, an increase of $5,275,161.

Uinta County Herald, July 25, 1986.

Also that month the city stepped up the campaign to inform voters that on Tuesday, July 15th there would be an election to vote on the proposed Sulphur Creek Reservoir enlargement to supplement the city's water supply. Mayor Martin and members of the city council made an extra effort to encourage folks to get out to the polls and vote in favor of the project.

Due to the water shortage that year, the city council went ahead and limited watering during the summer by putting the odd and even house number system in effect. Even though there was actually a water shortage, and the right thing to do was to limit the use of water, some folks didn't agree with the city. They didn't feel the water shortage was as bad as the city indicated. They accused the city officials of putting the limit on water use to help encourage the citizens to realize the importance of voting in favor of the Sulphur Creek project.

There was a lot of criticism concerning the location of Sulphur Creek. Most of the folks would have rather seen a new dam and reservoir on the Upper Bear River, because they felt that the water would be much cleaner than Sulphur Creek, but at this time it was too late to change, because the Wyoming Water Development Commission had already approved the project, contingent on how the citizens of Evanston voted.

On July 15th the citizens of Evanston voted overwhelmingly in favor of the project – a project that would be essential to the City of Evanston and give the community and area a significant supply of water that would be needed in the future and for further growth. There would be no need for rationing water once the project is completed.

After the election, Mayor Martin and the city council got the project moving by signing all the necessary papers with the State of Wyoming and starting the process of draining the reservoir. Actual construction would not start until after hay season was over, by the ranchers' request. The city and state officials agreed to honor their request, and it was the consensus that the project would not be completed until sometime in March of 1988.

Other projects going on during this summer season were the beautification of downtown Evanston with new decorative street lights and the planting of trees, and the construction of the new Evanston Post Office.

Evanston, Wyoming 82930   Friday, July 25, 1986   Volume 52, Number 60   Price 25¢ Per Copy

Trees and lights will line downtown Evanston

A proposed tree planting and lighting proposal for the downtown historic area was discussed at the DIC (Downtown Improvement Corporation) meeting held at the New Paris Café Wednesday morning.

Paul Knoph, assistant city planner, and Virginia Mahaffey of TLC Landscaping, along with other volunteers, looked at the downtown area and drew up a possible plan for the planting of trees and placing of decorative lighting.

The design for the trees and light fixtures was selected to minimize visibility problems and loss of window space for the merchants.

The trees would be planted in pits cut in the sidewalk, approximately 3 feet square. City volunteers and equipment would be used to cut the concrete for the planting pits.

Volunteers from the community would assist in planting the trees.

The merchants, if they agree, will be responsible for watering the trees, while the city will provide assistance in pruning, fertilizing and mulch to cover the bases.

The cost to the merchant for the trees is approximately $150 for a two-inch diameter tree.

Tree varieties were picked for their size, color, and flowering ability as well as a lateral tap root system that would grow down rather than outward, causing problems with sidewalks and water system. Those varieties selected were crab apple, hawthorne, purple leaf plum, mountain ash and thornless honeylocust.

The green ash species can be used for placement around larger buildings.

Knoph told the group there would be no need for consultants or planners because of the experts who had volunteered their time to work on the proposed project.

A committee was appointed to talk to individual merchants in the downtown area.

A report was given on the Moonlight Madness promotion with special appreciation given to Evanston Police Officer David Schultz, Kelly Sather, KEVA-KOTB Radio, Shawn and Karen Lundberg, and Rick Sather for their work on the project.

Crazy Days promotions for August 1 and 2 were discussed.

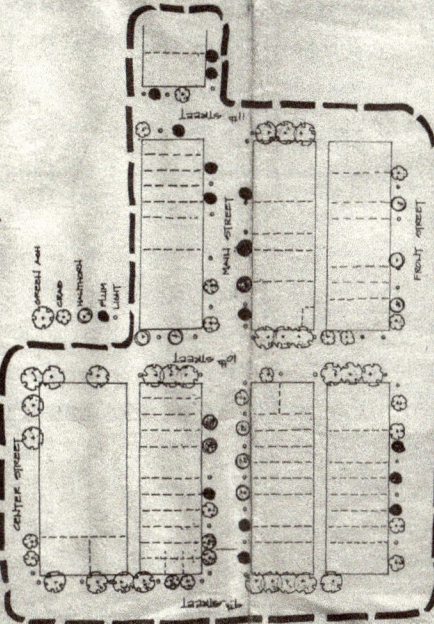

DOWNTOWN HISTORIC DISTRICT

This proposed plan shows approximately placement of trees and lighting fixtures planned for the downtown historic area.

Uinta County Herald.

Also, depot square was becoming what I always called "A people's place": a place for folks to hang out. The Depot Square Committee, Frank Swan, Mildred Palmer, Diane Martin, Carol Stephens, Chuck Straw and Michael Matts, were busy with plans and had added a new cedar roof onto the old U.P. train depot, and they were planning to renovate the interior and clean the exterior, bricks and so on, of the depot.

They were also making plans for the preservation of the Beeman-Cashin Building (the Old Barn, as some called it) that had been donated by J. R. Broadbent and moved to the corner of 10th and Front Streets near the depot. More plans were being made for depot square for the future. Evanston was trying very hard to preserve the history of a community that was started in 1868 as a railroad and mining town.

The morning of July 24th Andrew W. Armstrong, City Engineer, tendered his resignation to the mayor and city council. He had come to work for the city in December of 1984 as assistant engineer, but was promoted when the previous engineer had resigned.

According to his letter to the mayor, he stated: *"I would like to take this opportunity to inform the Mayor and Council that, effective August 7, 1986, I will be leaving the employ of the City of Evanston. I have enjoyed working for the City, and it is with regret that I leave my position and the City of Evanston.*

"I wish the Mayor and Council success in the future."

Mayor Martin and members of the city council accepted his resignation with regrets. They complimented him on his work as an excellent engineer in getting the city projects completed as scheduled. They also wished him and his family the best of luck in the future.

After talking it over with my wife and sons we came to the decision to take up Elaine Michaelis' offer and file for the office of mayor, but I was still concerned with the present economy and how my business would do. My oldest son, Randy, also a real estate broker, said he would help me as much as needed to operate Uinta Realty, Inc.

The position of Mayor for the City of Evanston appeared to be more popular than I had ever seen it before. Seven people filed for the office of mayor; besides me were Miles Alexander, Denice Wheeler, Marvin Bollschweiler, Lance Voss, Clarence Vranish and Willie Cason.

The entire election appeared to draw a lot of interest all the way around. Even the city council had more than the usual filings for the various wards, such as Ward 1, William Davis, Ken Lee, Thomas Marsh and Jay D. Schofield; Ward 2, Merrill Bowman, Jon Lunsford, Thomas Norton, Richard Pryor and Jerry Wall; and Ward 3, Francis Bettinson, H. William George and Darrell Staley.

My slogan *"He's Back!!"* was suggested by my daughter-in-law, Kerri, because I was returning for re-election from four years prior. It was a good slogan and got a lot of attention. There were those that kind of mocked it, but I didn't pay much attention; I just figured no matter what I did in my campaign those same people would have something to mock. I guess that's what they call politics.

In my interview with the local newspapers, *Uinta County Herald* and *Evanston Post*, I stated, *I am concerned about what has happened to Evanston during the last 3½ years. The state of our economy is the number one thing. I feel I did a good job when I was in there before and I feel I can get the people of Evanston out of this slump.*

I continued, *I know I can straighten out the city administration and general services as well as the budget. The economy will go up when we can take care of the sales tax and budget. I think we need to try to increase and diversify industry in this area to promote a better business climate.*

For a long time we've been working at trying to find the best way to get the community to work together. The Chamber and the City should be working for the same thing, but I feel they are shooting in two different ways. If we can work together for the same things, we can gain more.

I went on to say that, *For the past 30 years, Evanston has been my town. Sandy and I have raised four sons, Randy, Dave, Tib and Cody, and we plan to live here for the rest of our lives.*

Before the primary election I had a lot of support with people and friends contributing money for my campaign and I wanted them to know that I appreciated it very much, because it gave me a lot of confidence and a good feeling about running again.

After the primary was over it was clear that Uinta County voters were not apathetic in this run at the polls. A record 71 percent showed up to vote in Tuesday's primary.

In the mayor's race I was the top vote receiver with a total of 1,038 votes, while Denice Wheeler was second with 744 votes. Miles Alexander came in third place with 349 votes, followed by Clarence Vranish with 275, Marvin Bollschweiller with 139, Lance Voss with 98 and Willie Cason with 97. It looked like I would be running against Denice Wheeler in the General Election this coming November.

In the City Council race, the results were as follows. Ward 1: Will Davis – 276 votes, Jay Schofield –245, Thomas Marshall – 123, and Ken Lee – 65. Davis and Schofield would be running in the General Election for Ward 1. Ward 2: Jon Lunsford – 446 votes, Jerry Wall – 363, Richard Pryor – 115, Merrill Bowman – 97, and Thomas Norton – 92. Lunsford and Wall would be running in the General Election for Ward 2. Ward 3: Darrell Staley – 318 votes, Francis Bettinson – 229 votes, and H. William George – 192. Staley and Bettinson would be running in the General Election.

We would have a new governor with Democrat Mike Sullivan and Republican Pete Simpson, the top two vote getters, running in the November election for the governor's seat.

And with two County Commissioner seats open the candidates with the top votes were Republicans John Stevens and Clark Anderson and Democrats Ken Bloomfield and Bob Burns would be running for the two open County Commission positions in November.

I was very pleased with the mayoral results and told the local news, *I feel good about the returns, and I thank all those who supported me. I plan on sitting out for 30 days to relax and then going after it again. I came away from this one with a good feeling.*

My biggest supporter and very good friend Elaine Michaelis received the Business Person of the Year award that summer from the Wyoming Board of Realtors, presented by local Realtor Lisa Burridge, President of the State Board.

Elaine was one of the hardest-working people I have ever known and she worked very hard in building a growing business. She was an honest, upfront and one of the most considerate people I had ever known. The award was well deserved and a long time coming.

Once again in September the city faced another budget shortfall. The city faced this budget problem shortly after the 1986-87 fiscal year budget had passed. It was a real problem to come up with a shortfall that early in the budget year.

The *Uinta County Herald* of September 26th ran an article titled, ANOTHER BUDGET SHORTFALL FACES THE CITY. The article started out: *"This should be proof beyond a shadow of doubt that Evanston and the State of Wyoming are both in a severe economic crunch." Mayor Martin said of the news that the city's general fund will be in shortfall if revenues continue to decrease the way they have been doing.*

"Although, when the budget was being established for the current year the city council projected the budget lower than ever before, the revenues are still an average of 30 percent less than budget requires," Martin said.

Al Hayes, administrative service director, told the council that property, sales, severance, royalty, gas, cigarette and motor vehicle tax revenues were all below what had been projected.

He told the council there would need to be approximately $478,000 cut from the budget to balance with revenues at the end of the year.

The article continued: *In staff meetings held on Thursday morning, the Mayor asked for cuts in all capital construction projects that have not already been started as well as asking for cuts in all departments.*

He is hoping to be able to gain $500,000. "I'd rather cut more so we can have a cushion," he said.

On the bright side, the city's water, sewer and garbage budgets are approximately $250,000 ahead.

Spirits at City Hall are definitely changed from the elation exhibited when the new census figures were announced recently which is expected to bring in more revenue for the city. Unfortunately, that won't help the budget this year, the *Herald* concluded.

The same *Herald* edition announced that the city planner, Bruce Wright had submitted his resignation to Mayor Martin on Wednesday of that week. He stated that he would be leaving on October 3rd and that he had felt that Evanston had been good for him and he had learned a lot and accomplished many programs in the past four years.

Wright was hired by me as City Planner during my administration four years ago and was instrumental in completing the city's comprehensive plan. Now he was leaving and Paul Knopf, his assistant planner, hired recently by the Martin Administration, was taking over the position as City Planner.

I hated to see Wright leave, because he had done a good job, but the mayor and council thanked him for getting the comprehensive plan completed and for his interest and the hard work he had provided the city since he came on board, and they all wished him well in his future plans.

The tree planting project for downtown Evanston had started in early October of 1986 with Assistant Planner Paul Knopf spearheading it. A total of 26 trees were planted that week on Main Street. Businesses owners that participated in the program signed the tree adoption agreement with the city and paid $110.00 for a 2-inch diameter tree.

The trees that were planted were Washington hawthorne, green ash, green spire linden and two varieties of crab apple. These trees were known to be acclimated to the Evanston area.

In *The Evanston Post* dated November 6th it was reported *that "Uinta County unemployment was 2nd highest in the State of Wyoming at 10.8 per cent."* The only county higher was Big Horn with 11.4 percent. The Uinta County rate had nearly doubled the previous year's rate, which last year at this time was 5.7 percent.

The Post's article stated: *The falling oil prices are the major reason unemployment here is so high. Oil service businesses, as well as all services and stores in the county have felt the impact of the declining prices.*

People were leaving Evanston and the economy was declining. The city was having budget problems, employee problems, and many other problems with a "lame duck" Mayor and three council members that were not running again. However, they continued working hard toward budget cuts and keeping the ongoing projects alive.

After several weeks of tough campaigning, speaking to several organizations and talking to people asking for their vote, I was awfully glad to see November 4th, the day of the election, finally arrive and be over. I was elected to be the next mayor of Evanston.

The *Uinta County Herald* of November 7th ran an article titled, OTTLEY BEATS WHEELER FOR MAYOR. The article went on to read: *Ottley carried all three precincts that saw a total of 2,778 voters cast ballots for the Mayor's seat, vacated by Gene Martin this year.*

Campaigning strongly with a slogan that "He's Back, And Evanston Needs Him," the former Evanston mayor garnered a total of 1,531 votes to Wheeler's 1,247. "I was real pleased with the outcome," Ottley told the Herald Wednesday. "We were hoping we would win and I'd like to thank everyone who supported me, especially my family. I commend Denice Wheeler for running a fair and clean campaign. She was a good opponent. Now the work starts. I'll be looking at the problems of the city and searching for the answers. It's going to be quite a chore."

The Herald article concluded: *Ottley will begin as Mayor in January but has had the experience before when he served as Mayor four years ago. He sought re-election but was beaten by Gene Martin who did not choose to seek re-election.*

It was reported that voters turned out in full force with over 70 percent showing up at the polls. In other city elections, in Ward 1, Will Davis beat Jay Schofield by a vote of 494 to 298; Ward 2 was a real squeaker with Jon Lunsford only beating Jerry Wall by 5 votes (569 to 564); and in Ward 3, Darrell Staley beat Francis Bettinson by a vote of 507 to 299.

The Uinta County Clerk had to call for a recount of Lunsford and Wall because of it being such a close race, but after the recount there was no change and in the end Lunsford still won.

In other county elections, Clark Anderson and John Stevens, both Republicans, narrowly beat Ken Bloomfield and Bob Burns, both Democrats, for the two Uinta County Commissioner seats. Kathryn Cue, Republican and former real estate broker for Uinta Realty, Inc., beat out Eyvonne Osborn, Democrat, in a close race for County Assessor, and Leonard Hysell, Democrat, beat Forrest Bright, Republican, for County Sheriff.

On the Wyoming state level, Mike Sullivan, Democrat, beat Pete Simpson, Republican, for Governor, and Kathy Karpan, Democrat, beat K. C. Thomson, Republican, for Secretary of State.

Also, Ron Micheli and Jerry Parker, both Republicans, beat out their only opponent, Democrat Jeff Carlton for State representatives.

I felt bad for Denice Wheeler for her loss, and I really appreciated her for running such a clean race. She was a good and pleasant opponent and probably would have been a good mayor.

I would be going in as mayor with three new city council members: Will Davis from Ward 1, Jon Lunsford, who had been a member with me previously, from Ward 2, and Darrell Staley from Ward 3. They would be joining the standing council members; Clarence Vranish of Ward 1, Craig Nelson of Ward 2, and Tom Hutchinson of Ward 3.

Not too long after the election results came out in the newspapers and were finalized, someone asked me what I intended to do when I take over as mayor. I answered, *One of Evanston's old timers and a supporter of mine told me this, "Just do the best you can with what you've got, that will be enough."* That old timer was Robert "Bob" Mitchell.

I said to the inquirer that I was going to do just that. I said, *I'm going to do the best I can with what I have to work with, and I hope that will be enough. And if I don't have enough of what I need, I will look elsewhere for whatever it takes to get the job done.*

Right after the election, I started thinking about my appointments. I first approached Attorney Dennis Lancaster to take the position of City Attorney, who was city attorney during my first term as mayor. He had worked hard and did a great job for the city at that time. I was hoping that he would consider it again, but he declined and indicated that he wanted to concentrate on his private practice. So I had to look elsewhere.

I contacted a relatively new Evanston Attorney, Dennis M. Boal, who had been highly recommended to me by other attorneys and associates, so I asked him to meet with me. During our meeting we talked about the position and what the city would expect of him. He seemed to be very interested and I was very impressed with him after hearing what he had to say and his reactions toward the job. I told him that he would have to go on retainer and wouldn't be an employee of the city. He said he was interested, but would have to talk to his associates, and if they agreed, he would send me a letter with his proposal.

We shook hands and he thanked me for considering him and that he would get right on it. Dennis at that time was affiliated with the firm of Vehar, Beppler, Jacobson, Lavery & Rose, a well-known and accredited Wyoming law firm.

On November 20th, Dennis sent me a letter accepting the position of City Attorney if the city agreed to his proposed terms and rates, as described in the letter, for his services to the City of Evanston. I accepted his proposal and nominated him for City Attorney, but it would have to wait until the January meeting, after I was sworn in as mayor, and then the city council would have to confirm his appointment along with several others.

Monday morning, December 8th, I held a news conference to announce my appointments for the positions in my new administration.

People keep asking me what I will be doing, I told the news staff; and that was why I called for this news conference.

I announced that I named local attorney Dennis M. Boal as City Attorney to handle the legal affairs of the city, and that he would be hired on a retainer basis and not as a regular employee.

I said, *He's had a lot of high recommendations. He's good, young, energetic, and will do Evanston a lot of good.*

I named another local attorney, Thomas F. Mealey, as Police Justice/City Judge, and Steve Snyder as my Administrative Assistant again.

As Administrative Assistant he would help me, not only to manage the city's affairs, but also as an adviser, a mediator when necessary, and as a communications person. He would also be a liaison to the employees for me, and accompany me in various meetings with outsiders and act in my behalf when I am absent. In other words, Snyder would work very closely with me on running the city; he would be my in-between.

Someone asked me if I was going to have a Director of Administrative Services, but I told them that all I need is someone to help me directly and keep me on the straight and narrow, and that would be Snyder. He and I worked closely together before, and got things done, and I didn't need a Director of Administrative Services; I didn't need a Director of General Services, and I didn't need a Financial Manager, a Public Relations Person or a Communications Person, or any separate person or individual to be Budget Director. All I need is what I had before and that was Snyder, a city clerk and a city treasurer. The budget will be taken care of through the treasurer, Snyder and the mayor.

Boal

Continued from page 1

1979.

He worked in the Natural Resource division of the Attorney General's Office in Cheyenne for three years. He also worked for approximately a year for a private attorney's office right out of law school.

Boal will be working for the city on an hourly reduced rate of $65 per hour. His normal rate is $75 dollars per hour.

According to Boal, he and incoming Mayor Dennis Ottley discussed his rate and duties. He will be required to keep track of his time along with what he did during that time and give a report to the City Council.

He has named Rick LaVery as his assistant. Both are involved with the local law firm of Vehar, Bepplar, Jacobsen, LaVery and Rose.

"In the lawsuit with the sewer treatment plant, the city has retained an outside specialist attorney to represent them,"he said.

Ray Hunkins will remain as the principle attorney on that action, but Boal will be monitoring the work and helping when needed. His major responsibility will be to act as contact person to advise the council on the proceedings.

Boal and his wife Mary Jane have two children, Craig who is seven and Kara who is four.

UINTA COUNTY HERALD   Wednesday, December 17, 1986

Boal excited about serving Evanston as city attorney

by Ann Curtis
of the Herald Staff

"I am looking forward to and I am excited about working for the city. I'm interested in developing my skills in that division of the law," newly appointed attorney for the city, Dennis Boals, stated.

"I can give something back to the community and use my legal education for the city."

Boals is 33 years old and has been living in the community for four years.

He graduated from the University of Wyoming law school in

Continued on page 16

Dennis Boal

Evanston, Wyoming 82930   Friday, December 19, 1986   Volume 52, N

Snyder will serve as assistant to Ottley for City of Evanston

Steve Snyder is not a new face at city hall. He has been working for the city through several administrations. He has lived in Evanston for ten years, eight of it working with the city.

He was named as administrative assistant by Dennis Ottley, mayor-elect.

Under Mayor Gene Martin, his title was primary grantsman for the city.

As administrative assistant, Snyder says "I will have added responsibilities of carrying out policy for the mayor and council, implementing the day-to-day functions of the city." He will be coordinating the existing departments, keeping communication lines open to prevent duplication of work. He will be working for ways to make city government more cost-effective.

According to Snyder, a large part of his duties will be getting grant money for such projects as the water treatment plant which will be a continuation of the Sulphur Creek Reservoir project and obtaining grant money which will complete County Road.

The County Road project already has $1.6 million in its coffers, which will build the new bridge and complete the new roadway to the Maverick station. Snyder will be working on finding the money to finish the project.

"Mayor Ottley wants to get money for economic development," he added. Grant money comes from state as well as federal sources. He explained that the Federal HUD (Housing and Urban Development) program makes money available to states for economic development. The states then make the money available to cities.

Working in the city's behalf, he makes a proposal to the state and lobbies them for money to do individual projects. "We have been successful in the past," he stated. "We have good rapport with elected officials in Cheyenne, it has worked out well."

"In the spirit of friendship and cooperation, I have also been assisting Uinta County in some grant work such as in county roads and the Veterans Memorial," Snyder explained. Other projects in the future may be helping find money for the proposed jail or a new fair grounds.

Steve Snyder

I told the group in the news conference that I would appoint Albert Hays as City Treasurer if he accepted the position, and Don Welling would remain as City Clerk, and Dennis Harvey would be appointed to the position of Chief of Police.

The position of city engineer would not be filled immediately, but I would keep Assistant Engineer Frank Smith on until I can advertise for an engineer. I told the press: *I am looking for a city engineer with a public engineer's certificate and who ideally has been in the business five years or so.*

I hoped to find a local engineer to fill the job who knew Evanston's problems. I did talk to John Proffit of Uinta Engineering and Surveying about taking the position of City Engineer, but he declined and said he had other plans.

I also told the press that I was very concerned about the Sulphur Creek Reservoir project, the water treatment plant and the improvements to County Road, and I wanted to advertise for a city engineer shortly after I was sworn in.

I said that my policy would be to stick with the basics. I would eliminate the position of Public Works Director and name Allen Kennedy as General Superintendent of Operations, although this is not an appointed position.

I also said at the news media conference that I would appoint or re-appoint board and commission positions as they expire. There would be no immediate changes in those positions unless someone quits or resigns. I also told them that I wasn't as concerned with the budget as I had previously been, because I plan to freeze all expenses to help take up the shortfall, since revenues are not as much as anticipated.

I continued: *When I left office four years ago the city had a reserve fund in the amount of approximately $4 million, but when I go back in office that fund will be dwindled down to approximately $200,000. That is something I will have to think about. I have always felt good when I had a sizeable reserve fund on hand. It's there if you need it.*

I said that I planned to be very aggressive in pursuing economic and industrial development. I would work closely with the Chamber of Commerce to bring highway travel into Evanston.

I would also encourage existing business expansion with Industrial Development Revenue Bonds if the applicants have the right credentials. *I am very much aware of these funds being available,* I told the group. *I will look at all aspects to increase the economy, not just for Evanston but for the whole area.*

I said that Snyder and I would be planning trips to Denver and Cheyenne to talk to members of the oil industry and get acquainted with the new Wyoming State Administration: Governor Sullivan, Secretary of State Karpan and others. I planned to spend a lot of time with the Wyoming Highway Department, because we have a big need for their assistance.

Finally, I told the press that I promised to welcome the media and any questions they might have, and if there were to be any additional council meetings, they would be notified and the meetings would be held in council chambers. As for city employees, I said, *I will be doing a lot of shuffling but I do not intend to get rid of anyone right now.*

The Depot Square and green belt are two projects which were started during my previous administration and I would continue to work on. *Evanston is in a good location and has a lot to look forward to,* I promised.

The *Uinta County Herald* of December 24th ran an article titled, SULPHUR CREEK BIDS OPENED. The article went on: *Larry, Inc. of Gillette, Wyoming, is the apparent low bidder for the dam construction portion of the Sulphur Creek Reservoir project with a bid of $7,995,862.85. Bids were opened and read Friday, December 19th.*

The awarding of the bids will tentatively be made on Feb. 4th, after the city staff and the staff of Woodward-Clyde, the engineering firm on the project, have had time to go over all figures and make sure no mistakes have been made on the addition of the bid.

The Larry, Inc. bid was substantially lower than most of the other five bids on the project. The engineering estimate for dam construction was $11,740,666, the article continued.

The *Herald* also said that the city had the right to reject the bid if they chose, and that the bid was for the dam construction only, and not the pipeline construction.

In the same issue of the *Herald*, Jim Wise, Evanston Postmaster, announced that the new 17,000 square foot Evanston Post Office was expected to be completed by April 1, 1987.

Mayor Gene Martin said that the new water well donated by Amoco Production Company was a good addition to Evanston's water system, and quoted Martin as saying, *I want to thank Amoco for the $78,000 donated to produce this well and Chuck MacIlvaine, Public Works Director, for his efforts in producing this well for the City of Evanston.*

"The new well, plus the new water lines that have been constructed in the area, will now loop the Overthrust and Centennial Valley with the main part of Evanston, and will help with the water pressure in those areas," the mayor said.

PART FOUR

"HE'S (OTTLEY) BACK"

"Before everything else, getting ready is the secret of success."

— HENRY FORD

CHAPTER 21

1987.... 1987 was the year that I would be taking over as Mayor of Evanston once again. Four years ago while being mayor, Evanston experienced one of the largest booms in the history of Wyoming. But now it appears I will be looking at the problem of improving a depressed economy.

I read a comment once, by an unknown author, that reminded me of being mayor of the city, though I changed the wording to fit my position. The comment went something like this:

The people of a City may spread itself over the entire community...But the average person will almost always form a judgment of it through contacts with one individual, the Mayor. If the Mayor is discourteous, inefficient or ineffective, it will take much time and energy to overcome that bad impression.

Each citizen of that City who, in any capacity, comes in contact with the public is an agent, and the impression made is an advertisement, good or bad, which will make an indelible impression on the mind of the public.

I also read another quote, also anonymous, that read:

"I am of service,
everything I do makes a difference in people's lives.
I am a success."

All those words meant something to me and I was looking forward to being Mayor of Evanston once again because I always tried to be courteous, efficient and effective, and I had hoped that I could get the folks of Evanston to do likewise.

Other than the economy and the budget shortfall, we had two ongoing projects that we had to look forward to: the Sulphur Creek Dam and the improvements to County Road. Both were just starting and were approved by the state. Sulphur Creek dam engineering had just been completed and we were in the process of calling for bids for construction of the dam, and we were just starting on the County Road project. An engineer had just been hired by the Martin Administration from an engineering firm out of Casper.

The budget was showing a deficit and had to be adjusted. Our revenues had a shortfall over the past few months. I wasn't too worried about the budget, because I knew I would not have positions such as Director of Administrative Services, Finance Manager (Budget Director), Director of General Services, or a Communications Person. I would be going back to basics and wouldn't be appointing any more high-priced outside help, and that would help a lot in balancing the budget. According to reports from the previous administration, the shortfall or deficit was under $400,000.

All of the top personnel that the Martin Administration had hired that were still employed during Mayor Martin's last year of his term had quit prior to the election in November or right after the election. I know some of them quit because they had been told that I would be going back to basics and would not be hiring for those positions.

But I did immediately start advertising for the City Engineer position and received one application from Brian Honey, who had been with Forsgren-Perkins Engineering for several years and had worked on a number of projects in and around the City of Evanston. Forsgren-Perkins's head office was in Salt Lake City, but they had established an office also in Evanston.

I was very impressed by Honey's resume and after my interview with him I was even more impressed, and decided that he was the right person for the position of City Engineer. I spoke to the council members, new and old, one on one, and none of them had a problem with him being appointed.

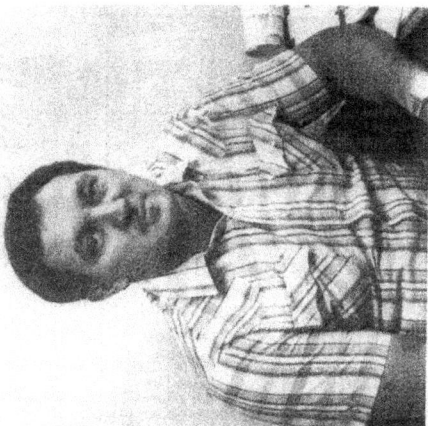

Brian Honey

Mayor impressed by new engineer

UC H   1/7/87

"After looking at his resume and talking to him, I was impressed," Mayor-elect Dennis Ottley said of his newly appointed city engineer, Brian Honey.

"He's a young engineer with a public engineer's license and treats the public good. He's a person who will work for the public," he continued.

Honey, 38, was born and raised in Kanab, Utah, and came to Evanston four years ago. He graduated from Utah State Univer-

sity in 1974 with a B.S. degree in civil engineering.

According to Honey, he joined the staff of Forsgren-Perkins Engineering at the Salt Lake office before coming to Evanston with the firm.

During his tenure with the office, he has worked on a number of projects in and around the city of Evanston. He was engineer on the storm water master plan in Centennial Valley and Brook Hollow. Also on his list of credits

are the detention basins for Grass Valley and Brook Hollow.

He is now working on engineering designs for the West Interchange which will make the water system loop from Sheridan St. across the Interstate to Kentucky Fried Chicken to improve the water pressure for the businesses on the hill, such as the Dunmar Inn and Whirl Inn on that end of town.

"I have a lot of experience with the city water systems and a technical understanding of the utility system as well." Honey said.

He added that he hoped to add stability to the city engineering department. "In the time I have been in Evanston, I have worked with four or five engineers at the city," he said.

He feels he can technically provide the expertise the city needs to complete the Sulphur Creek Reservoir and the proposed water treatment plant.

"One of the first projects I worked on was the Phase II of Sulphur

Creek Reservoir for the Wyoming Water Development Commission. I understand a lot about what the city needs to achieve and what it hopes to gain from the Sulphur Creek project," he added.

When he relaxes from his time at the drafting table, he likes to fly fish. A new hobby is river rafting.

He and his wife ZoRae have five children ranging in age from 15 to 4 years of age.

He feels the new position with the city will help him grow professionally with other aspects of engineering.

According to Ottley, the position will not only cover the engineering department but Honey will be responsible for the public works department as well.

The position will pay $40,000 plus benefits for the first year with a chance of a further raise after a year's time.

Frank Smith will remain as assistant city engineer.

Uinta County Herald, January 7, 1987.

Brian Honey was 38 years old and was born and raised in Kanab, Utah and had moved to Evanston four years prior to taking the city engineer's position. He graduated from the Utah State University in 1974 with a B.S. degree in civil engineering. He and his wife ZoRae had five children ranging in age from 4 years to 15 at that time.

The first council meeting was on January 14th and was called to order by Outgoing Mayor Gene Martin. Following the Pledge of Allegiance, he called for roll call and for a motion to approve the minutes of the previous meeting, and to pay all outstanding bills.

After business as usual was completed, Martin gave his final State of the City speech, listing his accomplishments during his four-year term as mayor, which he indicated he was very proud of. He had reason to be, because he did get most of the projects that had started prior to his term completed.

His administration formed the Parks and Recreation District in Uinta County School District No. 1, and the Evanston Voluntary Fire Department as a Uinta County Fire District under the county commissioners. By redistricting both of these departments it saved the City of Evanston a ton of money. They both would primarily be funded by the district and county mill levies now in place. I had to admire Martin in that respect, but he did have a lot of inside problems with the employees and members of the council.

After his speech he presented City Attorney Mark Harris with a plaque and thanked him for his services during the past four years. He also presented the outgoing city council members each with a plaque.

He explained to them that those plaques were *so you will know that you were here, because in three or four days everyone will have forgotten all about you.*

Each of the recipients told of their pleasure at working for the city and representing their constituents, and showed their appreciation for the opportunity to be of service to the community.

Mayor Martin then presented me, as incoming mayor, with a toy alligator in a bear trap, saying, *Every administration has its alligators – problems that come up from nowhere and plague you – so I want you to have this trap. Please pass this trap on to the man or woman who follows you.* Everyone kind of chuckled, including myself.

25¢

the evanston

post

January 15, 19887

The Alligator Trap

Former Mayor Gene Martin handed new mayor, Dennis Ottley, an alligator trap at last night's City Council meeting where Ottley was sworn in. "I've seen alligators around here for the past four years," Martin said, adding "I think you might need this too." Photo by John Bowers.

And then Council President Lance Voss presented Mayor Martin with a plaque saying, *There have been some tough times for the seven of us sitting here; it's not always been fun, but we've done the best we could for the city.* He also gave Martin his gavel, saying, *When you get to feeling lonely you can use this to beat up Di's [Martin's wife Diane] furniture.*

Following the presentations, City Clerk Don Welling swore in the new city officials: me as mayor, and the three newly elected councilmen, Jon Lunsford, Darrell Staley and Will Davis. They would be joining the three holdover members of the council, Julie Lehman, Tom Hutchinson and Clarence Vranish.

After the swearing-in ceremony, Gene Martin, as outgoing mayor, handed his position over to me and wished me luck and offered me his support. I thanked him and wished him well.

But as I took the mayor's seat, I told everyone that it felt good to be, as the old saying goes, *"back in the saddle again,"* and thanked everyone for giving me this opportunity to serve them once again, and promised them that I would do my best to get the economy back on track. I explained that the economy has always been number one with me, and should be with any elective official, and that I had always taken the Oath of Office, that had just been administered to me, very seriously and promised to uphold it.

I stated my goals and objectives for the next four years. We would get the budget straightened out and try our best to keep a balanced budget. *I have always been a believer in fiscal control, and maintaining a reasonable reserve that we can fall back on in case of an emergency or unexpected change that could happen.* I also said that I would follow through with the completion of ongoing projects such as the Sulphur Creek Dam and improvements to the County Road.

I added that, *I'm looking forward to being able to work with the Evanston Chamber of Commerce, and all other organizations and groups in the community, to assist in making the economy better. I want to work with the Chamber especially in trying to attract and increase our tourist traffic. Also, with the help of the Chamber, I will do my best to try to encourage local spending and keep our money in town.*

I spoke of the history of Evanston and Uinta County and said, *I will continue to encourage the preservation of our history and to keep downtown Evanston the heart of the community. There is an enormous amount of history that we should never let go of in Evanston and the area.*

I continued, *I will also work very hard to locate new industry and needed businesses for Evanston. Through available programs such as the Industrial Revenue Bonds and the Greater Evanston Industrial Corp., which I am currently President of, I hope to use these programs to obtain new industry and additional businesses that will provide more jobs and opportunities for the folks in Evanston: new, old and for our youth.*

I added, *I will work very closely with all my top employees in the various departments, and I will also work with city boards and commission, including the Joint Power Boards, and stay informed of what's going on. My office will have an open door policy for all city employees and all citizens of Evanston. I will move my office to the front of the city hall area as I did before, which was a better position to observe what's going on and a better opportunity to communicate with office personnel and the public. I like to know what's going on in the city, and my door will be open to all, with no exceptions.*

I will take a hard look at all city ordinances, especially building, zoning, and subdivision. I will be looking at them to see if we can't allow more flexibility in them which, I believe, will encourage more construction for folks to improve or expand their present businesses, and to encourage more new construction, whether it be housing or business, I added.

I continued: *I promise to give the folks in Evanston the best service possible in all areas; keeping the streets in good condition, clean and open by removing the snow when necessary. I will continue to improve our water supply and follow through with the Sulphur Creek Dam project, and I plan to change our garbage pickup system as soon as possible to give our city employees some relief and make it easier for the public to dispose of their garbage. I also promise that there will be no immediate increase in any city rates at this time.*

I will work on upgrading our police department by communicating with them and keeping a good relationship, as well as work on improvements in the department to curb crime in Evanston. I will also be working closely with the Uinta County Fire Department because, although they have now gone countywide, we will still be concerned with their operation within the City of Evanston, and the same goes for the Parks and Recreation Commission. We must keep close communications with both the fire department and the recreation board because we will still have a fiscal responsibility to both.

I ended by saying, *I will strive to encourage continuous planning for the short term as well as long term. I have always tried to look ahead and plan for the future, but at times, I do look back once in a while to improve and correct any mistakes the city may have made to be sure we don't repeat them, and sometimes to get additional ideas for the future.*

Communications is the key to any successful program. My major goal is to successfully give the folks of Evanston the community that they can be proud of and the community they desire and deserve.

After my comments I made my staff appointments: Dennis Boal, City Attorney; Tom Mealey, City Judge; Steve Snyder, Administrative Assistant; Don Welling, City Clerk; Al Hayes, City Treasurer; Dennis Harvey, Chief of Police; and Brian Honey, City Engineer.

I also named, although they are not appointed positions, Frank Smith as Assistant City Engineer, Allen Kennedy as General Superintendent of Public Works, and Paul Knopf as City Planner and Community Development Director.

After these appointments I asked for confirmation from the council. A motion was made and seconded, but there appeared to be some concern, so I called for discussion.

During the discussion Councilwoman Julie Lehman said she had no problem with the qualifications of the people named, but she did have reservations concerning the $65 hourly rate promised to the new attorney, and expressed some concern about the $40,000-plus salary of the city engineer.

I felt that Julie Lehman had questioned the attorney's hourly rate because her husband, Larry Lehman was also a local attorney, and she felt she may have a conflict, but nevertheless she voted in favor of all appointments.

Councilman Clarence Vranish said that he thought Brian Honey was well qualified for the position of city engineer, but objected to the salary figure. The starting salary for Honey would be $40,000 annually, plus a 10 percent increase in 6 months with deferred compensation.

When asked for the vote to confirm these positions as named, Vranish was the only dissenting vote. Lehman and all other council members voted in favor.

Councilman Jon Lunsford was unanimously elected as President of the Council. Also named were members to fill vacancies on several boards and commissions. I named myself to the Airport Joint Powers Board, the Human Services Joint Powers Board, and to the Sulphur Creek Joint Powers Board.

At that time I felt that it was very important that I be on these boards because they were all relatively new boards that shared powers jointly with County of Uinta, and it gave me an opportunity to work closely with the board-assigned county commissioners. I also felt that these projects were essential to the city and I wanted to be concerned in the decision making by the boards.

In addition, I appointed Councilmen Lunsford and Vranish to the airport board; Councilman Staley to the human service board; and Councilman Davis to the Sulphur Creek project board. Councilman Vranish was already on the Sulphur Creek board as a holdover and had been named Secretary/ Treasurer of the board previously.

On January 7th, Vranish distributed a written financial statement for December 1986 showing that the cash investments pledged to the Sulphur Creek project were doing very well accruing interest during the month. He said that it was imperative that we receive Uinta County's contribution as soon as possible, because of the likelihood that the project may be finished earlier than we had anticipated.

On January 23rd, the *Uinta County Herald* ran an article titled, CHAMBER SURVEY SHOWS LOCAL BUSINESSES FAVOR GAMBLING BILL. The article read: *The Evanston Chamber of Commerce Board of Directors voted yesterday at their regular Board meeting to endorse Wyoming HB174, which is a local option gambling bill. The Board of Directors based their endorsement on a recent survey of the Chamber members.*

According to the *Herald* article, the Wyoming House of Representative Bill 174 was a full gaming bill similar to Nevada and New Jersey, with certain limitations. If passed by the state legislature, it would be the county or municipality's option to have an election where the people could vote on whether or not they would be in favor of gambling.

To screen the members of the Evanston Chamber of Commerce on their thoughts about whether or not the gambling bill would be good for Evanston or not, the Chamber did a survey of their membership by sending out a questionnaire with four questions to each member. The results of the survey showed overwhelming support in favor of House Bill 174. The fourth question of the questionnaire was, *"Do you think gambling would be good for Evanston?"* 95 members said yes, 15 answered no, and 14 had no opinion.

My opinion of this was that the main reason the Chamber of Commerce members voted so heavily in favor of the gambling bill was because of the present economy, but to be honest, I never was in favor of gambling in the State of Wyoming at this level, and I did vote against it as a Chamber member. I had more confidence that our economy was going to improve, and improve quite rapidly. But, then I could be wrong.

However, the Wyoming House of Representatives voted down House Bill 174 at that time. Another gambling bill would come up again in a few years and would be passed by the state legislators, but it would be a bill allowing a referendum for a vote of the people of the entire state of Wyoming to allow casino type gambling only by local option.

During the meeting of January 14th Councilman Lunsford made a motion directing the mayor to write a letter to the Wyoming State Legislature in support their bill pertaining to cabooses on railroad trains. At that time the Union Pacific Railroad, among other railroad companies, was considering removing the cabooses from all trains, but for safety reasons, the state legislature had a bill opposing the railroad's decision. I sent a letter stating that the City of Evanston was in favor of the legislative bill opposing the removal of cabooses from over-the-road moving trains, but the railroad companies were successful in getting approval from the U.S. Congress to discontinue the use of cabooses on their trains.

We were opposed to it for safety purposes, and it would eliminate more jobs in Wyoming. The state was already having economic problems and we didn't want to see it get any worse.

Also during the meeting I announced that the Wyoming Association of Municipalities (W.A.M.) had assigned me to two W.A.M. committees: Legislative Steering Committee and Economic Development Committee, and they assigned Councilman Hutchinson to the W.A.M. Utility Committee, and City Clerk Don Welling to the W.A.M. Joint Powers Insurance Committee.

Our next regular City Council meeting was on January 28th, which the *Uinta County Herald* claimed was a quiet meeting with only a few items on the agenda.

The *Herald* article stated that I had announced my appointments of council members to act as liaison with respective department heads. They would work closely with the assigned departments and report back to the mayor and full council concerning problems and questions the department may have. This was a system that had been used by previous mayors for years, up until Mayor Gene Martin decided to stop it during his term of administration. Why? I did not know.

I wanted to go back to the system of assigning council members to various departments, because I always felt that it was a good idea to delegate council members to something other than just going to meetings. I believed it was good for department heads to have someone with authority to talk to, and I felt that the appointments gave city council members more responsibility and a feeling of having a more definite part of the city administration.

My appointments made during that meeting were: Tom Hutchinson, streets and alleys; Darrell Staley, water and sewer (including the plants); Will Davis, sanitation; Jon Lunsford, fire department; Staley and me, recreation; I would act as Police Commissioner with Davis and Hutchinson serving with me on the Police Commission; Clarence Vranish and I were assigned to Planning and Zoning; Julie Lehman, Urban Renewal and Beautification; and I would be assigned to the Evanston Housing Authority and oversee the administration department.

This year, 1987, was the Bicentennial of the United States Constitution and during the meeting Councilwoman Julie Lehman made a motion that Hight and Dorothy Proffit act as city representatives to the Bicentennial Celebration of the United States Constitution scheduled for September 17, 1987. Motion was seconded and passed unanimously.

During the meeting a motion was made and passed unanimously to direct City Attorney Dennis Boal to prepare a resolution to change the city council meeting dates to the second and fourth Monday of each month, and change the starting time to 7:00 p.m. This was to give city staff a reasonable amount of time to prepare minutes, treasury reports, and so on for the meetings, and it was thought that by starting the meetings at 7:00 p.m., council members and the public would have time to go home and change, if needed, and have dinner, because sometimes our meetings would last late into the next day. Our intentions were never to purposely rush through any of the meetings; we felt that council members and those present from the public should have the time to say what they had to say.

It was also announced in the news article that there would be a special city council meeting at 5:00 p.m. on February 4th to discuss Sulphur Creek Reservoir and several other matters. This was also stated in the news article for the public's benefit.

<hr>

The Greater Evanston Development Corporation, dba Western Wyoming Certified Development Company, was still very active under Director Bill Frisby. He was working continuously trying to entice new businesses and industry to Evanston and Western Wyoming. Businesses already operating were also eligible for the 504 program for expansion purposes, as well as new construction. He also helped in getting some companies in operation in other parts of Uinta, Lincoln, Sublette, Sweetwater, and Teton Counties. The SBA-504 loan program was working very well for the area.

However, Frisby wasn't doing enough to keep him on board as director and in a couple of years, when our money ran out, we had to let him go; but through his efforts Evanston did gain several business-es that created dozens of jobs. Therefore, it wasn't a total loss to hire Frisby. He was doing his job and it was too bad we couldn't afford to keep him on longer.

Later on the Greater Evanston Development Corp. dissolved its corporation, because with the economy as it was, everyone lost in-terest in trying to keep it active, because we didn't have any more income for operating purposes, and there was nowhere to go to get more unless we went for public donations. No one on the board wanted to do that and I was too tired to worry about it after 21 years as president of the corporation.

Michael Matts, Evanston's Director of the Urban Renewal Agency announced in late January of 1987 that the Beeman–Cashin Building had been completely refurbished and was now ready for community use.

Uinta County Herald

Evanston, Wyoming 82930   Wednesday, January 28, 1987   Volume 53, Number 7   Price 25c Per Copy

Beeman-Cashin building now ready for community use

The Beeman-Cashin building and Depot Square are continuing to receive their facelifts with the removal of the overhead wires and poles and the installation of the historic Sternberg lights.

"It is a long-term goal to install them throughout the downtown area," Paul Knopf said.

Additional lights will be installed at Depot Square and along the underpass, along 11th and Center and near the new Post Office, according to Knopf.

He has been questioned about the lighting along the underpass.

"The lights going in there will be whiter and more brilliant than the yellowish ones along Depot Square for security of the pedestrians and traffic. It will be the same lighting intensity as the other lights," Knopf said.

Michael Matts, Evanston Renewal Agency, affirmed that the Beeman-Cashin building was near completion and ready to be used for community activities.

A steering committee has been formed to schedule and plan activities for Depot Square this summer.

The building now has its new windows, insulation installed, barnwood siding installed on the interior walls, heating and water outlet and light fixtures have been hung.

"It's ready for community activities," Matts confirmed.

Anyone interested in having an activity in the building or on the site can contact Matts or Mildred Palmer at the Chamber office to get on the schedule.

On June 6, the Renewal Ball is tentatively scheduled to be held on the Depot Square site. The theme this year will be the period of 1900 with a subtheme of Chinese dress during the same period.

The funds generated at the ball will be earmarked for renovation of the depot.

The Beeman-Cashin building has already begun its use with a wedding being performed in the structure.

It will be available for use with a fee structure of $50 for any non-profit agency who wants to hold an activity that will not be charging a door admission. If an admission will be charged, the fee will be $50 plus 25 cents per ticket sold.

For private use, the fee will be $75 and if a ticket price is charged, 50 cents per ticket will be added to the fee.

This will help pay the power bill and for maintenance and operation of the building.

The Depot Square Committee has planned an open house for the building in April so the community can see the work that has been accomplished.

Refreshments and activities will be planned for the celebration.

According to Matts, it will be geared toward thanking people who volunteered their labor, materials and expert advice on the project.

The Beeman-Cashin building is ready for use by the public. Anyone wishing to hold an activity in the building can contact Michael Matts at Evanston Renewal Agency or Mildred Palmer at the Chamber office.

The Depot Square Committee, headed by Mildred Palmer, said they planned to hold the open house for the building in April when the weather was nicer so the folks in the community could see what has been done and to hear some of the history of the building. She also said they plan to hold the 1987 Annual Renewal Ball this year on the Depot Square site on June 6th.

Not too long after I resumed office as Mayor of Evanston, an interested group of local citizens, Willis Barnes, Elmer Danks, James Butcher, Curt Ellingford, Clarence Lowham and Marvin Bollshweiler, asked to set up a meeting with me. These men were all old-timers of Evanston and all very concerned with what was best for the city.

The reason they wanted to meet with me was to talk about the Sulphur Creek Dam project. First of all, they didn't feel good about the enlargement of the dam. Like a lot of other folks, they would have rather seen a new reservoir and dam on the Bear River, because they all thought that the water would be much cleaner.

One of the group members said: *That's why they call it Sulphur Creek, because it has a bit of Sulphur in the water.* But I told them that it was too late to change the location of the dam because the State of Wyoming had already accepted the project and all the engineering on the enlargement of the dam, and that we were now closing deals with the ranchers to obtain additional property for the enlargement and the roadways. Also, I said, the bids for the dam are now out and we will be looking at them very soon.

But I added that I did not like the approved plans with the intake on Bear River being almost 20 miles south of Evanston, and having a 30-inch pipeline running from Bear River to the east across Hilliard Flats and entering into Sulphur Creek waters miles before the creek reaches the reservoir. I told them that our city engineer didn't like it either. We thought there should be a better way of connecting the Bear River to the reservoir than that. And that the whole purpose of involving the Bear River was because of the large amount of water rights we had from the Bear, and the river water would help to keep the reservoir full if and when Sulphur Creek got too low and with much cleaner water.

I explained that City Engineer Brian Honey was now working on a new proposal to relocate the pipeline that we can present to the State Water Commission when we meet with them in Cheyenne next month.

After talking to Honey about the conversation that I had with the interested group, he immediately continued to work on his proposed idea on the pipeline from the Bear to the reservoir coming up with a new plan that would serve the same purpose in providing additional water to the dam from the Bear River.

Brian's plan was to bring the intake on the Bear further to the north near the old Wes Myers ranch and install a 36-inch pipeline from the new site of the intake from the Bear River to the Sulphur Creek Reservoir in a northerly direction, crossing the Wyoming State Highway 150 near the old Broken Circle Ranch home, and installing a Y-type pipe connection in the pipeline with a valve controlling which way the flow from the Bear would go: to the reservoir, or directly to the Evanston Water Treatment Plant.

With this plan we would not have to run the proposed 30-inch line from Bear River to Sulphur Creek across Hilliard Flat. The Bear River water would never enter the creek, but would, with the valve turned right, flow from the Bear to the southeast to enter the reservoir.

We were scheduled to meet with the Wyoming Water Development Commission (WWDC) next month concerning the dam project, but when we got there, as I was relatively new to the project, I had Councilman Tom Hutchinson, Chairman of the Sulphur Creek Joint Powers Board, represent the City of Evanston. After explaining that we had come up with a new proposal changing the pipeline from the Bear River to the reservoir, and noticing that there was surprise in some of the commissioners' faces, he then introduced Evanston's new City Engineer, Brian Honey, to the Board to explain the proposed change.

Brian told them, *The new intake will be constructed with a 36-inch pipeline at an elevation whereby water can gravity-flow directly from Bear River into Sulphur Creek Reservoir, and the 36-inch pipe would also feed into the 24-inch line a short distance below the reservoir so that Bear River water can flow to the city without going first into the reservoir. Reservoir water would be used by the city only when necessary.*

He continued, *In addition to the benefit of providing direct flow from Bear River to Sulphur Creek Reservoir, the quality of the water will be better because most of the water used by the city will flow directly to the water treatment plant from the Bear River and not go through the reservoir.*

SCENARIO THREE:

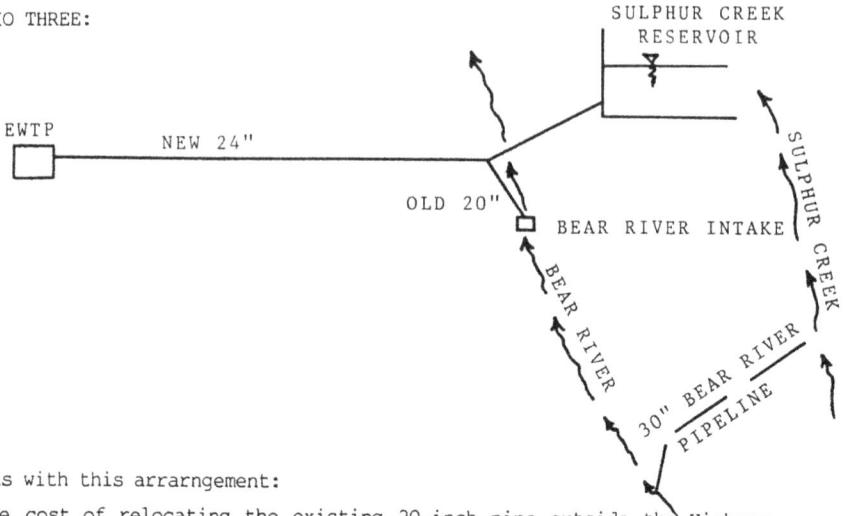

Concerns with this arrarngement:

1. The cost of relocating the existing 20-inch pipe outside the Highway right-of-way may be too expensive for the City.

2. Plans have been suggested, to connect the old 20-inch intake line to the new 24-inch line.

3. If this connection is made, the City can use all it's river diversion until water stored in Sulphur Creek is needed then the intake must be shut down so Sulphur Creek water will not run back into the River. While we are using stored water, the Bear River rights go down the River. Also, we will have to draw from stored water, the amount going down the River; hence, depleting stored water faster.

4. Forseeable ways to rectify this situation is for the City to relocate its diversion up-stream or put pumps at the present intake to boost the head such that Sulphur Creek water does not run back out the intake.

5. Pumps on the intake line would be labor intensive due to the variable level in the Sulphur Creek Reservoir.

6. The City (under this option) is faced with expenses to build the sump, provide pumps and power to improve the intake works and provide daily manpower to check and adjust pumping head.

7. Again; we still have Bear River pipeline easement problems, plus (I believe the pipeline is too small).

***

This is the scenario of the original plan of the Sulphur Creek Dam pipeline, prior to City Engineer Brian Honey's suggested change of plans.

SCENARIO FOUR:

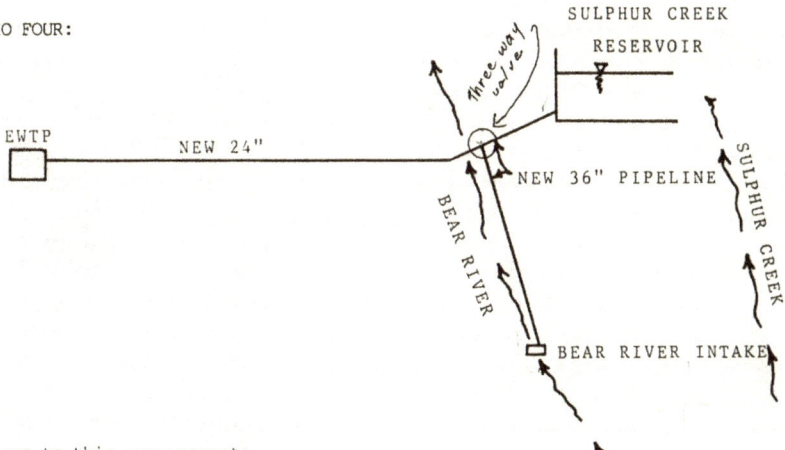

SULPHUR CREEK
RESERVOIR

Three way valve

EWTP

NEW 24"

NEW 36" PIPELINE

SULPHUR CREEK

BEAR RIVER

BEAR RIVER INTAKE

Advantages to this arrangement:

1. The City has one intake to maintain. The new one will eliminate the problems associated with the present intake.

2. The existing 20-inch line does not necessarily need replaced in that the head from the new intake will allow full use of the City's Bear River Diversion rights.

3. The new 36-inch line can be constructed within an existing County road easement which will eliminate the potential conflicts with the Hilliard Flat Irrigators, in that the Bear River pipeline is eliminated.

4. The new 36-inch line will carry more water in that the flow will be 20 CFS when the reservoir is at maximum height of 7187 feet, and 44 CFS when the reservoir livel is low, near 7147 feet. This will facilitate filling the reservoir faster in the Spring vs. the fixed 20 CFS Bear River pipeline.

5. We will still want to negotiate with the canal companies and have a working relationship with them.

6. The filtered intake water will be less costly to treat at the Treatment Plant.

7. The water stored in Sulphur Creek Reservoir will be used only as needed and the water not used will be available for carry over to the next year. This eliminates the losses of water associated with having to shut the existing Bear River Intake off when Sulphur Creek water is needed because Sulphur Creek water would run out the intake, back into the Bear River.

***

This is the scenario of City Engineer Brian Honey's change of plan of the Sulphur Creek Dam pipeline. NOTE that he eliminated the 30" pipeline from Bear River to Sulphur Creek cutting the project costs tremendously, plus making it a lot less costly for the City of Evanston to treat the plant.

He emphasized that this option would allow the city to construct an intake for all of the city's water supply in the Bear River, and that the new intake, an infiltration gallery placed under the bed of the river, will eliminate maintenance problems of ice buildup in the winter and silt and trash in the pipeline during spring runoff.

Honey stressed that with the relocation of the intake, the city will be able to use all the city-appropriated water rights from the Bear River and Sulphur Creek Reservoir. The 20-inch pipeline, then in place, did not have the capacity to conduct the flow of water needed for city use. Relocating the pipeline and the intake it could save the project as much as $1.5 million by eliminating the 20-inch line and an additional $1 million in expenses by building a new intake upstream at a later date.

After a lengthy question and answer period with the WWDC, they sounded very interested in the proposal and directed the state water engineer Mike Purcell to look into the proposal and work with Evanston's city engineer concerning the feasibility of implementing this proposed change into the project.

Our timing was so tight in presenting the change to the reservoir pipeline project that we didn't have time to present it to Purcell before the commission meeting. Because of that he was very upset and pissed off about not having the opportunity to look at it first.

After the meeting was over, he caught us in the hallway and was so mad and upset about not knowing about the proposal prior the commission presentation that he jumped all over Brian Honey and started cussing him out until, when I noticed what was going on, I told him to leave Brian alone, and if he wanted to blame someone to blame me, because I was the one that asked Brian to come up with a better system.

I told him we were sorry about presenting the proposal to the commission first, but we didn't have the time to meet with him first. We scheduled a flight to get us here just in time for the meeting as it was, and it didn't give us time to meet with him first. I said we were sorry this happened and that he was probably right to be a little upset, but it wasn't our intention to leave him out. He left in a huff and appeared to still be a little pissed off.

To make the story short, the proposal was accepted in the end, and Engineer Purcell was so angry that he resigned from the position. But was rehired for the same position several months later, so I would say he must have been a pretty good engineer.

In the *Uinta County Herald* dated February 27th there was an article titled, SULPHUR CREEK PROJECT WILL FACE MAJOR PIPELINE CHANGE. It began: *The new city administration is going full steam ahead with the Sulphur Creek Reservoir enlargement and pipeline project, but they will be making some changes in a few of the "nuts and bolts" of the project.*

The article continued: *The original plan was to run a 24-inch pipeline from Sulphur Creek Reservoir to Evanston. The project previously approved by the Wyoming Water Development Commission included the construction of a 30-inch line and intake constructed almost 20 miles south of Evanston off the Bear River to the Sulphur Creek stream across Hilliard Flat, according to Brian Honey, City Engineer.*

This would have consisted of five-and-a-half miles of 30-inch pipeline. Construction would also include approximately 10 miles of 24-inch pipeline from Sulphur Creek Reservoir to Evanston as well as the continued use of the existing 20-inch line from the old intake to town.

"The new plan solves quite a few problems," Honey said. "At the present time, the city is losing water because the water can't be diverted from the present intake and Sulphur Creek at the same time. The water runs from Sulphur Creek out into Bear River, losing water in both directions."

"A feasibility study was conducted by the engineers who designed the project on the pipeline and reservoir. They agreed that the new project would be feasible and would not add any expense to the construction of the dam nor will it exceed the original cost of the $25 million project," Honey added.

After Willis Barnes and the group that met with me in early January read the news concerning the dam, they were all much more satisfied with the plan that Brian had come up with. Willis told me that I needed to give Brian a raise because it looked like he was going to be a good engineer.

In early February I met with the Evanston Planning and Zoning Commission. I wanted to speak to them of some changes I had in mind. I felt that it was not right for members of the commission also to be on the Board of Adjustment, which is an appeal board for variances and other requests that were denied by the commission because they didn't quite meet the ordinances. I said that I would assign the city council members and mayor as the Board of Adjustments for the city. I said that there should be another group of people to hear someone with a request for a variance or deviation, other than members of the P & Z Commission. The way the Board of Adjustments is set up at the present, the only alternative for people now is to go to District Court.

The Uinta County Herald quoted me as saying, "I feel it hurts the economy to be too tough on ordinances. We must have flexibility – control, not dictate."

"The reason this was dumped on our necks in the first place was to keep the public off the council's neck," Andy Mullhall, a member of the commission, said. "If you feel we're scaring people away, ask for our resignations and change the board," Mullhall suggested."

I explained to the commission that my goal was not to have anyone quit, that I was not upset with the commission or any member of it. I said, I only wanted to have the opportunity to let you know how I felt, that we were not dictators, and all I ask of you is that you be reasonable and, where possible, use a little flexibility. After all, we are here to help the folks, not make it tough for them. I will be appointing the mayor and council as the Board of Adjustments and I hope that when we disagree with the commission nobody takes it personally.

And Mr. Mullhall, I said, The mayor and council are elected to do a job, and we shouldn't mind if you dump things on our necks— that was what we were elected for. However, it is your choice if you want to resign, nobody is going to stop you or beg you to stay, and that goes for anyone else that feels the same way. I continued, I want you all to know that I'm not here with the intention of releasing anyone from the board. The city needs you and I appreciate all of you for your service to the city by accepting the appointment to serve on the commission. I realize it is a gratis position, but I assure you that the council as well as the public all appreciate you very much. I would really appreciate it if you would all think twice before resigning. As I remember, no one resigned at that time or for that reason.

That edition of the Uinta County Herald also reported that the city council had approved the police department's K-9 program. Officers participating would be Ray Varner, who had 14 years of experience training dogs, was certified with the Wyoming Police Officers Standards, and he spent 6 and a half years with the Air Force canine program; Chet Alexander, who had spent five years with the Army's K-9 Corps; and Forrest Bright, who had been in law enforcement for several years and training dogs for quite some time.

These three officers had been training three dogs named, Sarge, Trouper and Remington on their own for quite a while—hoping that, in the future, city officials would give them a chance to prove their worth.

The city council approved the program at our last meeting, and I know that the K-9 program is still in effect and going strong. It has been a well supervised program over the years, and the dogs have appeared to have been a lot of help in solving and preventing crime in the area.

That month I also named another board organized as a Public Service Advisory Board to work on changes in ordinances and listen to complaints from the public on water and sewer changes. *This board will have no real teeth at this time but will listen to complaints and advise the council. The board will consist of three members from the council, three citizens from the public and one staff member,* I said. *They will meet once a month to review problems.*

According to an article in the *Uinta County Herald* of February 27th the Evanston City Council opened bids for the construction of the Sulphur Creek Dam Enlargement Project. Ames Construction, Inc., of Burnsville, Minnesota was the apparent low bidder of $8,879,697, after Larry, Inc. of Gillette, Wyoming withdrew their low bid of $7,995,863 because a number of errors were discovered in their calculations.

Jerry Eberson of Ames Construction was on hand to sign the contracts with the City of Evanston.

City Engineer Brian Honey asked the council to release the bid bond from Larry, Inc. as soon as possible in order for the company to be able to bid on other projects.

The council agreed to the proposal but withheld $10,000 to cover the costs to the city by Woodward and Clyde, project engineers, and the city engineer to review the low bid of Larry, Inc.

Brian Honey also brought up to the council something he and I talked about and hoped the council would agree to: giving Honey and the engineering department the authority to enter into negotiations with Uinta Engineering and Surveying for the design and construction of the planned 24-inch pipeline connecting the Evanston water treatment plant to the 36-inch pipeline.

He will also, with the permission of the council, negotiate with Forsgren-Perkins on the 36-inch pipeline connecting the Bear River to Sulphur Creek dam, intersecting with the 24-inch pipeline at mid-point.

Honey and I had talked about involving the local engineering firms and giving them a chance to bid on public projects, because Mayor Martin and his administration had refused to give local engineer firms an opportunity to do business with the city during his 4-year term as mayor. Again, I don't know why. All I know is the two local firms told me earlier that, for unknown reasons, Martin had denied them any city work.

Therefore, Honey and I agreed to request permission from the council to give these two firms some local business. The council agreed unanimously on both firms.

Also during this meeting the city council members gave me, as mayor, the authority to sign agreements negotiated with landowners involved with the Sulphur Creek project, either for acquiring additional property or for easements so that construction could begin on the dam.

A news item was released on February 12, 1987 by the O.I.A. stating that they had *donated to the University of Wyoming more than twelve boxes of files, documents and other materials related to its extensive mitigation activities in Southwestern Wyoming during the boom days of Over-thrust oil and gas development.*

The news release went on: *The materials were presented to the university by Chevron U.S.A., Inc. Regional Vice President Owen Murphy. Also attending the ceremony were former O.I.A. Presidents Murray Roney and David G. Dwight. Murphy, President of the O.I.A., said, "The O.I.A. helped us learn that local and state officials and industry can work together to solve the problems of rapid growth in a constructive non-confrontational way. I hope these records will help others to understand this unique public/private partnership."*

The release continued: *Accepting the donation on behalf of the University was Acting Vice President for development, Peter K. Simpson. Dr. Simpson stated, "The University of Wyoming is proud to be the recipient of these O.I.A. documents. The activities of the O.I.A. represent a significant period in the history of the state and it is appropriate that this history be documented so that future generations may benefit from the lessons learned."*

Dr. Donald L. Veal, President of the University of Wyoming, was the guest of honor at the donation ceremony. "The O.I.A. materials provide a wonderful opportunity for students of public administration, public policy and business to study an innovative public/private effort," said Dr. Veal.

The news release read: *State Senator John Fanos agreed, adding, "The O.I.A.'s mitigation program was instrumental in assisting local communities deal with the impacts of rapid growth." Senator Fanos (D-Uinta County) was Chairman of the Uinta County Commissioners during the height of the boom period. Senator Fanos also was Chairman of the O.I.A. Impact Coordinating Committee, which coordinated all mitigation programs.*

The O.I.A. was active in a three state area surrounding Evanston, Wyoming, during the energy boom which occurred in the late 1970s and early 1980s...The mitigation effort provided assistance to affected communities in Wyoming, Utah and Idaho by providing cash grants, technical assistance, loans and matching funds...at the end of the boom in 1984 more than $110 million had been generated for communities in the area.

The O.I.A. documents will become a part of the University of Wyoming's American Heritage Center, and will be made available to the general public. In addition to the O.I.A. written materials more than 55 video tapes also will be donated to the University. These video tapes include coverage of Impact Coordinating Committee meetings, news conferences, interviews, feature stories and television clips, the news release concluded.

It was no secret that Evanston and Western Uinta County were the center of the boom period and had received most of that $110 million, because we were faced with the most and the fastest population growth, but donating all those materials and documents to the U. of W. was a great move to give future booms an idea on how we mitigated our growth problems. Evanston and Uinta County were very fortunate to have major oil and gas companies care enough to form, at their expense, an organization like the "Overthrust Industrial Association." As mayor at the time, I will never forget the problems we incurred during one of Wyoming's most challenging boom periods, and I will never stop thanking the oil and gas companies, the O.I.A. and the Denver Research Group for what they did for Evanston during that period of the boom.

The March 25th edition of the *Uinta County Herald* reported on the past council meeting in an article titled CITY COUNCIL GEARS UP FOR BEGINNING OF SULPHUR CREEK RESERVOIR CONSTRUCTION. The article stated: *The City Council is gearing up for the beginning of Sulphur Creek Reservoir project and doing housekeeping to make the project possible.*

The article continued, *Dale Davenport, as coordinator of the project, was recommended to the council by a selection committee appointed by Mayor Dennis Ottley. The committee consisted of Clarence Vranish, Tom Hutchinson, Brian Honey, Jon Lunsford and Steve Snyder.*

The council accepted the recommendation pending the writing of the contract for his services. He will be the coordinator for the city and responsible for reporting to Brian Honey, City Engineer, on the project.

Davenport will be asked to coordinate the project between the three contractors and three engineering firms, on the dam itself, the Bear River pipeline and the Evanston pipeline, the *Herald* continued. The three engineering firms would be Woodward-Clyde on the dam, and Uinta Engineering and Forsgren-Perkins on the pipelines.

The *Herald* continued: *The council authorized Honey to execute all the necessary changes in the documents and acquire water rights and change the points of diversion for the water stored in the reservoir enlargement project.*

The *Herald* also reported that during the council meeting, *James M. Montgomery of Consulting Engineers, Inc. was given the go-ahead to prepare the documents to apply for funds from the Farm Loan Board for funding to expand the water treatment plant for the city.*

The firm was hired by the previous administration at a cost of $7,300 to study and determine if the existing plant should be expanded or a new facility built. It was determined the existing plant with updates was needed.

The *Uinta County Herald* reported in their issue of March 25th that Evanston still ranked among the cities and towns in Wyoming with the lowest property taxes collected per capita the past year. It was also reported that all taxes for the City of Evanston had taken a drop, causing revenues to diminish from all sources.

Councilwoman Julie Lehman, appointed from the council to select a committee for the Bicentennial of the United States Constitution celebration for the year of 1987, called a number of representatives from the community to meet with her on Monday, April 6th. The meeting was to select and organize a committee to put together a program to help re-educate people on the Constitution, as well as celebrate the Bicentennial.

During the meeting Maurene Ellingford was elected to act as chairman of the Evanston committee and would be selecting her full committee and giving her report at the next meeting on Monday, April 20th, concerning the committee's activities for Evanston.

Hight and Dorothy Proffit, Bicentennial Representatives of Uinta County, gave their report during the meeting on their attendance at the state meeting and said they will be available to help with the project whenever needed.

On Wednesday, April 8th, I raised the new Bicentennial Flag over City Hall commemorating the nation's Constitution. The dates on the flag are 1787 to 1791 which represent the beginning, when the Annapolis Convention was held to address various concerns of the states about the Articles of Confederation, to the time when Virginia ratified the Bill of Rights and the amendments became part of the U.S. Constitution. The nationwide observance would be celebrated in Evanston with a number of different festivities and programs.

On April 13th, the Evanston City Council's first regular meeting of the month had a full agenda and ran very late. The *Uinta County Herald,* in their article on April 15th, printed: CITY COUNCIL BURNS MIDNIGHT OIL.

After a long agenda, including action taken concerning the K-9 unit of the police department and the insurance cost: each dog would cost the city $816 per year for insurance. The dog would still be owned by each of the police officers, and they would be responsible for housing and feeding their dog. Carrying insurance on each dog would be the only responsibility the city would have.

Very late in the meeting, the mayor and council members went into executive session and retired to the conference room to discuss the continued negotiations concerning their lawsuit with Eckhoff, Watson and Preater (EWP).

EWP, a Salt Lake engineering firm contracted to design and construct the city's wastewater treatment plant, had been involved with the city in a lawsuit that was filed by the administration of former Mayor Gene Martin, and has been ongoing since.

The suit by the city alleged that the company (EWP) was involved in "deceit, trickery and misrepresentation, along with destroying and altering documents" amounting to a breach of contract.

Offers and counter-offers have been taking place for the last few weeks. Both parties have made offers to settle, but so far all offers have been rejected. As it stands now the City of Evanston has once again made another counter-offer with new figures just waiting for EWP's reply. No final decision was made from this night's meeting, but if a compromise cannot be reached soon both parties will be involved in a court action in Federal District Court in Cheyenne.

As every year, I signed proclamations for various events, starting with the Winter Carnival Committee proclaiming February 20, 21 and 23 as Evanston Annual Winter Carnival Days. Dick Stokes, Chairman of the Committee was present.

We also had Student Government Day, when the Evanston High School students would take over city government for a day. Kristen Bergeson joined me as acting mayor to oversee the proceedings. During the meeting that evening I handed Miss Bergeson my gavel and told her she was in charge, but I helped her along. Other students sat with their designated council members and proceeded to act in their place. This was a program instigated by the school to help teach students the process of government.

After all other business during the meeting was completed, Acting Student Mayor Kristen Bergeson asked help from the city council and the mayor to raise money for the girl's track team to participate in the Castle Rock Invitational in the State of Washington.

Within minutes, other members of the student council started asking for financial help in a number of other athletic programs.

I told the group of students that the city could not help them by donating money to their causes, but we would be happy to give our support by writing letters to a number of civic organizations within the city asking them to help support your programs.

Other proclamations I signed that spring declared the month of March as Developmental Disabilities Awareness Month, sponsored by the Uinta County Rehabilitation Center; March 16-22 as War on Drugs Week sponsored by Southwestern Wyoming Alcoholism Rehabilitation Association; the week of February 15-21 as Agri-Business Week; April 19-25 as National Coin Week, sponsored by Troop 9 of the Evanston Boy Scouts; the month of April as Child Abuse Prevention Month sponsored by the Evanston Exchange Club; May 10-16 as Nursing Home Week, sponsored by the Rennie Nursing Home; May 11-16 as City Wide Pride Drive Week sponsored by Evanston Beautification Committee; and May 6th as National Nurses Day, sponsored by the American Nurses Association and the Wyoming State Nurses Association. It seemed like every month there were one or two, sometimes more, proclamations to sign, but that was okay because it showed that the people of Evanston were very active in the community and willing to help promote various programs. Having the citizens take part in city programs by various sponsors is good for the community. It is, like a good recreation program, the sign of a pleasant and healthy community.

It was reported in the *Uinta County Herald* of May 8th that, on Wednesday, May 6th, during a special city council meeting, the City of Evanston finally settled its lawsuit against Eckhoff, Watson and Preator Engineering, Inc., over the design and construction of the city's wastewater treatment plant. Attorney Ray Hunkins, who was representing the City of Evanston in the lawsuit with EWP, presented the council with a settlement check for $400,000.

According to the *Herald*, Hunkins said to the council *"The settlement was to have been kept confidential, but the settlement agreement was placed inadvertently in the public records,"* and he cautioned the council to answer *"no comment"* to any questions about the settlement. And, as far as I remember, no one questioned me or any member of the council.

The settlement money would be used to pay for all expenses occurred by the lawsuit, to complete the project, and to be used for the treatment plant as needed.

On May 15th Councilman Tom Hutchinson, Chairman of the Sulphur Creek Reservoir Joint Powers Board, received a letter from State Examiner R. W. Poulson from the Wyoming State Examiner's office with a statement showing the financial position of the Board between March 1, 1986 through March 31, 1987.

The statement showed, after expenditures, that there was a balance of $2,204,822 in the Sulphur Creek project funds, with $1,660,300 of the amount being held in certificates of deposit (CDs). This balance indicated that the project was doing financially well and Hutchinson and Councilman Clarence Vranish, Secretary/Treasurer were doing a fine job in controlling the funds and reporting to the State Examiner's office.

It was announced during the month of May that water restrictions would go into effect once again on June 1st. The City of Evanston Public Works Department reminded Evanston water users that city ordinance prohibited the use of water for irrigation purposes between the hours of 10:00 a.m. and 6:00 p.m.

In the department's public announcement, published by both local newspapers, read as follows: *"Due to the warm spring weather we are experiencing, we will proceed with caution asking that users to conform to the hours stated for restricted irrigation use and also that users exercise voluntary restraint meaning – AVOID EXTRAVAGANCE."*

The announcement continued by requesting, more or less, that the public abide by the requested irrigation periods and use good common sense in their use of city water, because there would be, once again, a shortage and probably would be every year until the Sulphur Creek Reservoir project is completed.

The announcement from public works ended with *"Thank you for your help and cooperation."*

At this time there seemed to be full pages of foreclosure notices published in every issue of the local papers indicating that more people were leaving Evanston and just letting their homes go back to the mortgagees (home lenders) to be foreclosed on. This was really hurting residential home sales and the overall economy.

Over the past several months many small businesses had closed their doors, leaving town with regrets, according to Letters to the Editors that had been printed in the papers. Most mentioned how much they loved our community, but because of the economy, they just couldn't make a living anymore.

That spring the Depot Square Committee had raised enough money to construct two public restrooms (men and women) next to the Beeman-Cashin Building for use by Depot Square visitors and downtown shoppers. Years ago a request was made by a group of older folks that Evanston should have public restrooms in the downtown area, and now they had them, maintained and kept up by the city.

Also, because of such a cold winter this past season, a good share of the water lines in the Centennial Valley had frozen up, especially on Independence Street. Public works checked the depth of the lines, only to find that they had not met the city specifications. The lines had not been laid deep enough, causing the city to have another project that hadn't been budgeted for. When Centennial Valley was annexed, the City of Evanston did not check if the subdivision had met city specifications or not.

It probably wouldn't have made any difference in annexing, because the folks residing within the area wanted to be part of Evanston. But at least we would have had a chance to apply for more money from the State of Wyoming and get it in our budget, but like they say, *"If you can't make a mistake, you can't make anything."*

Therefore, the city was stuck with the mistake, but with the State of Wyoming's help we were able to get some funding, and that summer we had to go into the subdivision and tear up the streets, where we discovered that the streets had also not met city specifications. So it turned out to be a bigger and more expensive project than we anticipated, but we had to do it for the benefit of the folks within the subdivision. We did owe it to them and with some additional funds we got the job done, though the residents had a very inconvenient summer of construction. All I could say was, "lesson learned."

That spring Evanston finally got the Bear River Information Center and State Park opened. A big ribbon cutting ceremony took place on May 15th with Governor Mike Sullivan, State Recreation Commissioner Al Pilch and former State Senator Hight Proffit cutting the ribbon.

Governor Sullivan told the crowd, "This is the kind of facility that makes the people want to visit Wyoming." He commented on the meadow larks, the state bird, singing in the valley. "Those are the kinds of things that make people want to stay and enjoy our great state longer."

Former Senator Hight Proffit, one of the originators of the idea said, "Ideas, dreams, the impossible take a little longer and a little more effort."

He gave Al Pilch of the Recreation Commission most of the credit because the project was actually Pilch's idea. It was his dream and his quest to make Wyoming's Bear River State Park and Information

Center become a reality, and Evanston could be proud because it would do nothing but help the economy of our community.

During that month I signed another proclamation declaring May 21-24 Lions Club Week, because the Evanston Lion's members would hold the Annual State Lions Club Convention in Evanston, which would bring approximately 250 Lions Club members to visit our community.

It woud be a great time to promote our Depot Square and the new Wyoming State Park on the Bear River. Timing couldn't be any better.

Also during that month the Wyoming Public Employees Association Convention was held in Evanston on May 15th with the State of Wyoming's newly elected Secretary of State Kathy Karpan as the special guest.

Secretary Karpan sent me a letter dated May 27th praising the convention, and thanking me for attending and being a part of the very warm and receptive audience, as well as presenting to her one of Evanston's lapel pins and paperweights, which my administration had made up to have something from Evanston to present to dignitaries that visited our community.

Bids for the Sulphur Creek project pipelines were opened during the afternoon of May 20th by City Engineer Brian Honey and personnel from the Wyoming Water Development Commission. There were 12 bidders submitting bids on four alternatives, either ductile or steel piping, and 24 or 30 inches in size.

After the city engineer and personnel from the WWDC made a determination of which alternative the project can afford, and after checking out all specifications, Honey would present the bids to the city council for a decision at its next meeting on Tuesday, May 25th, at 7:00 p.m.

The *Uinta County Herald* of May 29th headlined: FLORIDA GRIZZLY WILL CALL TRAVEL CENTER ITS HOME. The article stated: *On April 1, Game and Fish Director Bill Morris was visiting with Governor Mike Sullivan when their conversation was interrupted by a phone call from the Florida Oceanographic Society asking if the state would have use for a bear.*

Governor Mike Sullivan, Al Pilch and Hight Proffit cut the ribbon at the dedication of Bear River Travel Center Friday afternoon.

Uinta County Herald, Spring of 1987.

BEAR RIVER RECREATION AREA

TRAVEL INFORMATION CENTER

DEDICATION
EVANSTON, WYOMING
MAY 15, 1987

PROGRAM

May 15, 1987
4:00 P.M.

MASTER OF CEREMONIES

Ken Collins

FLAG CEREMONY

Evanston High School Band
Boy Scout Troup #9

INVOCATION

Pastor Richard Meyer

HISTORICAL PRESENTATION

Denise Wheeler, Uinta County
Museum Committee

HONORED GUESTS

Governor Mike Sullivan
Governor Ed Herschler
Hight Proffit, former Senator
from Uinta County
Albert Pilch, Recreation Commission

RIBBON CUTTING CEREMONY

BENEDICTION

Rulon R. Osmon, President
Evanston L.D.S. Church

REFRESHMENTS

Sponsored by Utah Power & Light Company

BUILDING TOUR

Hosted by Evanston Chamber of Commerce
Red Carpet Committee

According to reports, the *Herald* continued, *Bill Kruckenberg, Chief of Game and Fish Communications Division, jumped at the chance to take the bear off their hands. There was only one question: "How do we get him here?"*

Within 20 minutes the Florida organization called back to say they had been given a $2,500 anonymous donation to ship the grizzly home.

The article continued: *When the word got out in Stuart, Florida – where the animal had resided since 1970 – that animal would be making its trip back to Wyoming, a number of people got on the bandwagon to give him a glorious send-off.*

Since we now had the Bear River Center and State Park, those in Cheyenne decided that a grizzly bear would be appropriate to have in the information center of the new state park.

When news got back to Evanston concerning the bear, Councilman Tom Hutchinson, who contracted with the Wyoming State Tourism Board to manage the park and center as an independent contractor, made the trip with Governor Sullivan to Stuart, Florida to receive the bear and attend the "big bear bash" of the grizzly's departure put on by the Florida Oceanographic Society.

After Tom Hutchinson called to let me know about getting the old grizzly back to Wyoming, I called the mayor of Stuart, Florida and thanked him for the bear. During our conversation we decided that Stuart and Evanston should become sister cities.

Due to a prior commitment I couldn't make the trip to attend the grand send-off in Stuart, but Tom Hutchinson was able to go with the Governor. Before they left, I signed a proclamation declaring *"Stuart, Florida a sister city of Evanston, Wyoming."* Councilman Hutchinson was to deliver the proclamation to the Mayor of Stuart, and bring back a similar proclamation signed by the Florida mayor declaring *"Evanston, Wyoming a sister city of Stuart, Florida."* Both documents had been displayed at the state park center near the "griz".

The Oceanographic Society paid the cost of shipping the bear to Salt Lake City, Utah by air. Tom Hutchinson, after he got back to Evanston from Stuart, drove his truck to the S.L.C. airport to pick the grizzly up. The full mounted bear was in a see-through container where the bear was visible to traffic.

The Evanston Post, May 28, 1987, Page 12

The following story was submitted by Mayor Ottley. It appeared in the May 18, 1987 *Wyoming Government Report.* We thought it would be of interest to our readers.

An 'ol griz finds his way home

By Tim Harms
WGR Editor

Once upon a time in the West, there roamed a griz. Not a particularly special griz — at least no more special than any other griz, except this one had a date with fate.

Now this griz spent most of his time like those of his kind, wandering around the landscape near Jackson, foraging for food and perhaps scaring the you-know-what out of an insolent tourist or two. Not knowing any better, this ol' griz continued to wander about the landscape a scrapin', a snortin' and a rootin', all the while with a big bull's eye stuck to his carcass.

To make a long story short, this particular grizzly bear wound up in Florida, and that is where the real fairy tale begins.

About three or four years ago, plans for the new Bear River Visitor's Center near Evanston began taking shape. Several state agencies, including the Game and Fish, the Travel Commission, and the Recreation Commission, were involved in the planning and despite that fact, the building was dedicated on May 15. Anyway, during initial planning for the center, officials from the agencies decided that some sort of wildlife display would be a nice addition to the interior of the building. As a matter of fact, these planners thought a bear would be a nice addition to the interior of the Bear River Visitor's Center.

Well it just so happened that an animal fitting the description of a bear was located in the wildlife display area in the Game and Fish Department headquarters in Cheyenne. They decided against taking the G&F bear, and that posed a problem. They still wanted a bear — a grizzly bear — but as Larry Kruckenberg says, "They aren't exactly easy to come by." Kruckenberg is the chief of the G&F communications division and a prime player in this true-life fairy tale.

The main problem in finding a bear was the fact that not just any bear would do. A polar bear might be appropriate as a representation of a Wyoming winter, but the thing was going to be placed in a visitor's center, not the ideal place to point out the arctic nature of a Wyoming winter. It had to be a griz. Well they figured a griz might be too hard to find, so they almost resorted to a crusty old black bear mount instead. Not nearly as effective as a griz, but a black bear would certainly fit the description. All hope was nearly gone when fate began to snowball like, well, like a snowball.

Once upon a time in Cheyenne, April 1 to be exact, G&F Director Bill Morris was chatting with the governor in the governor's office when an urgent phone call interrupted. It seemed there were these folks in Florida who had this stuffed griz they didn't quite know what to do with, so they asked if someone in Wyoming might have a use for it. And it just so happened that this particular bear was the same one that had wandered around the landscape near Jackson with a bull's eye on its hide.

Needless to say, someone did indeed have a use for it. "I said bingo ... you bet," Kruckenberg exclaimed. He was happy. It wasn't just the fact that he had found a griz, this griz was a Wyoming native. The way the bear is mounted even makes it look like the bear pictured on the sign at the visitor's center.

Kruckenberg called the Florida Oceanographic Society, the people with the bear, said "bingo you bet," and asked one question: "How do we get it here?"

The next thing that happened was a monumental clue, Kruckenberg said, that this bear was indeed a special breed. After posing the question to one Donna Dupuy, who handles public relations for FOS, Kruckenberg waited only 20 minutes for a reply. Within that time span, an anonymous donation of $2,500 mysteriously appeared, more than enough to move the bear back to its home on the range.

When word got out in Stuart, Fla., where the bear had resided since 1970, that the ol' griz was leaving town, the folks there could barely contain their excitement. From the time it was decided to send the bear and the June 1 sendoff, the town of Stuart and a few enterprizing people made the best of the situation. Kruckenberg said it not only helped them, it garnered a great deal of free press for Wyoming and Wyoming grizzlies.

The Travel Commission got requests for Wyoming posters and the G&F got requests for grizzly brochures. A restaurant owner in Stuart displayed the bear and sold Grizzly beer to raise funds for the FOS and the list goes on and on. The Sun Cooler people — the ones with the bear in the TV commercial — got in on the act, and so did Southern Bell, the telephone people.

Kruckenberg said stories about the bear appeared in the Miami Herald just a few days before equally momentous stories about Gary Hart giving bear hugs to women appeared. All major TV networks around the Palm Beach area near Stuart were on hand when the bear was moved form the FOS headquarters to the restuarant. Kruckenberg said the story has been submitted and may appear in an upcoming issue of Newsweek magazine.

The people in Stuart are even holding a "Name the Bear" contest. Kruckenberg graciously told the kind folks in Stuart that "the bear's name stays in Florida." Wyoming folks know of course that the only name for a grizzly is "griz."

"The whole thing reads like a love story or plays like a soap opera," Kruckenberg said. "We should never underestimate what Wyoming has to offer. (The people in Stuart) think Wyoming is the greatest place on earth."

The moral of the story is simple: Wyoming is a great place, and thanks to an ol' griz that happened to be wandering around a scrapin', a snortin' and a rootin', a great many more people understand that fact. And the price of all this notoriety is darned good — not one nickle of Wyoming money was spent.

Of course the ol' griz paid a pretty dear price, but if he had to go, we all ought to be glad that he finally came home.

Florida Oceanographic Society

Stuffed grizzly soon to return home to Wyoming

Drivers were looking at the bear as they drove, which got a Utah Highway Patrolman concerned. He followed Tom for a ways before running him down. He told Tom that he was going to cause an accident if he didn't cover the bear, because the traffic was getting so excited when they saw the grizzly. So the patrolman went and got a tarp from somewhere and between them they got the bear covered.

When Tom tells the story he gets a big laugh out of it and admits that the patrolman was right, because some drivers were looking so much at the bear that it was causing them to pay less attention to their driving.

The bear was a Wyoming grizzly that was shot near Jackson, Wyoming by an out-of-state hunter and was mounted in full, ending up in Stuart, Florida in 1970, where a restaurant in Stuart displayed and sold Grizzly "Beer".

The *Herald* concluded: *The public relations of the whole enterprise has been fantastic for the City of Evanston and the state as a whole, and the cost of all this publicity has not been one nickel for either the city or state.*

"Urrus Horribilis Bear-a-cida Faux Pas Griz" had a party on Wednesday, June 8th at the Bear River State Information Center for the unveiling of the "griz", and the public was all invited.

I presented Tom Hutchinson, Manager of the information center, with framed copies of the two proclamations issued by Stuart, Florida and Evanston, making the two "sister cities."

The party was the first of two events planned for "Griz's" return.

A second event was a "Welcome Back Bear Bash" held at the Legal Tender Lounge on Wednesday of June 17th. It was a community celebration for the return of a native son with free hors d'oeuvres, home-brewed *"grizzly beer"* (bear-hug drinks), a *"bearabation"* cake to celebrate the return of Bear-a-Cuda. Both events were well attended by an interested and excited public. Among those in attendance were State Senator and former Uinta County Commissioner John Fanos, State Representative Jerry Parker, former State Senator and Uinta County Commissioner Hight Proffit and his wife Dorothy, all there to welcome the animal home to the state that *"Griz"* was originally from.

Florida grizzly will call

Mayor Dennis Ottley signs a proclamation making Stuart, Florida, the sister city of Evanston. Councilman Tom Hutchinson will be going to Florida to accompany the donated grizzly bear home and deliver the proclamation.

The Wyoming Bear River Information Center will soon be receiving a mounted grizzly bear from the newly-claimed sister city, Stuart, Florida.

The story of how this original Wyoming bear — shot near Jackson, as the tale goes — is now coming home is a fairly complicated one.

Several state agencies which were involved with the Bear River Information Center — the Game and Fish, Travel Commission and Recreation Commission — decided that some sort of wildlife display would be a nice addition to the interior of the building.

Since it was the Bear River Center, it was decided that a grizzly bear would be appropriate.

On April 1, Game and Fish Director Bill Morris was visiting with Gov. Mike Sullivan when their conversation was interrupted by a phone call from the Florida Oceanographic Society asking if the state would have a use for a bear.

According to reports, Bill Kruckenberg, Chief of Game and Fish Communications Division, jumped at the chance to take the bear off their hands. There was only one question: "How do we get him here?"

Uinta County Herald, June 10, 1987.

Grizzly unveiling is scheduled Wednesday

Tom Hutchinson and Ken Collins of the Travel Commission removed "Bear-a-Cuda" from his crate Tuesday in preparation for today's celebration in his honor. Everyone is invited to the "Welcome Back Bear Bash" at 2 p.m. at the Bear River Information Center.

"Urrus Horribilis Bear-a-cuda Faux Pas Griz" is having a coming out party on Wednesday. Everyone is invited.

The Bear River Information Center will be holding an unveiling of the "griz" which was recently returned to Wyoming from Stuart, Florida.

On hand for the ceremony will be Ken Collins of the Wyoming Travel Commission, Senator John Fanos, Rep. Ron Micheli and Mayor Dennis Ottley.

The bear was shot in 1970 near Jackson Hole by Jamie Taylor and then taken to Florida. The 800 lb. bear was housed at the Florida Oceanographic Society (FOS) for a number of years.

When the FOS moved to new headquarters, there was no room for the large bear.

In the meantime, the Wyoming Travel Commission was looking for a bear for the newly opened Bear River Information Center in

Evanston.

City Councilman and information center manager Tom Hutchinson went to the Stuart, Florida, "Bear Bash" to receive the bear an bring him back to Wyoming.

Today at 2 p.m. he will be officially welcomed home by local residents.

The bear has also brought back to Wyoming a proclamation from Stuart's Mayor Jeffery Krauskopf making Evanston and Stuart sister cities and helping to cement relations between the two states.

PROCLAMATION

WHEREAS, the City of Stuart and the City of Evanston, Wyoming, share a common bond and heritage, in the form of one Urrus horribilis, more commonly known as a grizzly bear;

WHEREAS, said grizzly bear has attained residence in the City of Stuart and has been warmly received as one of its own;

WHEREAS, the State of

Wyoming and the City of Evanston are directly in need of a grizzly of Wyoming origin;

WHEREAS, the City of Stuart feels a strong sense of kinship with the City of Evanston;

WHEREAS, the City in an extreme moment of generosity and fellowship is willing to forego the joys, pleasures and benefits of having its own resident grizzly bear;

NOW THEREFORE, be it resolved and proclaimed that the City of Stuart recognizes the City of Evanston as its sister city; and in an act of compassion and sharing does bless the return of its resident Wyoming grizzly bear to its sister city;

To this document BEARING the seal of the great City of Stuart, Florida, I hereby affix my signature confirming the sistership of our two cities on this the 31st day of May, 1987.

Jeffrey A. Krauskop
Mayor

Uinta County Herald, June 10, 1987.

Also that month, on June 13th, the *Celebration of Freedom* was held at the Uinta County Courthouse to celebrate the addition of two black granite walls. One wall commemorated the names of those from Uinta County serving in the United States military during the Korean War and the other wall was for those who served during the Vietnam War.

Uinta County Commissioner John Stevens was Chairman of the project while Mary Lou Norris, who did a terrific job in the planning and completion of the project, was Project Coordinator.

Mary Lou not only spearheaded a fundraising program for the project, she also had the old Doughboy Statute, that had been dedicated in 1920, cleaned up, and had the World War ll Uinta County veteran names, cast in bronze, added to the statute that already had been dedicated to those who had served in World War l and the Spanish American War.

The celebration included a downtown parade with WWl veterans, John Mills, Joe Rasmussen and Oscar Dahlquist as Grand Marshalls, a barbecue lunch and the dedication of the new granite walls, and the addition of the WWll veteran names on the Doughboy Statute.

To top the program off, Mary Lou had invited General William C. Westmoreland as the special guest speaker. He arrived in at the Evanston Regional Hospital landing pad by helicopter where Project Coordinator Mary Lou Norris and the Uinta County Commissioners met him and brought him to the courtyard. As mayor, I also met him at the hospital, welcoming him to Evanston and presenting him with a large gold-painted Key to the City, adorned in red, white and blue ribbons. The program was a big success with other special guest speakers in attendance such as U.S. Senator Alan K. Simpson and U.S. Congressman Dick Cheney.

On June 6th the Evanston Urban Renewal Agency sponsored their 5th Annual Renewal Ball held at the restored Beeman-Cashin Building located on Evanston's new "people's place," the Historic Depot Square. The theme of the ball for the 5th annual event was *"Evanston...1900."*

Uinta County Herald

Evanston, Wyoming 82930　　Wednesday, June 17, 1987　　Volume 53, Number 47　　Price 25c Per Copy

War Memorial dedication
A day we will never forget

by Ann Curtis
of the Herald staff

"It was a day in Uinta County's history that those of us who participated will never forget," Uinta County Commissioner John Stevens, chairman of the War Memorial Committee said Monday.

The day dawned a beautiful, shiny summer day and by the time the parade started, the patriotic feeling was so strong in the air you could almost touch it.

Ret. General William C. Westmoreland and a contingent of the committee flew into Evanston on a helicopter which landed at Evanston Regional Hospital.

After debarking from the aircraft, he was greeted by Evanston Mayor Dennis Ottley and presented the "keys to the city."

The general then mingled with the small contingent of people who were on hand to greet him.

He signed autographs and talked to a number of young people on the site.

Saturday began with a military-oriented parade headed by veterans of World War I Dave Dunning, John Mills, Joe Rasmussen and Oscar Dahlquist who acted as Grand Marshals for the parade.

The parade consisted of a number of bands, floats, horse groups and other entries.

blood-stained areas of our history, and our people would go again. We are a special breed of people. I hope there is no need to ever gather here again."

Representative Dick Cheney said that it was appropriate to write the names in stone from the same quarry as the Vietnam Monument in Washington, D.C. "As you read the names, you see your own reflection, which is appropriate because it reflects the best in all of us."

Pat O'Hara introduced Gen. Westmoreland who delivered an address along with leading the unveiling of the three monuments and the laying of the wreath by WWI veteran Dave Dunning, WWII veteran William Reitz; Korean veteran Darius Eardley, and Vietnam Veteran Gary Roper.

A 21-gun salute was performed by Fort Bridger American Legion Post No. 36.

Bob O'Hara and David Blackwell presented a stirring rendition of "Echo Taps."

Following the dedication ceremony, many of the crowd proceeded to Depot Square to enjoy the music of the Marine Corps Band and to enjoy a feast of barbecued beef, potato salad and baked beans.

Saturday was a time for family and friends and for reunions of old

Ret. Gen. William C. Westmoreland exchanges salutes at the Celebration of Freedom ceremonies held to honor all the Uinta County veterans from World War I, World War II, Korea and Vietnam.

In memoriam ....

A General visits

John Stevens, Gen. William Westmoreland, Pat O'Hara and Sheriff Leonard Hysell arrive in Evanston by helicopter.

Mayor Dennis Ottley presented General Westmoreland with the key to the city.

Grand Marshals of the parade were WWI veterans John Mills, Joe Rasmussen, Dave Dunning and Oscar Dahlquist. They were riding in a "White" truck which took inductees to board the train.

Uinta County
Herald

Photos by
Ann Curtis

Also on June 20th, the Overthrust Chili Cookoff Committee held Evanston's 6th Annual Chili Cookoff. *There will be something to please people of all ages,* Chairperson Joan Wilson (Nixon) said. This was another of Evanston's very successful annual events and once again showed that the local folks are actively involved and concerned with the present economy.

There was a question why the city was using the water truck to wash down the streets instead of using the street sweeper broom when the city is having such a water shortage.

In the local newspaper, Public Works Supervisor Allen Kennedy told the public, *"Washing the streets down is cheaper than using the street sweeper; it also cuts down on dust and makes the city cleaner. The city is not using treated water for this operation. The water used is taken from the Yellow Creek ditch."*

"Deb Wagstaff of the city crew, runs the water truck from 4:00 a.m. until about noon to push the dirt off the center of the street into the gutter. The dirt is then picked up with the broom to keep the debris out of the storm sewer," he continued.

"We still use the broom to maintain clean gutters," he stressed.

That month Kilburn Porter announced that he was no longer in a position to continue maintaining the translators that were providing television to those in Evanston and rural areas throughout west Uinta County.

When the Century Cable T.V. Company bought out Western Cable Television, it did not include the television translators that had been owned and operated by Kilburn Porter for many years. These translators were the only means of providing television for rural areas outside of the City of Evanston. Kilburn Porter originally put the system in as a business venture, but since cable came to Evanston, television viewers became fewer and fewer. His system had always been funded by folks voluntarily donating to keep the system up. Porter said that because his users were paying less and less, he had lost money the past few years and could no longer continue to pay out-of-pocket to keep the system operating. His system was not on a subscription pay basis, as the Century Cable T.V. Company was; therefore, Porter offered to donate all the transformers and other equipment to the Parks and Recreation Commission, thinking that the district could find the funding to keep the program operating for those folks who did not have access to the new cable TV system.

Since the cable company ran their cable lines only within the limits of the city, they had no plans to extend any further. Therefore, folks residing outside of the city in western Uinta County and those in Evanston that hadn't subscribed to Century Cable would be without television if the translators are shut down.

A group of the folks using the Porter translator system to receive television had organized, and requested that the new School District No. 1 Recreation Commission look at the possibility of forming a Joint Powers Board and finding funds within its budget to maintain and upgrade the system so that those who did not nor could not subscribe to cable TV would be able to receive television as they had been.

As mayor, I had received dozens of letters from citizens of Evanston who were using the Porter system, and a number of letters from folks outside the city asking the city to support their request to form a Joint Powers Board to take over Porter's translator system and fund it through the Recreation Commission.

The folks residing in the areas of Upper Bear River and Almy called a meeting to advocate that the Recreation Commission take over the Porter system. They had recently formed a group named "Save our Stations" (SOS), chaired by Debra Litz and Hight Proffit, to save the translators that Porter had proposed to donate to the Recreation Commission.

Century Cable T.V. Representative Bob George said during the well-attended meeting, *We want the translators to stay on, because we can't afford to go out of the city limits and there are a few places within the city we can't reach without spending a lot of money.* Among the large attendance at this meeting were myself, City Councilman Clarence Vranish, Uinta County Commissioner John Stevens and District No. 1 School Board Chairman Craig Welling, who all voiced enthusiasm for the project. I suggested that the Recreation Commission take over the translator system until another plan could be devised, possibly with the intercession of the legislature.

The city budget for fiscal year 1987-1988 that was passed and adopted by the Evanston City Council was down 2.1 percent with a carryover from the previous year of approximately $1,148,000.

The total budget would be $29,556,708 with over $20,000,000 pledged to be used to construct Sulphur Creek Reservoir and other projects, such as reconstruction of County Road, expanding the water treatment plant, additions to the Uinta County Airport and Human Service Center, paving downtown parking lots, and other smaller projects. Most funds for these projects were from the Wyoming Water Development Commission, the Wyoming Highway Department, and the Wyoming Farm Loan Board.

A two percent cost of living wage increase was given to city employees along with a 1 percent merit increase which could be authorized if the city council feels revenues are sufficient.

The County Road construction had started first with the enlargement of a new bridge located across from the old Jolly Roger Restaurant and Lounge (presently known as the Old Mill and The Painted Lady Bar & Lounge). The bridge would be expanded from a two-lane bridge to a four-lane, with sidewalks on each side. CEI, Inc., the engineering firm on the project, stated that the bridge would take approximately 60 days for completion.

The bridge portion of the project would be the first phase of the new construction on County Road from Bear River Drive to Wyoming State Highway 89. A new roadway would be lowered, because of problems with the drainage and build-up of asphalt, and the road would be made wider with new storm drains and sidewalks on both sides. Phases two and three were scheduled for the next summer of 1988.

CEI, INC., the engineering firm, only had the bridge portion of the County Road under contract, which was given to them by the previous administration. However, because of some dissatisfaction of the assigned engineer from CEI, the city council, at my suggestion and city engineer Brian Honey's, the council provided a provision in the contract with CEI that their agreement would only concern the first phase (the bridge). Phases two and three would be rebid at a later date.

Other projects started that summer included the Gazebo in the new downtown city park (later to be named Martin Park), the Bear River Walkway from the new proposed Bear Project to the Bear River State Park, and the reconstruction of the old Red Bridge that crossed the river where most local kids went swimming years ago. The Bear Project would also include work on the two ponds that the railroad used, years ago, to freeze and cut ice for the refrigeration cars for shipping perishables. This property was purchased from the railroad during my first term as Mayor of Evanston.

Uinta County Herald

Evanston, Wyoming 82930   Friday, August 14, 1987   Volume 53, Number 64   Price 25c Per Copy

Sulphur Creek project moving along

The work on Sulphur Creek Dam is proceeding well; when completed it will be approximately 30 feet higher than the present dam. In the foreground are the new spillway and intake structures.

The Sulphur Creek project is humming along on several fronts with pipeline from Evanston being layed; roads being built and the interior work on the dam itself being done.

Work on construction began last April with Ames Construction, based out of Minnesota, winning the bid.

At this point in the construction, Ames has 13 Wyoming employees below supervisor level working on the site. The subcontractors, Construct Tech, also has 13 Wyoming employees and Rocky Mountain Trucking employs four Wyoming employees. Each of those companies have supervisors and management people who have come with the company.

The men on the site are constructing the large morning glory (intake) works and the outlet.

Along with the morning glory there is a flip bucket and still basin to handle the overflow of the reservoir. The outlet, a 48-inch piping system, will house the gate valve to regulate the flow of water into and out of the reservoir.

According to construction manager Dale Davenport, the concrete structures are molded by a new process. The mold is on wheels and can be raised to the height desired. When a section is completed the mold is rolled to the next section.

The work on the dam itself began with a cement and bentonite slurry wall the full length of the structure. The slurry wall is an eleven to thirteen foot thick structure which is placed three feet down in the bedrock and will prevent any seepage of water behind the dam.

As the construction work pro-

ceeds it will incorporate the existing structure and continue on to an additional height of approximately 30 feet. Davenport stated the dam was designed to take care of the worst possible problems.

At the same time, work is being done to replace the section of county road which will be under water when the dam is complete.

Two 60 inch pipes have been installed to allow water to run under the road. The new exit will be near the Aaron Martin ranch turnoff.

Materials for the road will be taken from areas owned by the city. The pipeline which will carry water to the treatment plant is being installed at this time along Hwy 150. This part of the project is being done by High Plains Construction, a Wyoming contractor which employs 12 people.

Yet to be started is the Bear River pipeline which will bring water into the dam. It will also be connected to the pipe going into Evanston.

During spring runoff, water will be run into the reservoir. As the year goes on the water will be diverted straight from Bear River to the treatment plant.

Uinta County Herald.

On Monday, July 27th, during their regular meeting, the city council gave permission for Assistant Engineer Frank Smith to purchase additional 10-and 8-inch piping to be laid in the same trench with the water pipeline coming from Sulphur Creek Reservoir.

The extra pipe will return treated water from the treatment plant up the line to those families now using untreated water. Approximately 10 residents south of the Aspen Grove Subdivision had given the city access to their property when the original pipeline was installed from the old Bear River intake to the treatment plant about 25 years ago; in return, the city agreed to supply them with water.

The council determined that the money for laying the additional line would be picked up by the Wyoming Water Development Commission as part of the Sulphur Creek Reservoir project, and the cost of the pipe could be paid for by the city through future hookups to the system.

After the Gazebo was constructed in the new downtown city park, during the meeting on August 24th, the Evanston City Council voted to officially name the park "Martin Park" in honor of former Mayor Gene Martin, because of his interest in the park.

Councilman Jon Lunsford suggested the name of Martin Park after City Planner Paul Knopf gave the council a list of names suggested by the planning department. The motion was made and seconded to name the park as suggested by Lunsford. The vote was 5 in favor with 2 voting no.

Councilman Will Davis and I voted against the motion. I have no idea why Davis voted no, but I did because Gene Martin had no part in obtaining the old Y.M.C.A. property from the railroad. The property was obtained and the park was started during my administration during my first term as mayor. I guess you could call that sour grapes, but I had my reasons and I didn't think that the name was either appropriate or deserving.

But the park was a great addition to the downtown area and I was proud to see the gazebo (which was Mayor Martin's idea) added to the park. It was going to be good to see the local city band playing there every week. It brought back a lot of old memories for the old timers of Evanston and others who remembered when the gazebo was on the courthouse yard and the local band played every Wednesday evening.

Gazebo brings back a bit of "old time" to Evanston

A bit of "old time" has been brought back to the city in the form of a gazebo recently constructed between the police station and Depot Square. The structure is part of the redevelopment plan for Depot Square.

"Years ago there was an old gazebo in the Courthouse yard," Mayor Dennis Ottley recalled. "They used to have concerts there every Wednesday. Everybody in town would come to that thing. The Courthouse lawn would be full.

"That's what I think we're try-ing to get back to," he said. "Even though the town has grown, we want to keep that small town atmosphere."

Ottley said the gazebo was designed for use not only by the general public but by local bands, choirs and groups who'd like to use it for meetings in the summer months.

Kimes Construction, from Bridger Valley, was low bidder on the project which was built in only a few days' time. Total cost of construction and materials was about $6500, according to City Planning Director Paul Knopf. He said the City's Parks and Recreation Department did the landscaping and irrigation.

Knopf said a weather vane needs to be added to the roof of the structure and a few ground lights and inside lights still need to be installed.

Next spring, he said, there are plans to add some historic lights like those which have been put in at Depot Square already.

Lighting and a weather vane is all that remains to be added to the gazebo at "Martin Park" as it will be called. Being 31 feet in diameter, it was designed to accomodate a full-piece band, according to City Planning Director Paul Knopf.

Uinta County Herald, November 20, 1987.

In August the City of Evanston was recognized as one of 1104 communities in the United States as *"A Designated Bicentennial Community"* by the Commission on the Bicentennial of the United States Constitution.

The active involvement and willing participation of our nation's local governments will be a key to the success of the Bicentennial, said Chief Justice Warren E. Burger, Commission Chairman. *A major goal of this Commission is to educate the American people on the historical significance of the Constitution,* he added.

Maureen Ellingford was appointed the chairperson of the Evanston Bicentennial Commission when it was formed earlier this year. *The task of this commission will be to plan and coordinate Bicentennial activities in Evanston,* she said. *We are looking for any suggestions from our citizens to assist us in this endeavor.*

I signed a proclamation declaring the week of September 14th as Constitution Week, when Chairperson Ellingford and her committee would invite the public to attend a celebration to commemorate the signing of the United States Constitution.

The patriotic ceremony was held on Thursday, September 17th at the Depot Square. A short program was held, followed by an old-fashioned ice cream social with a great turnout.

During the city council meeting on Monday, September 14th a 10-day extension was requested by City Engineer Brian Honey for the County Road Bridge project. David Berg, representing CEI Engineering, Inc., told the council that the main reason for the delay was problems relocating utility company lines. The council reprimanded him for not contacting them earlier about the problem. Berg reminded the council that the city had a representative on the project two hours per day with the responsibility to keep them informed. It was then found that all communications between Clark Ready-Mix, the contractor, the engineering firm, and the city representative had been verbal, leaving no paper trail to confirm variations in their stories. Neither the city council nor I was very happy with the way the project was going, but we did get those involved straightened out.

The City of Evanston had a street repair project that summer starting in August, because of the way the streets had been neglected recently, mostly because of revenue shortfalls. When streets are neglected and in need of repairs it is not good to ignore them because the repairs get worse and much more costly. However, sometimes it's understandable when revenues become short and funds are no longer available.

Streets on the list to be repaired, sealed and overlaid that summer included a large portion of the Overthrust Road, Cedar, Birch, part of Roosevelt, part of Morse Lee, Center, Summit, part of 14th Street, part of West Uinta, Pine, Ash, Lincoln, Grant, "C" Avenue, and a large portion of Main Street.

The streets were an important part of the infrastructure that needed to be attended to every summer, because of the hard winters, but we had to wait until the fiscal year budget was adopted before we had the funds to proceed.

In the September 24th edition of *The Evanston Post,* it was reported that a manufacturing company named Ehman Engineering, Inc. had opened up about 6 miles north of Evanston on State Highway 89. They manufactured computer peripheral equipment for the Apple Macintosh line of computers. They also manufactured and sold a line of external disk drives, and would employ over 20 full-time employees.

The Wyoming Economic Development and Stabilization Board approved a loan package of $101,000 to Ehman Engineering to assist them in the start-up of their operation. These were funds from the Board's $10,000,000 which was set up by the state to encourage business development. The loan request was submitted by the City of Evanston, and would be paid directly to the city to be used for local needs.

In late September the city, county and school district jointly form a new board to oversee the Porter T.V. translator problem. The new board was called the T.V. Translator Non-Profit Board. It was supposedly a temporary board to work with the Recreation Commission in helping to raise money through donations and payments by users.

During the city council meeting of September 28th I named Mary Lintz, Tom Norton and Betty Smith as the city appointees to the board to represent the City of Evanston. At this point it looked like Kilburn Porter finally got shed of his T.V. Translators, and now those folks that were using the system would be able to continue having T.V. service.

At that meeting I named my wife, Sandy, as chairperson for the newly planned "Sister City Committee" to coordinate a number of festivities and promote Evanston and Sister City Stuart, Florida. Other members of that committee to assist Sandy were City Planner Paul Knopf, Councilman and Manager of the Bear River State Park Tom Hutchinson, Pat Rhode, John Bower and my daughter-in-law Kerri Ottley.

During the same meeting Doris Peterson, a widow and long-time resident of Evanston, submitted bills to the council for cleaning expenses incurred when a sewer backup, resulting from city crews cleaning a blockage suddenly became unstuck, forcing several inches of water and sewer into her basement.

As reported in the Wednesday, September 30th edition of the *Uinta County Herald*: *Allen Kennedy, Superintendent of Public Works, told the council the problem happens every once in a while. "We've unplugged the same line twenty times, usually the plugs go slow—this one was different," he stated.*

"If there is nothing we could have done, or nothing we can do in the future to prevent the problem I don't see how the city was negligent," Councilman Jon Lunsford stated.

Five members of the council and I voted against her request to pay for her bills. Councilman Tom Hutchinson was the only vote in favor of her request. I felt bad about not paying her, but for years when we have had similar incidents we have never paid for anyone else' damages, and I was afraid that we might just be setting a precedent if we paid for Mrs. Peterson's. I have thought many times about that situation since then, and I think if I had it to do over again I may have just voted in favor of her request.

I felt bad for her, but it wasn't like she didn't have the money; it was just the idea of her being a widow and alone. I kind of wished that

I had voted differently, but then, after things are all said and done, it seemed like a lot of folks at times wished they had done differently.

A quote I once read said, *"Good judgment comes from experience, and often experience come from bad judgement."*

However, during the years that my agency, Uinta Realty, Inc., had been renting the Old Town Hall Building from owner Gene Harter, we had the sewer line on Harrison Drive, between Center and Main Streets, plug up three times, causing raw sewage to back up into the basement level of the building. One time I had subleased space for a sporting goods store in the lower level when about two to three feet of sewer backed up, ruining a lot of merchandise, including small barrels of black powder.

Each time I called the city, all they did was remove the manhole cover and run a rod into the manhole, cleaning the sewer line out so it could flow freely. Two of the times this happened were during my term as mayor, but knowing what the policies of the city were, I didn't even approach the city for any reimbursement. Uinta Realty, Inc. paid to pump the sewage out of the basement and clean the mess up, and paid for some of the merchandise that the tenant's insurance wouldn't cover. All the time I had been a member of the council or mayor we had sewage back up in many areas of the city, but the city set up a policy, not by ordinance or resolution, that the council would look separately at each incident when it happened. If the problem was in the city main sewer line then the city might look at paying for damages, but if the problem was in the line from the building to the main then all the city would do was ream out the line to get the sewer running once again, but the cleanup and damages were the responsibility of the owner. In most cases the owner understood the city's position.

The City of Evanston operates on taxpayer dollars only, and by law city officials are required to be very much aware of how public monies are spent. They are required to keep a balanced budget without having a deficit. That is why they have public budget hearings once in a while, to adjust the budget based on the present revenues. Sometimes revenues drop unexpectedly during the fiscal year.

It was the first part of October when I suggested to the council something that I had been thinking about for several months: that in order to help get the economy going we needed a program in the fall to encourage folks to get active in the community, and also to entice them to shop in Evanston first for all their needs. I suggested that the last full week of October from Saturday through the following Friday would be a good time because it wouldn't be too long after the tourist season and it would be just before the holiday season for their Thanksgiving and Christmas shopping and would hopefully remind Evanston citizens of the importance of shopping at home.

The primary focus of the program would be to support ourselves better by communicating among ourselves and shopping at home, and building a stronger and more prosperous Evanston by working together.

"As I'm sure you are aware, a tremendous amount of business is done along the Wasatch Front by people of this area. If we can help ourselves by encouraging just a small percentage of those that are shopping elsewhere to shop at home, the results would be many-fold. The primary result would be the preservation of jobs that might otherwise be lost. Additionally, it's possible that new jobs could be created," the Uinta County Herald quoted me saying.

My idea was to build a program by using each day of that week for something different that pertained to supporting Evanston. We would have programs that would include folks of all ages, young and old. I also suggested to the council that the program could be an annual event. I suggested that we should make an opportunity to honor some of our senior citizens who had been active in the community over the years, without recognition, during a Friday evening banquet and dinner every year by requesting nominations from the public.

I also told the council that I also would mention this program to Jerry Wall, President of the Evanston Chamber of Commerce, and request their involvement as a co-sponsor. The entire city council agreed to the program, and the Chamber of Commerce also agreed to be involved by becoming a co-sponsor.

We all agreed to the permanent title of Support Your Community Week for the week-long program. In 1987, it was to be the week of October 26 through the 30th. The agenda included programs and fun events for school children of all ages, as well as having them write stories about the community and essays on "Why I Love Evanston." Evanston High School cheerleaders were invited to perform during certain events; included was a Prayer Breakfast with a featured speaker on Tuesday morning with the public invited. We also planned a program titled Lunch with the Mayor on Thursday, inviting the public to bring their favorite senior citizen(s) to lunch as their guest. As mayor I always invited two or three older folks to be my guests that I had a lot of respect for. I picked them up and brought them to the luncheon, and I was expected to say a few words; but to top the week off we held a Friday night banquet honoring senior citizens who had been nominated by the public for their active involvement in the community. We always ended up honoring three or four every year.

The first year of the program we honored former Governor Ed Herschler because of the enormous support he had given the City of Evanston during the boom period. Although he was from Kemmerer, the folks that nominated him felt that he should be honored by Evanston. Other nominations that year were Albert Pilch, retired local businessman and long-time member of the Wyoming Recreation Commission, and most instrumental in providing Evanston with the Bear River State Park and Information Center; former Wyoming State Senator, Hight Proffit and his wife, Dorothy Proffit; and former Wyoming State Senator, J. Wes Myers. Master of Ceremonies was performed by current Wyoming State Senator John Fanos.

On September 28th, during the second regular city council meeting of the month, the Liquor Dealers Association requested lowering the annual fee of a retail liquor license because of the downturn in the economy. The dealers requested a decrease far lower than the council agreed to.

In a memo to the city council I agreed with the liquor dealers and stated; *There is no doubt that the downturn in the economy of the past two years has affected your businesses, just as it has affected other businesses in town. However, I don't feel there is any way we can honor your request; I believe you are asking far too much.*

My suggestion would be to lower the full license from the present $1,500 to $1,000 per year, the resort licenses from $3,000 to $1,500, and the retail license holders with an additional dispensing room a fee from $2500 to $1,667. I believe we should keep the $100 annual charge to the private clubs [V.F.W. and the Eagles Club] the same, I continued.

The memo to the council stated that there were 21 retail liquor dealers in Evanston, and if the council were to accept the dealers' request, it would decrease net fees to the city as much as $26,750. But if the council accepted the suggested schedule mentioned in the memo it would decrease the net amount only $17,832.

After discussion, I introduced a resolution to adopt the fees suggested in the memo, followed by a motion by Councilman Will Davis, seconded by Councilman Tom Hutchinson with the motion passing unanimously.

In other business during the September 28th meeting, the city council granted a 12-month contract to *The Evanston Post* to publish the minutes, public notices and other legal business of the City of Evanston.

Uinta County Herald

Evanston, Wyoming 82930   Friday, October 16, 1987   Volume 53, Number 82   Price 25¢ Per Copy

"Support Your Community Week" is designed to encourage residents

Mayor Dennis Ottley has proclaimed the week of Oct. 26-30 as "Support Your Community Week," designed to encourage local residents to become involved in the community, shop at home and share in improved communications.

Ottley will kick off the observance with an announcement during the next couple of weeks of two or three people whom he feels deserve special recognition and will be honored at a banquet Oct. 30. The banquet will honor individuals whom he feels have supported Evanston "in a big way but people don't know about it because they have been low key." He will announce those names in the near future and details of the banquet time, place and ticket price.

"What we are trying to do is get the community involved in three ways: shop at home as much as possible; get involved in communi-ty projects and participate in open communications. We all seem to be heading for the same thing but some people are doing it in dif-ferent ways. We need to all get on the same route."

Ottley will place posters in the community encouraging action during the week and explaining the benefits of shopping at home. With the help of store employers he hopes employers will understand the importance of the week-long

celebration. He hopes to make it an annual event.

Ottley is working on the project with city employees and the Chamber of Commerce and its president, Jerri Wall. Though the recipients of the awards "have been selected in my own mind, I would welcome any suggestions from anyone else."

Following is the mayor's proclamation.

PROCLAMATION
Support Your Community Week
October 26 - 30, 1987

WHEREAS, involvement and participation in Community ac-tivities enriches the lives of our residents; and

WHEREAS, improved com-munications among ourselves will enhance the community in which we live; and

WHEREAS, the Evanston Com-munity provides many oppor-tunities to shop at home; and

WHEREAS, Shopping at home provides more local revenue, helps the economy and provides employ-ment in Evanston;

NOW THEREFORE, I, Dennis J. Ottley, Mayor of Evanston, do HERREBY PROCLAIM the week of October 26 - 30,1987, as "Sup-port Your Community Week", in Evanston, Wyoming.

Dennis J. Ottley
Mayor

Mayor Dennis Ottley proclaimed Oct. 26-30 as "Support Your Com-munity Week" a celebration to help the community understand the im-portance of shopping at home, to encourage support and volunteerism in the community and to work at open communications.

The above photo is of the Evanston City Council during the October 1987 meeting the week of the first annual "Support Your Community Week" with their "I Love Evanston" (*the program theme*) stocking caps.
Left to right standing is Council Members Julie Lehman, Clarence Vranish, Tom Hutchinson, Craig Nelson, Will Davis and Jon Lunsford. Sitting is Mayor Ottley.

The Evanston Post was a relatively new newspaper in Evanston, which had been established during the previous boom period. But after some discussion, the council thought that after all the years that the contract had gone to the only newspaper in town, the *Uinta County Herald*, they felt that it would only be fair to give the new paper an opportunity to publish the city's minutes and other official business.

Therefore, the city council passed a motion and seconded it to offer the publishing contract to *The Evanston Post*, a contract that would run from October 1, 1987 through September 30, 1988. Each year from then on the council would put it out to bid, providing there was more than one local newspaper in Evanston. By law the city was required to publish all city minutes and other businesses in the most local newspaper for the public to read.

The vote on the motion made by the council and seconded was passed with a 5–2 vote to offer the contract to *The Evanston Post*, with Councilmen Davis and Hutchinson voting in the negative.

During October the city had a request for a zone change on Front Street between First and Second Streets by Harold Holmes of Cheyenne, owner of Taco John's, a fast food franchise, so they could apply for a conditional use permit to construct a Taco John's on that location. Evanston Planning and Zoning had already approved the zone change subject to the city council action, but with approximately 20 residential owners in the area opposing the zone change, Holmes decided at that time to withdraw his request, but would be coming back at a later date to try again.

Holmes had bought the property from the Amoco Pipeline Company, who had had an office on that location for many years, because of the old Standard pipeline going through southern Wyoming from Sinclair, Wyoming to the refineries in Salt Lake City, Utah.

The northeasterly side of Front Street had already been zoned commercial, but the southwesterly side had not been officially zoned commercial, although there were some commercial establishments already on that side. It probably would become commercial in time, because of Front Street being a major thoroughfare off the Wyoming State Highway 150 S on and off ramp.

Another issue that came up during the city council meetings of October was a request from Mountain Regional Services (MRS) to purchase a home located at 330 Hansen Avenue, to be used as a group home for developmentally disabled people. The home would be used to house people who are handicapped, incapacitated, or physically or mentally challenged. Some teenagers would be included. Some would have police records.

MRS was relatively new to Evanston and was formerly known as Uinta County Rehabilitation Center (UCRC). The program had recently been dropped from the Wyoming State Hospital in Evanston. John Holderegger, Director of Mountain Regional Services, who would be representing MRS at city council meetings over the next few years, was requesting group homes in several other areas of Evanston.

This was a big issue to neighbors, who were concerned about the type of individual that would be residing in group homes. The council was told that there could be as many as six or eight handicapped people living in the same house with the idea of taking care of each other. Holderegger said the program was to help these people learn to live with the public through association and mingling with the community.

At first the city had some problems with the idea because of neighbors' concerns and the possibility of someone getting hurt by these people if they were not kept on their medication and closely watched over. But Holderegger explained that through federal housing regulations the city had no say, and zoning had no place in this kind of living.

For quite some time the neighbors were worried, especially because some group home residents had been convicted of very serious crimes, but were committed as mentally incapacitated and ordered by the courts to go into a rehabilitation program. To the best of my knowledge there never was a problem caused by anyone living in these group homes.

In October of that year Superintendent of the Wyoming Highway Department Leno Menghini announced that the west end of

U.S. Highway 30 S (Historic Lincoln Highway, but presently Harrison Drive) would be under construction the summer of 1988 for widening, curb and gutter, sidewalks and storm drains. He said it would be similar to what they had constructed on the east end of Bear River Drive, formerly U.S. Highway 30 South in the summer of 1986.

When this announcement hit the public all hell broke loose. Because of all the problems they had and the time it took them to complete construction on the east end, the business folks on the west end of Evanston got very upset. Some of these folks also had business on the east end that got badly hurt because of the construction. One of those businesses was owned by my brother Bob Ottley, who had a truck tire sales and repair shop that he had to shut down partly because of the construction, but partly because of the economy.

Menghini had been very supportive and helpful to Evanston over the past several years, and had been more than willing in our requests for assistance when we were in need of construction of new streets or the upgrading and improvement of some old streets. He was always very supportive in helping the City of Evanston with the engineering, the financing and in some cases actual construction of our needs in keeping our streets up.

At this very time the Wyoming Highway Department was funding improvements to the County Road from the underpass to the north, intersecting with the new Wyoming State Highway 89, including the new replacement of the Bear River Bridge which was being changed from two lanes to four lanes.

The council and I were very concerned with what had happened on the east end of Bear River Drive, because of the way it had been handled. The road was shut down most of the time and it took the construction company all of that summer and more to complete the job, causing a big loss in tourist traffic. I'll admit that it made the road a lot nicer and safer with sidewalks and all, but it did cause some to go out of business, and that concerned me.

I had no idea why it took so long for construction of the east end, or why it was shut down so often, and I had no idea who was at fault, but it did worry me. I worried that the same thing might happen on the west end, and I wouldn't feel good about that.

Some of the business people on the west end requested that the highway department hold off for two more years before they did the construction. Some didn't want it at all, but we needed sidewalks for the safety of our pedestrians. It had just been a few years ago that a child crossing the highway, with his parents going to the Whirl Inn Restaurant to eat, was hit by a car and killed, and we needed storm sewer drains very much in that area.

Uinta County Herald

Evanston, Wyoming 82930   Wednesday, November 18, 1987   Volume 53, Number 91   Price 25¢ Per Copy

Council deadlocked on highway project

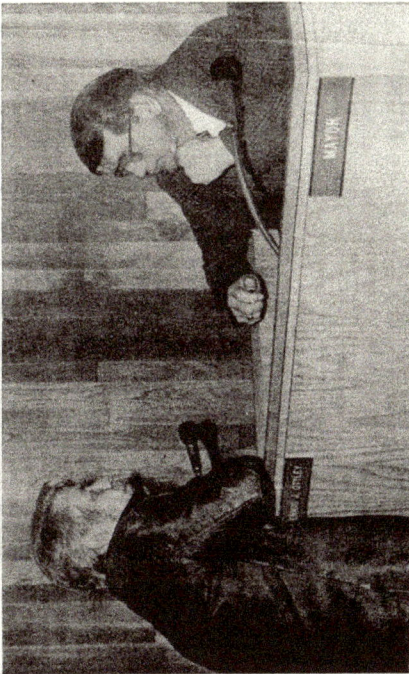

Mayor Dennis Ottley has two brothers in business on the west-end who were among those businesses requesting the City's support for delaying the proposed highway project there. Here he talks with brother Mack Lott during a recess in Monday nights City Council meeting. "I don't think it's fair to the people of Evanston to ask for a delay on the project," the Mayor said. "People elected me to represent them and that is what I'm trying to do."

City Council members Monday were at a standstill on the issue of whether to support west-end merchants in their quest for a two-year delay on the proposed highway project slated for construction next summer.

Council members voted three times with the same results. Jon Lunsford, Darrel Staley and Tom Hutchinson voted to support the two-year delay on the project while Clarence Vranish, Will Davis and Mayor Dennis Ottley voted for the 2.5 million dollar project to go ahead as scheduled. Councilwoman Julie Lehman was absent.

Before the vote, Staley pointed out to the more than 25 people in attendance that the council's vote was still only an opinion and the final decision on the project would be made by the Wyoming Highway Commission.

All council members present Monday said they favored the project but felt it would be better for local businesses if the project were delayed a few years, hoping the economy would be better.

"We really need this project," local teacher David Bills told the council "I'm in the kid business and I think we really need those sidewalks." Sidewalks, curbs, gutters, storm sewers and resurfacing along with new lighting will be included in the west-end highway project.

"Let's say we don't build it and three of four kids get killed. We'd all feel awful," Bills said, pointing out many children from Centennial Valley walk to school along the highway which currently has no sidewalks.

Again, west-end business owners pointed out they don't want to kill any hopes for the project ever being done, but want it delayed because most Evanston businesses are feeling the crunch right now.

"Right now the banks are working with most of us to help keep us open," Jae Dee Kindler said. "Since the stock market crashed, our businesses went to hell."

After meeting with the business owners from the west end and other interested citizens on November 10th, I announced that there would be a special city council meeting at 5:00 p.m. on November 16th with the issue of the west end highway construction as the only item on the agenda. The public was invited and would have the opportunity to speak prior to the meeting where the council would be voting on whether they were in favor of starting the construction next spring or requesting that the highway department hold off the construction for two more years. Approximately 50 interested citizens were in attendance, and representing the Wyoming Highway Department was Marlin Wright, Resident Engineer, and Tim McLeary, District Engineer from Rock Springs.

The Evanston Post issue of November 12th reported that *Wright told the group that the project is scheduled to be let in December and construction would start after the frost is out of the ground next spring. He said November 1, 1988 was the completion date, but the contractor would be working with an incentive clause for early completion. "The contractor would get $193,000 if the work is finished by September 1, 1988," Wright said. "There is a lot of storm sewer work that has to be done. That is why the project will take so long," he added.*

On November 16th we held the special city council meeting for the issue of the west end highway construction. After calling for the roll call it was established that Councilwoman Julie Lehman would be absent, reason unknown, leaving only five council members present and myself, as mayor.

According to the minutes of the meeting published in The Evanston Post on November 25th, after roll call I immediately opened the meeting up for discussion on the West End Highway Renewal Project.

A general discussion took place. Some of the business people from the west side of the city expressed their concern with the planned construction project once again. Some requested the support from the city for a delay of the project for two years.

Mr. J. D. Kindler, representing the Whirl Inn went on record, stating, *After two years, I would not ask for any further delay.*

Mrs. Diane Mills, representing the Dunmar Inn (Best Western), stated that they would like to see the project built as soon as possible.

More comments were made by the city council members, Marlin Wright, Resident Engineer of WHD, and several other business people and private citizens.

After a lengthy discussion Councilman Tom Hutchinson made a motion to support a short-term delay of one or two years for the improvements on the West End Highway, seconded by Councilman Jon Lunsford. The vote was called for with 3 voting yes (Lunsford, Darrell Staley and Hutchinson), and 3 voting no (me, Will Davis and Clarence Vranish). The motion ended up in a tie vote, causing it to fail.

Councilman Vranish then made a motion to support the street improvement project as planned for this coming summer, seconded by Davis with 3 voting yes (me, Davis and Vranish), and 3 voting no (Lunsford, Staley and Hutchinson). With a tie vote, the motion again failed.

Once again Councilman Hutchinson made a motion, with different wording, to support the west end business people in a request to the State Highway Commission for a two year delay of the construction project, seconded by Staley.

During discussion of Hutchinson's motion I stated that I thought the whole city would benefit from the construction because it would mean better lighting, sidewalks, storm sewer drains, curb and gutter and a generally better looking entrance into the city. I said I was very much in favor of the project and getting it completed as fast as possible.

After a little more discussion, I called for the vote on Hutchinson's motion with the same results, 3 yes and 3 no with the same turnout as the first two motions. It appeared that with only 6 members of the council being present, including the mayor, we were deadlocked on doing anything more during this meeting, and I stated that enough time had been spent on discussion of the highway construction project. I then ask for a motion to go into executive session to discuss the purchase of properties needed for the completion of the Sulphur Creek Project, another big issue.

Motion was made by Councilman Staley, and seconded by Davis, to hold an executive session to consider purchase of those properties, and the motion passed unanimously. Therefore, at that time, I adjourned the meeting at hand, and requested that everyone except the city clerk and city attorney clear the council chambers, and we proceeded to go into executive session.

Following the meeting and being very concerned about the construction on the west end, I decided to write a letter to Mr. Leno Menghini, who, over the years, I had gotten to know very well. Menghini had helped Evanston on many of their street projects.

The letter was dated November 18th and addressed the subject of doing the construction on the west end as he had recently announced. My letter read as follows:

> *Dear Leno,*
>
> *As you may know, there has been some concern raised about the planned construction project on Evanston's west end. In an effort to understand those concerns and to perhaps help mitigate those concerns, the City of Evanston has met with the local affected businesses several times.*
>
> *At the latest meeting, the City Council was asked to recommend to the Highway Commission that this project be postponed for two years. A motion to that effect was made, and failed. A second motion to support the project as planned was made. That motion failed. A third motion was made to support the West End Businesses in their effort to delay the project for 2 years. That motion also failed.*
>
> *As Mayor, I expressed my feelings to the concerned business people that I feel this project is a needed improvement to the whole city, and that safety concerns alone should justify this project. It is my wish that if this project continues, that a contractor be selected that will be sensitive to the special needs of business.*
>
> *In discussion with Marlin Wright he thought it may be helpful to you and the commission if we forwarded the above mentioned action, or lack of action, to you. I also want to let you know that Marlin has been most helpful and accommodating during the last*

few weeks while we have discussed and deliberated on this proposed project.

If you have any questions, please feel free to call me.

Sincerely,
Dennis J. Ottley (signed)
Mayor
cc: City Council

In answering my letter, Superintendent and Chief Engineer Leno Menghini stated in his letter to me:

As you might imagine, it was not an easy decision for the Commission to make, nor did they make the decision without a lot of thought and discussion.

The Commission was very sympathetic to the concerns voiced by the west-end business community. In the end, however, they felt that there is never a good time to build in an urban area, but that perhaps it might be better to do the project now when things are slow rather than in boom times which may return.

Leno Menghini (signed)

Word came back to us that the highway commission had noted that if the Kern River Pipeline, now in hearings in front of the Federal Energy Regulatory Commission, goes through. Evanston could see another boom period. Therefore no other action was taken towards the improvements of the west end highway project. The highway department kept their schedule to improve the west end during the summer of 1988, even though there was still some upset west end business folks.

The headline of the *Uinta County Herald* issue dated December 2nd read: HIGHWAY 30 WEST PROJECT IS A "GO". The article said, *Improvements will be made from the Kentucky Fried Chicken to Lombard Street, and will involve new curb and gutter, storm sewer, sidewalks and widening of the road.* Surprisingly, I also received a memo dated

November 19th from former Councilman David Bills commending me for my actions during the vote on the west end construction. The memo read as follows:

> To: *Mayor Dennis Ottley*
> From: *David Bills, Interested Citizen*
> Subj: *Memo of Appreciation*
> Ref: *Special City Council Meeting of 11-16-87*
>
> *I would like to write to you and express my admiration and appreciation for your actions at the referenced meeting.*
> *You were subjected to the most intense pressure I have ever seen. You did not waver. You did not hesitate. You resolutely advocated what you believed to be in the best interests of Evanston.*
> *I salute you. You made me proud you were my Mayor.*
>
> *Respectfully, David Bills* (signed)

I didn't know what to think when I received his letter because of the lies and innuendos that he said about me during the mayoral race in 1982, the year I got beat by Gene Martin. Bills was also running that year for mayor, but even after he got beat in the primaries, he continued spreading vicious lies and falsehoods to the public, helping Martin beat me in the general election.

However, I did appreciate the memo from him, because he did make an extra effort to treat me with a lot of respect from then on. However, I kind of felt it was his way of apologizing to me for the past, and that's great, because I am not a vindictive person.

In the latter part of October of 1987 the Evanston City Council introduced an ordinance to change the boundaries of Voting Wards l, ll and lll. Because of population changes in the three wards, it was essential that the adjustment be done. The ordinance received a lot of flak from some people, including Uinta County Clerk Joyce Holmes.

According to the news article printed in the December 17th issue of *The Evanston Post*, Joyce Holmes had said that the city council was *"gerrymandering of the ward boundaries within the City of Evanston."*

That comment, if it was correctly reported by the *Post*, upset some of the city council members. Some members of the council approached Bill Alexander, editor of the article and he claimed those were the words she used. I had never heard the word *gerrymandering*, and didn't know what it meant so I looked it up in the dictionary and found the following:

*Gerrymandering is to mean: *to divide (an area) into political units to give special advantages to one group,* such as a city.

Well, we all knew she had to be concerned, but it was her job to just do what she was supposed to do and that was to oversee the election. It was the city council's place to see that things were done fairly within the City of Evanston, including adjusting the election ward boundaries so that they are as even in numbers as possible. And that was exactly what we did, favoring of no one. In January, 1988, regardless of what the county clerk thought, the Evanston City Council acted on the third reading, and after a few adjustments, the ordinance to adjust the Election Ward boundaries passed by a unanimous vote. The ordinance would go into law immediately, and according to County Clerk Holmes, the new boundaries would be used at the upcoming 1988 elections.

⤙⤙⤚⤚

Another controversial issue came up in November concerning the changes of some street names. The biggest concern was that the Evanston City Council had included the previous named Uinta View Drive. This was the name of the road before annexation, but we already had a Uinta Street, so the idea was to change the name to City View Drive.

The name change requests were made by the postal department, the fire department and police department because there were so many similarities in the names of city streets. They claimed that in a

*Taken from Webster's Ninth New Collegiate Dictionary.

lot of cases when someone would report an emergency they wouldn't give the entire street name; as an example, someone might just say "there's an accident on Uinta," and hang up. According to these departments, that happened more than once and they indicated that it is very important that these street names be changed. The biggest complaints from the public were from businesses and offices, public and private, because of the expense of changing their letterheads, envelopes and business cards. Also, the Uinta County Clerk and Assessor's offices were concerned about how it would affect the street names already printed on city plats, deeds, and so on, and the workload it would cause to change those names.

But though there would be some problems for some people, the city council and others thought that the safety of the public came first, and was far more important than worrying about the cost of letterheads or additional work. Any action to change the street names would not take place or acted upon for another few months, probably not until the next year.

Also in November the City of Evanston was without a Director of the Urban Renewal Agency. Director Michael Matts had presented his letter of resignation to the city council in October. He stated that he was resigning because he was leaving Evanston. Matt had done a lot of good for the city and in accepting his resignation we all wished him and his family well and lots of success in his future endeavors.

Jim and Bonnie Davis had returned to Evanston in August of 1984 and had gotten very involved in the programs that the city was undertaking at the time. They were both natives of Evanston and had both graduated from Evanston High. They had left Evanston when Jim was employed by Allstate Insurance in Chicago until his retirement. With their family, they returned to their hometown that they both loved very much. They opened up a shop in downtown Evanston on Main Street, calling it "Home Décor," and it has done very well all these years.

After the resignation of Mike Matts, Jim Davis was hired in November by the Board of Directors of the Urban Renewal Agency for the next two decades and then some. Jim was very dedicated to the

City of Evanston and, in my opinion, did Evanston a great service. There were times that I didn't agree with him, but he did help build Evanston in many ways. Sandy and I worked with Jim very closely to help make Evanston a better place.

Another issue that came up late in 1987 was the announcement of AT&T, Inc. that they would be running a fiber optic line going coast to coast, which would be going through Evanston, and a few employees would reside here temporarily.

During the Evanston Planning and Zoning Commission's meeting in early January, the commission approved AT&T's request for a conditional use permit to build their regeneration station on Yellow Creek road near the already-built Mountain Bell Service building. They stated that the generation station was necessary to boost the signal for their fiber optic line being installed across the nation.

Also during the November meeting of the city council, the city approved the issuance of an oil permit to allow the Apache Oil Corp. to drill an oil well in the southeast area within the city limits, and Chevron USA announced that they had signed a Letter of Intent with the Kern River Gas Transmission Company to transport gas from this area through their new pipeline when completed. The pipeline would run from Opal, Wyoming to Bakersfield, California. They were now waiting for clearance by the U.S. Energy Commission to go ahead. This was all good news to Evanston and an indication that the oil and gas industry wasn't completely dead in the area.

Other action taken was that the Bear Project Ice Ponds, after purchasing the property from the U.P.R.R., was approved for recreational purposes, such as ice skating in the winter, fishing, swimming and possibly boating in the summer.

It seemed to me that if all these proposed projects went through it would help the economy a lot, including the reconstruction of County Road also in 1988. The City of Evanston contracted with Uinta Engineering and Surveying to engineer the construction of County Road.

The engineering firm that was hired during Martin's administration would be finished at the completion of the Bear River Bridge, which already had two extensions and change orders on it. Hopefully it will be completed soon.

~~~

Although 1987 was a very successful year in many ways, we received some unexpected news of a tragic and fatal accident that happened in December causing the death of a very good friend of Evanston's. Owen Murphy of Chevron USA had been killed with others in a commuter plane crash in California during a trip from San Francisco, Chevron Headquarters, to Los Angeles where Owen lived. The crash happened somewhere midway with no survivors.

Murphy had been President and was very active in the O.I.A. by assisting Evanston through the mitigation program and in many other ways through one of the most trying oil and gas boom periods in Wyoming history. He was a great guy and worked closely in assisting both the City of Evanston and Uinta County through those tough times. He was one of the most instrumental officials representing the oil and gas industry that assisted in Evanston's mitigation program. And he appeared to be very dedicated in seeing that Evanston met the challenges of the impact.

Administrative Assistant Steve Snyder announced at the December city council meeting that he and I would fly to Los Angeles to attend Murphy's memorial service, which was held on December 16th. He said, *I think we should do this because of Chevron and the work on the Kern River Project and because of Mrs. Murphy,* and the council all agreed.

When Snyder and I arrived at Murphy's memorial service, Mrs. Murphy was quite surprised, but very glad to see us. We had met her before when she would come to Evanston to meet her husband, so we were no strangers to her.

She appeared to be doing fine, but she and Owen had been together for quite some time and you could tell she felt very unhappy about losing him. She couldn't stop thanking us for taking the time to be there. I said to her, *Owen was a great friend and a lot of help to Evanston. We all felt real bad when we got the news about his accident, and there was no way that Snyder and I were going to miss being in attendance at his services.* She, with tears in her eyes, thanked both of us and gave us each a hug. It was a nice and well attended service.

<hr>

During the Employee's Annual Christmas Honor Banquet on Friday, December 11th, there were twenty-three employees honored. Gerald "Stubb" Julian, a certified operator at the city's wastewater treatment plant, and Sterling "Sterl" Mackay, a maintenance man with the city's water department had retired and were recognized for their service. Julian had been employed for 8½ years while Mackay had been employed for 10 years.

The Public Works Department gave special honors to Public Works Superintendent Allen Kennedy for his 36 years of service in that department.

Police Officer Michael Cole was noted for his accomplishments in graduating with honors from the Wyoming Law Enforcement Academy and being elected president of his class. Officer Doug Mathews was honored for saving a man's life with CPR after the man had stopped breathing on October 9th at the Bear River State Park Travel Center.

Fifteen year pins were given to Jack Day and George Morris. Four people received 10-year service pins: Frank Maioran and J. R. Dean of the police department, and Allen "Oop" Hansen and Ross Wilson of public works. Also, twelve employees were honored for five years of service with the city; Jake Williams, Colleen O'Brien, Robbie Edrington, and Doug Mathews, employees of the police department; and Robert Day, Ron Peterson, Jeff Martin, Dan Martin, Barry Constantine, Gary Bentley, Randy George, and Russ Robertson, all with public works.

It was to be a grand evening, and I made the statement that all of those honored were well deserved.

My first year back on the job had been another very busy year with its share of controversy and problems, and ups and downs, but in my mind, it had been another successful year with lots yet to come.

I once read a quote by Marie Curie, the great Polish–French physicist and chemist that went like this: *"One never notices what has to be done; one can only see what remains to be done."* She's right and, *"if you wait, all you do is get older."*

CHAPTER 22

1988....Here it is January of 1988 and after opening the first city council meeting for the year on Monday the 11th, I gave my State of the City address as reported by *The Evanston Post* of January 14th: *"I want to mention some of the past year's achievements,"* Ottley said, *setting the agenda aside for a few minutes at the beginning of the meeting.*

"We have a $900,000 carryover in the budget because of some cuts we made in early 1987. I am pleased with the current budget and I hope we can have a like amount of carryover next year," the Mayor said.

The *Post* continued: *He also commented that the Sulphur Creek Reservoir project was well on its way to completion. "We've got about two more seasons on it," he said, indicating the time that the dam expansion and the pipelines to Evanston would be completed.*

He said that the city finished the County Road Bridge project late last year and hoped that the $3 million County Road reclamation project might start this summer, "if we can find the money," he said.

The article said: *Ottley ended his comments with, "Economic development is a top priority right now. If we don't have a good economy, we can't have anything else." During his comments he thanked the council and the city staff for a job well done in 1987. He also mentioned that the Depot Square project was advancing, the Bear River Task Force had been formed to look at cleaning up the river and having a green belt [along the river] from one side of town to the other, and that the mayor and council were involved in the Kern River Pipeline discussions. "Maybe we can get word on this project this summer," he said.*

Ottley stated, the Post continued, *that in 1987 the K-9 Corps for the Evanston Police Department was started, the Water Treatment Plant Project [expansion], and that the city had sent a letter of intent to buy the old ice pond property from Upland. "The Treatment Plant is something we really need, and it will be a $4 million project. I hope we can move further on this project this summer," he said.*

After I gave my State of the City report I turned to the agenda. Following the approval of the previous minutes and outstanding bills, I made my appointments of the city officials with no change accept for City Planner Paul Knopf, who was also appointed to serve as Community Development Director, an appointed position. Paul would be wearing two hats through this year at the same pay rate. The city council made the usual motion and second to confirm the appointments of the city officials, with all voting in favor.

Appointments to the various boards and commissions were also announced and confirmed by the city council by a unanimous vote.

The article in *The Evanston Post* also read: *Miles J. Alexander of the Evanston Liquor Dealers' Association appeared before the council to ask for approval of the four extended hour days for the bars and liquor stores in Evanston. The four days selected, Alexander said, were May 29, July 3, September 4, and December 31. "The summer days all are three-day weekends and all days selected, except New Year's Eve, are Sundays," he added. December 31, 1988 is a Saturday. By state law the city council must approve the four days during the calendar year that the bars can ignore the 2:00 a.m. closing time and serve liquor all night. The council approved the four dates chosen by the liquor dealers.*

Under unfinished business during the meeting, *The Evanston Post* continued: *The council passed on third and final reading an ordinance setting the ward voting boundaries within the city. After much debate and putting the amended ordinance on the table at the last meeting, the council's original gerrymandering plan was adopted.*

In other business, the city council approved the P & Z Commission's decision on allowing the conditional use permit to AT&T for their regeneration station, which the council passed in favor by a unanimous vote.

Printed in the issue of the *Uinta County Herald* on January 13th was a resolution that read: *In a joint City-County resolution was adopted to pay a special tribute to Owen F. Murphy, the Chevron public relations man who died in the December 1987 PSA crash in California. "Throughout his career,"* the resolution stated, *"Owen F. Murphy provided substantial and significant public service to the citizens of Uinta County and earned the respect, admiration and high regard of those with whom he came into contact."*

The Resolution was not only recognition of Murphy's contribution to Evanston and Uinta County, but "an expression of the sincere appreciation of his dedicated performance and public service."

A framed print of this resolution was forwarded to Mrs. Murphy, his wife, indicating to her that the citizens of Evanston and Uinta County appreciated, respected, and recognized the services that Owen had given to this city and county, and that he would never be forgotten.

The *Uinta County Herald* of January 29th reported: CHEVRON THANKS CITY IN LETTER. The article went on: *Councilman Clarence Vranish commended Mayor Ottley this week for taking a delegation to Owen Murphy's funeral in December of last year.*

Vranish alluded to a letter of thanks written to the Mayor from Chevron's chairman of the board, George W. Keller.

The article continued: *The letter read, in part, "Owen was a close, personal friend and it is especially gratifying to see how much he meant to people outside our corporation as well," the letter said. The O.I.A. and Owen's work in Evanston was personally very important to Owen. In fact, it was probably the highlight of his career. He loved Wyoming and his work with you, and I know how much he thought of you and all the people who were involved in the O.I.A. process.*

"Please know that you will always have a friend in Chevron," the letter concluded.

In the *Uinta County Herald* issue of January 27th the headlines read: FARM LOAN BOARD WAS GOOD TO EVANSTON, UINTA COUNTY. The article continued: *City and county officials came home smiling from last week's state Farm Loan Board meeting in Cheyenne as Evanston and Uinta County received one million dollars each for the county jail construction and for expanding the city's wastewater treatment plant. On that same day South and Jones Timber Company, a local business, received $270,000 from the Wyoming Investment IV fund program, a loan to further construction on its wood pellet manufacturing equipment.*

The *Herald's* article continued: *City Administrative Assistant, Steven Snyder, who acted as grantsman for all three groups, said the city also received* *a $1.6 million low-interest loan for the balance of the cost of expanding the water treatment plant. The city received $445,000 at the state board's last meeting in October.*

Expansion of the water plant will double its capacity from 4 million to 8 million gallons a day and prevent the water shortages and restrictions city residents have had to deal with in the past, Snyder said.

The news article added: *According to one of the Timber company's owners, Dan South (former Evanston Mayor), production of the pellets will probably begin in a couple of months.*

"I got two calls from Colorado last week and each one of those guys would've bought a semiload apiece if they would've been ready," South said.

South pointed out he was unhappy about recent comments opposing the Wyoming State Investment IV funds and praised the program.

"It's making a lot of people think about all these different ideas," South said. "It doesn't matter how good an idea you have if you can't get the backing from the bank."

In other matters the Vietnam Veterans of Southwestern Wyoming sent a letter to me dated January 27th, *requesting Evanston's help in making the public aware of The American Citizens still missing or being held prisoner in Asia. You can help us by proclaiming the month of February as POW-MIA "Forget Me Not Month" in Evanston, Wyoming. You will be joining the Mayors of Rock Springs, Green River, Lyman and Mountain View who have already proclaimed "Forget Me Not Month" in their cities. We would also like to invite you as an honored guest to a candle-light vigil January 31, 1988, 7:30 p.m. at the Uinta County War Memorial in Evanston. Enclosed is a copy of the proclamation signed by other Mayors.*

Howard L. Combs (signed)
President V.V.S.W.

Calling for a special meeting of the city council, I read the letter from the V.V.S.W. to them and they responded with a unanimous vote to agree that I sign the requested proclamation. After signing we announced the proclamation and explanation to the local newspapers, and I also attended the candle-light vigil at the Uinta Court House.

It was reported to the Evanston City Council that Chevron, in conjunction with the Denver Research Group, was conducting a case study of what happened to Evanston during the oil boom of early 1980s.

In a letter addressed to me from Charles "Chuck" M. McLean, President of Denver Research Group, he stated: *Chevron U.S.A. is in the process of developing for distribution to colleges and universities a case study of the Overthrust Industrial Association (O.I.A.). The case study is a history of the O.I.A. and the experiences of and lessons learned during the Overthrust oil and gas boom. It is designed to help communities facing similar growth situations.*

We need your help to ensure that this publication reflects the opinions of local leaders.

We are inviting you to attend an informal workshop on January 26 at 11:00 a.m. The workshop will be held at the Dunmar Inn in the SAC room and will last approximately 90 minutes. Lunch will be provided.

The purpose of the workshop is to review the results of the O.I.A. mitigation program and compare these results to needs identified by the Community Advisory Groups at the beginning of the boom. We want to know what worked and what did not work. In an effort to keep the workshops informal and ensure maximum participation, we are inviting only a small group of individuals familiar with the issues as they affected the City. Additional workshops are scheduled to disclose other topics.

The letter ended with: *Thank you in advance for your participation. We look forward to working with you on this project.* I mentioned to the council that I thought this was a tremendous idea and that I would be making an extra effort to attend these work sessions.

Chevron's Wyoming Public Affairs Manager, Robert E. Quick, Jr. said, "The case study is to help people learn about the oil industry, for a new mayor or civic leader that may be faced with similar circumstances. 'How do you tailor your support services to deal with impact?' is one issue the study will address," he added, as stated in the *Uinta County Herald* issue of January 29th.

The *Herald* article also stated: *Chuck McLean, a consultant from the Denver Research Group in charge of spearheading the study, said Evanston has been chosen because the process developed with the O.I.A. during the boom worked well for Evanston.*

"It's important that an industry know that it can work with a community and Evanston has shown that it does that better than any community in the nation," McLean said. "If I were an industry coming in, I would want to work with a community like Evanston."

"It was very encouraging to hear that Evanston has built on its past experiences and really put itself in shape," McLean said after a day and a half in Evanston talking to local leaders. "I don't think there was one O.I.A. program that hasn't improved."

The Herald added: McLean and Quick pointed out that Evanston grew from a population of 6,420 in 1980 to an estimated 11,120 at the end of the boom in 1984. Some unofficial estimates were as high as 15,000 to 18,000 in population during the boom.

"The O.I.A. process is a tribute to the good common sense, the honesty and integrity of the leaders in the community," Quick said. "It's a process we would like to see replicated," he added, pointing out the major purpose of the study.

McLean said the benefits Evanston reaped by forming a working community-industry relationship through O.I.A. was manifold.

"O.I.A.'s budget was $12 million total," he said. "The committees and communities leveraged that into about $100 million in benefits in terms of capital improvements and programs. Evanston has really done well in becoming an excellently managed community," McLean continued. "That's what we hope to see come out of this study for other communities."

"This is not to say this [study] is the greatest thing since sliced bread," McLean pointed out.

The news article ended with: [Robert] quickly said, there are things that could have been handled better and these things will be well documented in the study and suggestions made for improvement.

During the Evanston City Council meeting on Monday, February 8th the council voted 6-1 with Councilman Clarence Vranish voting against the construction of a 35-foot roadway with a center turn lane and four-foot planning strip on both sides of County Road. Vranish said he was not against the new road, but rather against putting in the narrower road instead of an alternate proposal with a 39-foot roadway accommodating a parking lane on one side. Vranish said that he felt it was necessary to have ample room for vehicles to pull off the roadway in emergency situations, but the rest of the council, including me, thought that a center turning lane was far more important. Also, the proposal Vranish was talking about would only give emergency parking on one side of the road.

County Road was expected to be under the reconstruction this coming summer under the engineering firm of Uinta Engineering and Surveying.

During the meeting the renewable 10-year lease agreement with the Evanston Boat Club came up. This was a lease allowing them to continue using Sulphur Creek Reservoir for boating and keeping their boat dock and clubhouse. Some council members were concerned with the long-term lease of 10 years so City Attorney Dennis Boal added language in the new lease would allow the city to terminate the lease with a year's notification in case the city needed to move the boat club for any reason.

Also during the February 8th meeting, the City of Evanston came out ahead on a change order approved by the council, decreasing the cost of the Bear River Pipeline project by $14,969.16. Councilwoman Julia Lehman announced that she would be resigning from her elected position as a member of the city council in the near future, because her husband, Uinta County Judge Larry L. Lehman, had been appointed by Governor Mike Sullivan to the vacancy of the Second Judicial District Judgeship in Rawlins. She stated that her and her children would be leaving after the school year.

I had asked her to stay on and finish out her city council term which would have expired at the end of this year, but she said she would not be submitting her letter of resignation for few more months, and that she planned to leave sometime in June or July.

I said to the council, *We will not act on filling the vacancy until the council receives her letter, probably sometime this coming spring, unless she chooses to finish out her term. If she chooses not to, the council will then ask for the people living in Ward ll that may be interested in her seat to apply. The city council will have the responsibility of selecting the new council person from that list of applications.*

During the February meeting the Evanston City Council got word that Ehman Engineering had applied, once again, for additional funding from the Wyoming State Amendment IV Program to upgrade their business, which seemed to be doing very well.

After a short discussion, Councilman Jon Lunsford made a motion that a letter of support be sent to Ehman Engineering from the City of Evanston in support of their application to the Amendment IV Board, seconded by Councilman Davis, with all voting in favor.

After sending the letter of support to Ehman, I also sent a letter to Governor Mike Sullivan in support of the Ehman application.

A short time later I received a letter dated February 16th from Governor Sullivan in support of the application, but also a request that we, the City of Evanston, do whatever we can to encourage legislators to support that request, and assist the Board's continuing efforts to encourage companies like Ehman.

It was a very supportive letter and after reading it to the council, the council members thought that it was quite a nice thing to know that the Governor was also in support of Ehman's application.

During the council meeting, City Planner Paul Knopf reported on a meeting of members of a citizens' task force and officials from throughout the State of Wyoming that are participating in an effort to make possible a multimillion-dollar Bear River project which would not only clean up the river, but also help to solve the increasing problem of erosion of the river and stabilization.

Knopf reported that he introduced the presentation to several state agencies in attendance, including members of the Wyoming Department of Environmental Quality (D.E.Q.) and the U.S. Geological Society. He stated that all agencies present were definitely interested and enthusiastic about the project.

He also met with these state and federal agencies to brainstorm where the money will come from and what to do first. Along with that, several area businessmen and community members were present to work on the project, which would be years in the making.

Councilman Vranish, who was present at the meeting, stated that it was a well-organized, well-handled presentation and gave special commendations to City Planner Knopf. I expressed my appreciation to Knopf for being able to pull together so many state agencies for this special presentation.

There was no doubt that the project would become a reality, but everyone knew that it would be a long-range project. As I write this book, the project, I believe, is pretty much complete with a few exceptions. It has been a well worthwhile project that included a lot of funding, planning and hard work, but that is what it takes to make a worthwhile project become a reality.

The entire Bear River project was a dream. It was Paul Knopf's dream, among many others'. Quoting our great president, Abraham Lincoln: *"Always remember that your own resolution to succeed is more important than anything else,"* and Paul had done just that.

On February 16th I signed another proclamation declaring the week of February 28th to March 5th as *Agri-Business Week*, along with Tom Anderson, Mayor of Lyman; Steve Stucki, Mayor of Mountain View; and John R. Stevens, Chairman of the Uinta County Commissioners.

The Proclamation starts out: *WHEREAS, Uinta County, the City of Evanston and the Towns of Lyman and Mountain View had joined forces to call attention to the cooperative efforts of the Agri-Business Community.*

Agri-Business is an annual event that includes a county-wide banquet where a *Citizen of the Year* is named and honored from each community, and several other awards are presented to deserving folks throughout Uinta County. It had been a worthwhile program that had been sponsored during the months of February/March for the past few years and hopefully it would continue each year in the future.

During the council meeting on Monday, February 29th (Leap Year Day), the Evanston City Council voted to endorse Governor Mike Sullivan's proposal to aid local governments and an increase of one percent in the sales tax.

Last meeting the council unanimously voted against the increased sales tax, but after receiving a letter from the governor and giving it more thought, I urged the council during the meeting to support the governor and the Wyoming Association of Municipalities (W.A.M.), who were both very much in favor of the increase. After more discussion a motion was made and seconded with five voting in favor and two opposed. Motion passed with Councilmembers Clarence Vranish and Julie Lehman casting the dissenting votes.

The city council's motion to support the one percent sales tax increase also included supporting Governor Sullivan's proposal to shift $21.5 million in various tax monies to local governments, which was a good proposal and I was very glad that the city council voted in favor. It was monies that would be needed by local governments in the future.

The Evanston Post, dated February 25th, quoted Councilman Clarence Vranish as saying, *"Right now we are in pretty good shape but we seem to have a tendency to spend money if we have it and that makes new jobs. The increased tax would give us a surplus that we would spend, but then someday we might have to cut back and that makes it real bad."* Councilman Jon Lunsford countered, saying, *"We're only in good shape because the county took the landfill and the fire department, and the parks and recreation department formed a district. If that hadn't happened we would be in a hell of a shape."*

The *Post* added: *Mayor Ottley interjected, "I don't think the legislature is going to increase taxes this year, and I don't think we should stand apart from the other cities in the state. I want to support W.A.M. We should show we are behind W.A.M. and other cities, whether we need the extra money or not. Other communities may need the increase. We need to support the governor and W.A.M."*

The Post's article continued: *In other City Council action, the Council granted a limited malt beverage permit for two days to the Spirits of Red Mountain for the Evanston Ambassador's Winter Carnival. Dick Stokes of the Ambassador's appeared before the Council and requested the permit and said, "This is our fifth carnival and this is the first time we have ever had to do this [going through a liquor dealer for the permit]. In past years the council has just given us the permit."*

Mayor Ottley said that the council could not issue any sort of a malt beverage permit to a Chamber of Commerce according to state law. The Ambassadors are an arm of the chamber, the *Post* article continued.

Also, during the meeting, I appointed Dr. John Doidge and Pat Alexander to the Urban Renewal Agency to complete the terms of Beth Carlson and Jim Davis with both appointments being confirmed by the council unanimously.

The public meeting concerning the changing of some of the street names in Evanston was held on the evening of February 29th at City Hall. Approximately 15 local residents were in attendance as well as various city officials. The proposal recommended by the city included name changes on approximately 33 streets in different areas of the city.

Residents who were in attendance raised questions concerning street names being changed causing other problems, including their address changes on vehicle registrations, mortgages and other legal papers. City officials tried to explain to them that the changes were to eliminate duplications and near-duplications where the street names conflict with other street names, and that the primary purpose of making those street name changes were for safety purposes, as requested by the Evanston Police Department and the Uinta County Fire Department, and other emergency agencies. They had all stated that there had been times when they arrived at the wrong address on emergency calls. Also, the Evanston Post office had requested the changes because sometimes mail would not include the complete street name in the address.

A list of the proposed name changes were handed out to each of those in attendance by City Public Works Specialist Michael Klein, who had been assigned to make the study on street name changes. Klein said that the proposed name changes were not, at this time, set in stone. He said that the city would be more than willing to take suggestions and recommendations from those who were not happy with the changes, but if you were not satisfied, then you must get with your neighbors on your street and collectively decide on a name to offer the city as an alternate.

If they come up with a name, we will certainly give it priority over the one we have proposed, Klein said. *But if they come up with a name, they need to check to see if it's something we already have or similar.*

The group was told towards the end of the meeting that any suggestions they may have in street name changes must be submitted to the city by the end of March, because the city council will be acting on the proposed changes during their April meetings.

Sandy, a great "First Lady," was always involved with the city helping me on many city projects. During my first term as mayor, Sandy came up with the idea of displaying all of the Evanston's mayors' pictures, from the year of 1888, the year Evanston was incorporated as a town the second time, to the present. Her idea was to display a picture of each mayor on the wall of the city council chambers in City Hall. Sandy was able to locate a picture of almost every former mayor of Evanston from June 23, 1888, the date Evanston was incorporated as a town, through 1982, my first term as mayor.

The mayors' pictures that she first had hung up included Evanston's first Mayor, Dr. Francis Harrison, through my first term. There were a few of the former mayors' photos that she couldn't find, but she had a framed poster hung up with their names and other information printed on them.

Sandy had our daughter-in-law Tammy Branch Ottley, who was an excellent printer, do all the printing of the names and the years in which they served on each picture, and then she had all the pictures framed. With the help of the staff, each picture was displayed high upon the wall starting at one end of the wall and going around the room until all were hanging in order the mayors served.

After I got re-elected in 1986, Sandy added Mayor Gene Martin's photo plus a new photo of me to the group. The new photo of me would replace the older photo.

A few weeks after Sandy completed that project, John Fanos, member of the County Commission, asked her to do the same thing of the Uinta County Commissioners. Judy Lawrence, one of the Uinta County Courthouse employees, helped Sandy locate pictures of former commissioners and complete that project.

After Sandy and the staff finished with the mayors' pictures, Jim Davis, Urban Renewal Director, and his assistant, Jane Law, encouraged Sandy to locate and frame historic pictures of Evanston. With the help of Davis and Law, they were able to find a lot of photos and had them framed. Once again, Frankie Workman helped them by hanging and displaying the pictures in the conference room. Many other pictures were hung up and displayed throughout City Hall, and Sandy was involved in doing so.

On a city trip to Jackson, Wyoming, Sandy and I spotted a bronze plaque, about 3 or 4 feet high, of a cowboy on a bucking bronc, and we both thought it would look Wyoming-ish and real nice displayed on the front of the mayor's bench. It would go well with the bronze city seal displayed above and behind the mayor's bench. So I bought it, I don't recall for how much, using the city credit card, to be charged against the mayor's contingency fund. We brought it to Evanston and had either Gary Bentley or Frankie Workman install it for the city.

On March 2nd a news report came out in the *Uinta County Herald* that with the weather being favorable, work on the reconstruction of U.S. Highway 30 West had begun, scheduled for completion September 1st of this year of 1988. The Wyoming Highway Department had announced that work on the storm sewer system had started on Monday of last week, and grading of the roadway is scheduled to begin on March 28th.

Todd Call of Bear River Contractors, the construction company contracted to do the project, made a request to the City of Evanston to lengthen the haul hours on Main Street from 11th Street (Harrison Drive) to the gravel pit located just west of the roundhouse. Currently the city had allowed hauling from the pit, which was near a residential area, from 6:00 a.m. to 6:00 p.m. because of the problem of the loud air brakes on the trucks interrupting the sleep of those living nearby.

Therefore, the contractor requested that they be allowed to begin hauling gravel from the pit at 4:00 a.m. from the 1st of April to September 1st. He told the council that there would be about four or five trucks per hour until 6:30 a.m. that would be traveling the haul road.

The contractor also requested that the city remove the stop sign on the corner of 12th Street and Main Street next to City Hall, so trucks would be able to turn more easily onto 12th Street, go around the new post office and then up 11th Street to the construction site. At that time Main Street was a through street from 11th to 15th Street and beyond to the gravel pit. The purpose for routing the haul trucks around the post office was to avoid any congestion since the post office only had a one-way entrance from Main Street. Another measure suggested to avoid traffic problems was changing 12th Street temporarily to a one-way street, going up from Main Street, during the construction period.

The city was very concerned with the noise from the air brakes in the early morning hours, so the city agreed also to remove the stop sign coming off of the haul road entering Main Street at the corner of 15th Street. We were doing all we could to help keep the trucks from having to use their noisy brakes, and we were also concerned about keeping the traffic flowing the right way for road and public safety.

I explained during discussion that the entire purpose of the one-way street on 12th Street was to avoid traffic accidents for when the stop signs are removed. The city council, by motion, unanimously approved the contractor's proposal, because they wanted to do whatever was necessary to get the construction completed on the west end business strip no later than the September 1st deadline. We didn't want to hold up construction any more than we had to.

In mid-February of that year, the City of Evanston received an announcement and an invitation to attend the Governor's Prayer Breakfast at Little America in Cheyenne on the morning of Friday, March 4th at 7:00 to 8:30 a.m. Thinking this would be a good time to get a chance to talk to the governor on a few of Evanston's problems, Steve Snyder and I decided we would attend.

The Governor's Prayer Breakfast turned out to be a wonderful program with some great speakers, and both of us enjoyed the entire program. The trip gave us the opportunity to meet with Governor Sullivan that afternoon and have a chance to talk to him about some of the Evanston area problems, and we also had some time to meet with Secretary of State Kathy Karpan.

Both Governor Sullivan and Secretary Karpan assured us that the State of Wyoming was ready to assist the City of Evanston in bettering their economy in any way they could, and both told us to keep in touch.

At that time there was a Wyoming state law on the books that mandated the right to have gambling operations run for the benefit of non-profit groups, but the City of Evanston had no ordinance pertaining to non-profit group gambling activities. And the state statutes regarding gambling did not seem to be very particular, saying basically the games can be run only for charities and non-profit organizations.

Currently, one bingo hall had been operating in Evanston at the Boomtown restaurant, owned and operated by J. D. Kindler, and sponsored by the Human Services agencies as beneficiaries of Kindler's proceeds. The operations did not only include bingo games, there were also pull-tabs involved.

During the regular city council meeting of March 7th, there was a new family in attendance. Marylin Romsa and her son-in-law, Todd Stock, of Wymar Management, said they had started negotiating a lease with the Cowboy Casino (formerly Billie's Club) to run a large-scale bingo operation in Evanston. Romsa said they were proposing a large-scale operation as part of an economic development plan for Evanston. She said they plan on busing people from the Wasatch Front to play the games. She agreed with the council that there needed to be some controls on gaming operations, and suggested that the City of Evanston obtain a copy of Cheyenne's ordinance pertaining to gambling by non-profit sponsored games.

She also stated that her and her son-in-law were in the process of developing a bingo hall in Laramie and planned on busing people from as far away as Green River to play.

After listening to Marylin Romsa, it prompted the Evanston City Council to consider implementing a city gaming ordinance. I told City Attorney Dennis Boal that he may want to obtain a copy of Cheyenne's ordinance so that we might have some idea of where to start. I also asked those that had any interest, and that may be affected by the proposed ordinance, to try to attend the city council meeting on Monday, March 21st, at which time we would be discussing the possibility of a new ordinance and we would appreciate all the input that we could get.

During the meeting, Urban Renewal Agency Director Jim Davis announced that Evanston's Annual Renewal Ball would be on June 4th of this year and the theme would be "Heritage 1888," which commemorates Evanston's past 100 years.

The council had reports on the progress of the Sulphur Creek Dam project and the pipeline. The project, with a few change orders, was progressing according to plans and was staying pretty much on schedule.

According to the *Uinta County Herald* dated March 16th, the city had accepted the low bid for the reconstruction of County Road to JBP Wyoming, Inc. after receiving six bids. According to figures from Uinta Engineering and Surveying, Inc., the engineering firm in charge of the project, JBP's bid was the lowest in the amount of $1,330,858.50. The job would involve constructing a three-lane road, with the center lane acting as a turning lane, sidewalks, curb and gutter from the newly reconstructed County Road Bridge to Wyoming State Highway 89. Bear River Contractors, who was contracted to reconstruct the west end of U.S. Highway 30, was second-lowest bidder at $1,335,214.

Uinta Engineering reported that work on County Road was expected to begin on April 1st with completion targeted for September 30th of this year.

An article in the March 16th issue had the headline: LEGIS-LATORS SAY BILL SHOWS STRONG SUPPORT FOR (Kern River) PIPELINE. The article read: *After much debate in the Wyoming legislature, state lawmakers passed a bill authorizing the Wyoming Pipeline Authority to negotiate a low-interest loan of $250 million of the state's Permanent Mineral Trust Fund money for a Wyoming to California pipeline. What does that mean for Uinta County? Nothing, for sure, but local officials indicate they are happy with the move which they say shows strong support of the pipeline—still awaiting approval by the Federal Energy Regulatory Commission (FERC).*

The article also quoted me: *"I feel the Kern River pipeline project could be the big boost Southwest Wyoming needs to get the economy up,"* Evanston Mayor Dennis Ottley said. *The proposed low interest loan "has already helped," Ottley said, pointing to Chevron USA and Union Pacific Railroad's letters of intent to support the Kern River pipeline.*

The article also quoted Uinta County State Senator John Fanos, Uinta County State Representative (I don't recall the name) and Uinta County Commission Chairman John Stevens as all being in favor of the proposed pipeline.

The pipeline, better known as the Kern River Pipeline, would run from Opal, Wyoming to Kern County, California, near Bakersfield, but still had a number of hurdles to jump over before it became a reality.

That month of March the Evanston Volunteer Fire Fighters kicked off their 102nd annual fund drive. Uinta County Fire Chief Jon Lunsford said that while the county government, through their budget, handled most of the operating expenses and purchases of major equipment, the department still relied heavily on donations it received from individuals and businesses in the City of Evanston. Donated funds were used for training materials, fire prevention aids and individual equipment for the firefighters.

At the time, the Evanston Volunteer Fire Fighters had 40 members, of whom 35 were volunteers and 5 were full-time employees paid by the county.

As in the past, the firefighters appreciate your past assistance and look forward to your continued support, Lunsford was quoted as saying.

The *Uinta County Herald* dated March 23rd headlined an article: AS A POSSIBILITY IN EVANSTON, OFFICIALS EYE JOB CORPS. The article continued: *Local officials are eyeing the possibility of a Job Corps center being located in – or very near – Evanston. They say the community would benefit by increased income from support services and shoot about $1 million in payroll monies into the local economy.*

City Planner Director Paul Knopf and Uinta County Industrial Development Commission Coordinator Ken Klinker are drawing up a proposal to give to the Wyoming congressional delegation. The legislators are lobbying the U.S. Labor Department to authorize a Job Corps center in Wyoming – one of eight states without a facility. Currently, Wyoming sends students to neigh-boring states to train at the Job Corps centers, like the Weber Basin Civilian Conservation Center in Ogden, Utah.

The *Herald* continued: *Many people, Knopf points out, have the mis-taken idea that a Job Corps center is for kids with criminal records. "That's not true," he said.*

"Job Corps is an opportunity for underprivileged kids," Knopf says. "They're low income… high school drop-outs. They're not juvenile delin-quents. They haven't had a brush with the law. This is not a reform school. These are just disadvantaged youths who are being given a second chance in life."

Job Corps is a youth employment program run by the federal government for young adults ages 16-22. The program offers training in vocational trades and also offers youths the chance to receive their high school diplomas by earn-ing their GED (General Educational Development) certificate.

"The Forest Service has a lot to gain from it (a Job Corps center) here," Knopf says, pointing out that students could be used for mending fences, build-ing roads and putting in culverts for the Forest Service."

Klinker says the government is expected to select a site in April sometime, with the decision coming from the U.S. Labor Department.

The *Herald* article continued: *Mayor Dennis Ottley and Councilman Will Davis have been in Washington DC since Friday attending a National League of Cities convention and were expected to talk to Wyoming's con-gressional delegation about lobbying for the Job Corps site to be located near Evanston.*

Knopf says, however, Evanston is one of many Wyoming cities vying for the spot, the *Herald* article concluded.

On Monday, March 28th, during their second regular meeting of the month, the Evanston City Council held Student Government Day. It was very tight quarters for all the high school students to fit with the mayor and city council behind the council bench.

There were 27 Evanston High School students participating: Brad Hatch was acting Mayor and sitting beside me, 6 students act-ing as members of the council were sitting near their counterparts, and the others were sitting with their counterparts, such as the city attorney, treasurer, clerk, chief of police, fire chief, engineer and so on.

All students were allowed to participate in any of the city's business and ask questions whenever they had a need to. Although the chambers were very crowded, I believe the students learned a lot about the way city government operates, and I know that the council enjoyed having them there.

On March 30th Public Works finally installed the new sign reading "Martin Park" on the new park next to the new fire hall, but when a group of long-time local citizens saw the sign they wrote a Letter to the Editor stating that the park should be named *Aunt Lou's Park, because Aunt Lou was one of Evanston's pioneer women, who spent her life helping Evanston grow.*

The letter also said that Aunt Lou was a registered nurse who had worked in the office of Dr. Holland (a former mayor and who Holland Drive was named for) for many years and was well known throughout the county. She had purchased the Sims Hotel, which stood right across the street from the new park, formerly the location of the old Y.M.C.A. building until sometime into the 1970s.

The letter was signed by Michael Sims, Russ Heward, Mary H. Smith, and Mary Lou Blakeman, all life-time citizens of Evanston. Mary Lou was the last owner of the Sims Hotel before the new post office was built. She was a close relative of Aunt Lou and she lived there with her family for years after Aunt Lou's death.

I thought that those who wrote the letter were right, that the park probably should have been named *Aunt Lou's Park.* There is no doubt that it would have been well deserved and Aunt Lou should have been honored, but the park had already been named and the council didn't feel it would be right to change the name at this time.

The *Uinta County Herald's* article of April 8th was titled: EVANSTON WASTEWATER PLANT RECEIVES STATE AWARD. The article went on to read: *Evanston's wastewater treatment plant received a state award recently from the Wyoming Water Quality and Pollution Control Association for excellence and safety for 1987.*

The article continued: *City Wastewater Plant Superintendent, Randy Roper said, "The award is given out each year to a water treatment plant in the State of Wyoming, and this is the first year Evanston has earned the top honors."*

Jim Davis, Urban Renewal Agency Director, reported that the old train depot, given to the City of Evanston by the Union Pacific Railroad for historic reasons, was being refurbished. He stated that David Haines, a native of Evanston and a retired architect, had been hired by the Depot Square Committee to help on the project.

During the regular city council meeting of April 11th, the second reading of the new gambling ordinance allowing bingo and pull-tabs to operate in various businesses sponsored by non-profit organizations, was first on the agenda. Motion was made and seconded by members of the council to pass the ordinance on second reading, but after a considerable amount of discussion the ordinance was defeated unanimously.

The gambling ordinance was patterned after the City of Cheyenne's ordinance, drawn up by City Attorney Dennis Boal. It was sponsored by me and introduced by a member of the council at the previous meeting. Motion and a second were made to pass the ordinance on first reading. After a considerable amount of discussion the ordinance passed on the first reading by a 6-1 vote with Councilman Vranish being the only dissenting vote. However, there were a lot of questions and concerns that the entire council and I had on the ordinance at that time, and most of the council thought that it would be a good idea to pass the ordinance on first reading so we could get it published in full for public input.

But when it was brought back on the floor on second reading for discussion during April's meeting I said, *We need to put the burden on the sponsoring organization, not the operating organization. Last meeting there were some that wanted to throw this ordinance out. Tonight I urge you to defeat it so if necessary we can start all over.*

Councilman Tom Hutchinson said, *We need some regulation, but we have to go in another direction than this ordinance. The state statutes say that the heavy burden should be on the sponsoring organization, not the operators.*

I think we are trying to regulate something that is basically illegal. I think the state needs more law on its books, but, I too, want to protect the town.

After more discussion and comments from other members of the council, I told the council and the audience that to amend the present ordinance, now on the floor for second reading, would be tougher than to just start over with a new ordinance. I once again requested the council to defeat the ordinance on this second reading, which they did by a unanimous vote.

In the same April meeting a change order on the Sulphur Creek Dam authorizing an additional $25,000 payment to Woodward-Clyde, consulting engineers, for "extra services" was discussed in an executive session.

After coming out of executive session a resolution to pay the $25,000 was introduced. Motion was made and seconded to pay the consulting firm the money, but during discussion I asked the council to table the resolution until the next meeting to discuss the situation with the parties involved.

But the city council requested that I call for the vote and I did. The vote was in favor by 4-3, with me, Tom Hutchinson and Julie Lehman voting in the negative.

At that time I announced that I might decide to exercise my veto power for the first time. After doing a little research on the decision to pay the additional funds to Woodward-Clyde, I was satisfied with my findings and sent notice to the Evanston City Council that I had vetoed the resolution authorizing a $25,000 increase in the contract on the Sulphur Creek Dam project.

City Attorney Dennis Boal said the council could override the mayor's veto with a two-thirds vote. But that might be difficult, given the fact that the measure only passed by a 4-3 vote.

"The reason for the veto is I feel that Woodward-Clyde has some responsibility for the difficulties experienced in the construction of the drain system for the dam," I wrote in my letter to the council. *"It is also my opinion that Woodward-Clyde ought to assist the city in reaching an agreement with the contractor in regard to the drain system. Until that agreement is completed, it is premature to approve the change order which is the subject of Resolution 88-26."*

Vranish told the press that the council had no chance to override the mayor's veto at the special meeting on Monday, April 18th. The only thing the council could do is either try to override the veto or re-introduce the resolution. Otherwise a new resolution would have to be drafted.

City officials and representatives from Ames Construction and Woodward-Clyde met with the Wyoming Water Development Commission in Cheyenne during the commission's regular session on Tuesday, April 19th to discuss the situation. The commission was funding 75 percent of the project through grants. After meeting with the state commission and finding out the information I needed I told the press that I was hoping to settle the situation and get an agreement in writing before the council's next regularly scheduled meeting on April 25th.

The *Uinta County Herald* of April 27th reported: *During the council meeting of April 25th the Evanston City Council reached an agreement with Ames Construction requiring Ames to compensate the City of Evanston up to $25,000 for engineering services related to evaluation of the drain materials so far. It also requires Ames to pay up to another $25,000 for any additional engineering services when the city installs a piezometer instrumentation system [to measure pressure]—also to be paid for by Ames—to monitor the drain materials in the dam.*

The agreement also called for Ames to extend its $2.5 million performance bond and warranty period so the city can monitor the dam's drain system and see if it is working properly, the article concluded.

I was glad that I had vetoed the resolution to pay an extra $25,000 for additional engineering because after meeting with the WWDC in Cheyenne, things turned around and the contractor had to pay the city the extra $25,000 so that the city could pay Woodward-Clyde the money they had coming, which was approved by the council.

During the April meeting I also read a letter of resignation from City Judge Tom Mealey. He had been appointed to the position of Uinta County Court Judge that was left vacant by Judge Larry Lehman, who had recently been appointed to a district judgeship in Rawlins.

In his letter Mealey said, *"I want to thank you, the Mayor and Council, for the professional courtesies and support you have always given the Evanston Municipal Court."* The city council moved to accept Mead's letter of resignation with all voting in favor, and wishing the judge the best in his new position.

In that same meeting, I nominated Attorney John C. Phillips to take the place of Judge Mealey, which was confirmed by the city council by a unanimous vote. With both Judge Mealey and Attorney Phillips being present we asked Judge Mealey to perform the swearing-in ceremony and deliver the Oath of Office to Mr. Phillips. Attorney John C. Phillips was now our new municipal judge, and we all gave him a hand.

Duane Shupe, past president of the Evanston Old Timers' Club, an organization of railroad employees, requested the donation of a now-obsolete dining car from the Union Pacific Railroad to the City of Evanston to be located on Depot Square near the old train depot.

The 90- by 15-foot dining car, built in 1949, was transported to Evanston and the Union Tank Car Company donated storage space for the car until it could be renovated and moved to Depot Square. Towards the end of April, City Treasurer Albert Hays submitted a letter resigning his position effective May 13th. He would be moving to Craig, Colorado where he would take over the position of finance director.

With a motion and second, the city council voted unanimously to accept Mr. Hays's resignation. The council and I thanked him for the fine service he had given to Evanston as treasurer, and all wished him well in his new venture.

During our first meeting of the month on May 9th, Ryan Barker, son of George and Norene Barker of Evanston, was honored for his fast action in saving his mother and his cousin's life during a near drowning incident at Bear Lake on a very windy day in August of 1987.

His mother, known to be a good swimmer, had her nephew, Brady Voss, Ryan's cousin, who would be turning 4 years old in a few days, floating with her on an inner tube on Bear Lake when a strong wind started up. Mrs. Barker tried to swim back into shore with her nephew on the inner tube, but the wind blew Brady off the tube. She grabbed him and tried to swim towards shore, holding on to the boy, but the wind was causing them trouble and her nephew was panicking. But Ryan, on shore, noticed them having trouble. He grabbed an air mattress and swam out to them in time to save both from drowning.

Mrs. Barker said, *We had not realized a strong wind had come up and blown us out so far.*

Therefore, Ryan, his parents and his cousin Brady attended the city council meeting during the presentation of the Honorary Citizens certificate from the city, and the Heroism Award from the Boy Scouts National Court of Honor. The Heroism Award is the second highest honor bestowed by the Boy Scouts of America.

During that same meeting local resident Joe Dobry walked into the meeting with a rifle in his hands to make a point about one of the city's ordinances. This startled many of those in attendance. He had been put on the agenda, but never mentioned bringing a rifle into the meeting. Chief Dennis Harvey was in attendance and immediate grabbed him and the rifle. I asked Mr. Dobry, *Why the rifle, and is it loaded?* He said it was not loaded, but he had given everyone a terrible scare. He said he had become aware of Section 15-8 of the city code concerning dangerous weapons after city police officers had taken a hunting knife from his son when his son was in a local restaurant. Dobry complained that Section 15-8 prohibits *"knives, pistols and revolvers"* from being carried in a public place but does not address rifles.

You're in violation of the city code if you carry a knife but not if you carry a rifle, he complained. *I don't feel the police have the right to take a knife off of me or anyone else.*

Councilwoman Julie Lehman reprimanded him for walking in unannounced with a rifle in his hand. *It was very dramatic and very anxiety provoking,* she said.

I think it takes a little anxiety to get your attention sometimes, Dobry said. He felt the ordinance needed to be rewritten and couldn't understand why it was put into effect in the first place.

We don't have any problems with people carrying rifles into public places as long as they are not loaded, Chief Harvey said. The chief assured us that the rifle Dobry brought into the council was not loaded. But he explained that smaller weapons and knives could be hidden and the intent of the law was to address that problem.

So, Dobry stated, *you cannot carry a knife in this town and that includes a knife this big,* indicating the size of a small pocket knife with his fingers.

I didn't know whether or not to hit the deck, Councilman Tom Hutchinson said of the moment Dobry walked in with the rifle.

Dobry did get the attention of the council and made us aware of an old ordinance that, no doubt, should be amended or done away with entirely, but there was no action taken on it during that meeting. We assured him that it would be looked into.

The Wyoming State Legislature had finally changed the alcohol drinking law back to 21 years of age. As of July 1, 1988 the 19- and 20-year-olds would no longer be able to buy liquor or any other alcoholic beverages in Wyoming. In the years since Wyoming dropped the drinking age down from 21 to 19 years old, we found that it was causing a lot of problems in many ways, and they decided it was time to change the drinking age back. The biggest problems were young people from border towns coming to Wyoming to do their drinking and causing trouble.

One incident occurred when a bunch of Utah kids (19- to 20-year-olds) came to Evanston to party. When they left Evanston to go back to Coalville, Utah, apparently they were too drunk to drive, and had a deadly accident near Coalville. It was a bad situation and Utah newspapers made a big issue of it because of Wyoming's drinking laws.

Personally, I was glad to see the Wyoming State Legislature change the law because it was causing big problems for Evanston and our police department, and some bar owners were complaining about the young people using false IDs, which could cause legal problems if that person were to get in trouble with the police or have an accident. Something like that could cause the bar owner to possibly lose their liquor license.

It was late May, the time of year when the Evanston City Council would be working many hours to come up with a budget for the fiscal year of 1988-89. Budget requests were being received by the various departments and looking good and acceptable for the most part. I initially requested that each department try very hard to keep their budget requests at least 10 percent below their previous annual budget of 1987-88. I told them by doing that the city shouldn't have to worry about getting into a deficit problem, and if we end up needing more money we can use some of the carryover amount or call for a public hearing asking for more funds. I said I would rather do that and not have to fight a deficit problem, which makes a city look bad with the public and the state auditors.

The *Uinta County Herald* issue of May 20 quoted me on the proposed budget for the fiscal year of 1988-89: *Requests total $24,255,674 for both general and enterprise funds compared to last year's actual budget of $31,224,005.*

The article continued: *[Mayor] Ottley said a carryover amount of 1.1 million from this year's budget is about $300,000 more than last year's carryover—mainly due to increased sales tax and severance tax revenues to the city. However, he said he still wants to cut out about half a million dollars from the general fund requests and also would like to see the two percent pay increase—already built into each department's budget request—eliminated.*

"I feel the city can't really afford that increase right now," Ottley explained. "Not only can we not afford it, but I don't think we can justify it. My concern is we have quite a few capital improvements … and although I don't want to cut anything out completely, I want to set priorities." Ottley said he wants to see a sizable budget for maintenance projects, street repairs and city services maintained so citizens are not deprived of those types of services which he said "they deserve."

The *Herald* article continued: *There are three areas in which Ottley said he would like to see funding cuts: the parks and rec division, police, and joint powers divisions. The police department request is up about $245,000 over this year's budget, parks and rec and the joint powers requests have each more than doubled over last year's actual allocations.*

One thing the city is facing this year is a request from the school district for the city to take over maintenance of the lawns for 128 acres—at North, Aspen and Uinta Meadows elementaries, plus the high school football field and practice field.

Ottley said the request includes the purchase of a new mower and pickup truck and estimates the total cost to be about $105,000. The school district is facing about a one million dollar shortfall in revenues this coming year because of decreased county valuation, and is seeking ways to cut back its budget, the *Herald* continued.

The county is also cutting out funding for E.C.D.C. (Evanston Child Development Center), Ottley said, which amounts to about $25,000 the city will have to make up.

The city budget needs to be finalized by the third week in June so it can be filed with the county assessor and the county clerk's office, the article concluded.

The issue of the gaming law concerning bingo and pull-tabs came up again, and after hearing City Attorney Dennis Boal and County Attorney Scott Smith's interpretation of state law, which indicated that although the state law was very vague, it still gave non-profit organizations the right to hold the games. However, the law did not specify any type of restrictions or controls.

Without an ordinance with some control or regulations Smith said, *I think it would be very difficult to enforce as far as the criminal code is concerned. The state statute on bingo games states that the games must be "conducted by" a non-profit organization. Unfortunately, there is nothing in the statute defining any control.* City Attorney Boal agreed.

Therefore, at the city council's request, Boal was directed to continue checking into ordinances of other cities and to write up a new ordinance that would benefit the city. After checking on several communities with ordinances pertaining to the control of the bingo and pull-tab games, he found Laramie's ordinance to be the nearest to what we were looking for.

During the May 9th meeting Attorney Boal had the new ordinance ready to be sponsored and introduced and to be acted on the first reading. After a long and weary discussion, it was passed on first reading by a 5-2 vote, with Councilmen Tom Hutchinson and Clarence Vranish voting in the negative, and now it was up for the second reading.

During the May 23rd meeting, after a few more amendments, the ordinance was passed on second reading with a vote of 4-2 and one absent. Hutchinson and Vranish had once again voted in the negative.

But with more discussion, Hutchinson stated that he would like the issue to be put on a referendum vote in this coming election. He said, *I think the community needs the opportunity to decide.*

Councilwoman Julia Lehman said she had heard only from non-profit groups concerned with how the bingo ordinance was going to affect them. *I can't seem to get a stir out of people that they do not want this,* Lehman added.

The *Uinta County Herald* of May 25th article reported: *However, City Attorney Dennis Boal said the ordinance's intent is to provide written guidelines for license applicants so the council can obtain enough information on whether or not to permit the organization. "They don't have to ask this council's permission. They don't have to ask the county commissioners," he said. Boal said the city's ordinance does not "create a right" to operate bingo in Evanston. He said the state statutes, which county attorneys across the state have indicated to him is unclear. It makes an exception to the state law for bingo operations by non-profit groups. He said the city is just trying to regulate that 'exception' through a written ordinance," the Herald* concluded.

During the regular meeting of Monday, June 13th, the ordinance came up for third and final reading with more discussion. During this meeting Councilman Vranish made the amendment to shift the burden of operating the games from the for-profit organization to the non-profit organization to conform with state statutes more closely.

This amendment had been discussed throughout the entire process of getting the ordinance passed. I don't know why it wasn't already a part of it, but I felt that this was an amendment that should have been in the ordinance to start with. Thanks to Councilman Vranish for recognizing the need to amend the proposed ordinance.

Motion was made and seconded to pass the bingo/pull-tab ordinance as amended on third and final reading by a vote of 6-1 with Hutchinson being the only member voting against the issue.

During the meeting, the Evanston City Council also acted on the first reading amending the city code allowing 19- to 20-year-olds to purchase or consume liquor or alcoholic beverages, to agree with the new state law that a person must be 21 years of age to purchase or consume liquor or any alcoholic beverages, or even enter a liquor establishment. This amendment was made to correct the previous ordinance and was passed on all three readings by unanimous vote.

During the meeting of May 23rd, I announced that I was appointing Steve Widmer as a new Manager of Finance and Accounting for the City of Evanston. He would be replacing former City Treasurer Al Hays, who had recently resigned.

I told the council that I had decided against appointing a city treasurer per se, because of the confusion it created at City Hall. I told them that I wanted to appoint City Clerk Don Welling as the clerk/treasurer and Widmer the manager of finance and accounting under Welling.

Widmer was 36 of age and was a graduate of Weber State College with a degree in business administration. He had held positions of controller for 6½ years with Big K Corporation and of divisional manager for an Ogden, Utah company for 9 years. He seemed to be well qualified and was very impressive during his interview with me, I told the council.

I said that I hoped they would agree with my idea of position changes, and that it was only temporary. But it would give Widmer a chance to get the hang of things, at which time I might want to appoint him as the city treasurer. I asked the council to please confirm my appointment of Don Welling as clerk/treasurer and Widmer as manager of financing and accounting under Welling. They did by motion and second, with a unanimous vote of 6-0.

During the second regular city council meeting of the month on Monday, June 27th, I read a letter from Wyo Jon Brown stating that he was resigning from Evanston's Parks and Recreation Board. Motion was made by Councilwoman Julie Lehman to accept the resignation of Mr. Brown, seconded by Councilman Will Davis, with all voting in favor.

I thanked him and said that he had been one of the original members of the commission when it was organized, and he should be well commended for his long and dedicated service. Members of the council also gave their thanks to him and wished him well.

I also re-appointed Kevin Smith to another three-year term, Susan Vanderhoef to replace Dan Wheeler, another original appointee, and Councilman Darrell Staley to replace Jon Brown on the recreation board. Motion was made to confirm the appointments by Lehman, seconded by Hutchinson, with all voting in favor.

I also extended our appreciation from the council to Dan Wheeler for his long and dedicated service, and announced that he was also one of the original appointees.

During the meeting it was reported that the city had a complaint concerning the noise at the gravel pit from the trucks unloading and loading early in the morning, but it was the only complaint that we had so far. Therefore the council felt we should let the truck continue at the early hours so they could get the west end highway project done by the deadline of September 1st.

Ordinance 88-6, changing the names of certain streets, was brought back on the floor for the third and final reading. Motion was made by Councilman Davis and seconded by Councilwoman Lehman. The floor was once again opened for iscussion.

Although we already had several lengthy discussion periods during the previous council meetings and also a few special meetings with the public I still opened up the floor for more discussion and gave those interested citizens another opportunity to speak. First, Councilman Clarence Vranish presented a petition signed by mostly west end business owners requesting that the west end of U.S. Highway 30 S, a part of the old Lincoln Highway, be named Lincoln Way. This apparently was the only street remaining that the public was concerned with.

The city council had proposed the west end highway from downtown Front Street to the west interchange be named Harrison

Drive in honor of the first Mayor of Evanston. Dr. Francis Harrison had not only been the first mayor, he had also been one of few doctors who served, not only Evanston, but also as far north as Jackson and Kemmerer, all of Bridger Valley, and south into the Hilliard Flat areas including Old Bear Town, an old railroad town that they hauled timber to for making railroad ties, and a town with a sizeable population.

As a matter of record, he was the doctor that went to Old Bear Town after the big OK-Corral-type shootout that occurred there. The town was located about 12 or 15 miles south on the old Piedmont U.P. railroad line north of the Sulphur Creek Dam.

Councilman Vranish made the comment, *I don't think old Doc Harrison was that significant in Evanston's history, and I think we have a real chance working with the citizens to create a name that they like.*

I disagree, I said. *Harrison did a lot of great things for this town. We've discussed this over and over. All residents have had a chance to select names for the streets. I don't think a name has anything to do with getting people into town.* I also mentioned that we already had a street called Lincoln Avenue.

The petition from the west end business folks that Vranish had presented had approximately 21 names, but I didn't see any name representing Lotty's Restaurant or Flying "J", owned by my two brothers, and that made me feel good.

One of the business owners from the audience spoke up and made a derogatory remark about Dr. Harrison and naming the street Harrison Drive, which pissed me off so much that I said in an angry voice: *It's just too damn bad that we can't name a street after someone that has done so much for the area,* and then I ended discussion and called for the vote. The vote on the motion to pass Ordinance 88-6 on third and final reading passed on a 6-1 vote. Councilman Vranish was the only dissenting vote.

The old railroad frontage road starting from the old Highway 89 (now County Road), near where the recycling building is at the present, to Avenue "A" in North Evanston was named officially *China Mary Road.*

⥈

As a part of Evanston history I might add that at one time China Mary Road was unofficially called *O'Neil Boulevard* named for an O'Neil family that once lived in North Evanston (platted as the Union Pacific Subdivision of Section 19 of the Evanston Township during latter part of the 19th century). The boulevard was the only access across the tracks to the new North Evanston area, and ran along the tracks, as it does at present, to connect with First Avenue—and that is why First Avenue is first: it was the first street you entered in the new subdivision, because there was no access from County Road to the avenue areas at that time. There was no underpass. The only way from the southwesterly side of town to the northeasterly side, where North Evanston is now located, was by crossing the tracks at a railroad crossing near the train depot.

⥈

Ordinance 88-9, titled: "Annual Appropriation for the Fiscal Year ending June 30, 1989" was the ordinance approving the fiscal year budget for the next budget year of 1988-1989. It was passed on an emergency basis with a motion by Councilman Jon Lunsford, seconded by Councilwoman Lehman, with all voting in favor.

Resolution 88-44 was introduced by Councilman Tom Hutchinson, dissolving the Sulphur Creek Reservoir Joint Powers Board, and authorizing the transfer of all assets to the City of Evanston. Motion was made by Councilman Jon Lunsford, seconded by Darrell Staley to adopt Resolution 88-44.

During discussion, Councilman Vranish, Treasurer of the Board, indicated he was against dissolving the board because he thought the board would and could better manage the money, reserved for payments of the dam project, by keeping it out of the council's hands. He was afraid that the funds pledged for the dam project would get thrown into general funds, but I thought that it could be used anywhere as long as it was for the water department. It would never be thrown into the general fund while I was in office.

After listening to remarks by Councilman Vranish, I told him that we all had appreciated the good work he had done as treasurer of the Sulphur Creek Joint Powers Board, but the State Commission who provided the 75% grant and 25% loan said that the City of Evanston had 100% ownership, 100% responsibility and the liability in the construction, the maintenance, and the payback of the 6-million-dollar loan.

Therefore, I didn't think we needed an extra board to help the council control city funds. I told him that was what the citizens voted us all in office for, to run and manage the city properly. I then ended discussion and called for the vote which turned out to be 6 in favor, 1 opposed. Motion passed with Councilman Vranish once again offering the only dissenting vote.

Resolution 88-49 was then introduced by Councilman Hutchinson, designating the use of funds received from the dissolution of the Sulphur Creek Reservoir Joint Powers Board. Resolution 88-49 under Section 2 read: *It is policy of the City of Evanston, Wyoming, that said funds and any income generated by said funds, shall be used exclusively to satisfy the debt associated with the construction of the Sulphur Creek Dam and Reservoir Enlargement Project unless otherwise approved by a majority vote of the City Council.*

Councilman Lunsford made a motion to adopt Resolution 88-49, seconded by Councilman Hutchinson. Motion passed with 6 votes, including Councilman Vranish. Councilwoman Julie Lehman had been excused earlier for personal reasons, causing her to be absent during the vote on Resolution 88-49.

$500,000 of the Sulphur Creek Dam project was donated to the City of Evanston by Chevron USA. They were funds that Chevron had received back from the State of Wyoming Revenue Department for overpayment of sales tax that the company had paid previously. When Chevron donated the funds to the city, the city council immediately pledged the funds to the Sulphur Creek project.

When the North Elementary School was built, the only access into the schoolyard for school buses or any vehicle was off of Wyoming State Highway 89. Highway 89 was at times a very busy road, making it unsafe for buses and other vehicles turning into the school, and it was also unsafe for children that had to use the access.

Therefore, School District Superintendent Ranta approached the City of Evanston, requesting the city extend Washington Avenue by having the street continue past North Elementary through to Highway 89, allowing buses and other vehicles to enter the schoolyard from Washington Avenue, and explained how much safer it would be for the children. The city immediately agreed with him.

The next day I had Administrative Assistant Steve Snyder notify the Wyoming Highway Department and make an appointment for us to meet with them in Cheyenne as soon as possible to talk to them about the extension of Washington Avenue.

Leno Menghini, superintendent of the department, firmly agreed with us and offered assistance, not only to obtain the right-of-way for Washington Avenue, but also to fund the project. But we needed to immediately apply for a grant through the Wyoming Highway Department.

When the news got back to Evanston and the city approved a resolution for Snyder to request funding, we immediately got some flak about building in that area, because it was considered wetlands, and some of the neighbors were against losing wetlands because their kids had a lot of fun playing in the area catching frogs and tadpoles in the swamps.

When one mother called me asking the city not to build the road, I explained to her the reason we were building it was for the safety of our kids and school traffic. She seemed to understand, because after I spoke to her, the city had no more complaints from anyone. So the lady I spoke to must have spread the word. The Wyoming Highway Department had no more trouble obtaining right-of-ways.

During the June 27th city council meeting City Engineer Brian Honey gave a report on three projects that the Wyoming Highway Department was engineering and funding. Those projects were all necessary for the betterment of the community and the safety of both road traffic and pedestrians.

The projects Honey was referring to were prioritized as:

#1. Extension of Washington Avenue project.

#2. 6th Street and Lombard intersection.

#3. Park Road improvements.

All three of these projects were started in 1988, and project #1 was completed before the end of the year.

During the meeting I extended our congratulations to Frank Sheets, Jeff Martin and Dan Martin for their recent certificates related to their jobs. They all went through the educational program related to their certificates with high honors. All very dedicated employees and well deserving of the recognition.

Another very heartbreaking tragedy hit Evanston on Monday of July 4th when the fire department was called out to get a cat down off a power line pole near the new Uinta County/Evanston Airport. Fireman and Councilman Darrell Staley, in trying to rescue the cat, was electrocuted by a live power line knocking him to the ground, but died while in flight to the LDS Hospital in Salt Lake City. It was a terrible accident that, like most accidents, could have probably been avoided, but that's hindsight.

The *Uinta County Herald* of July 6th quoted me as saying: *"It was one of those accidents that probably shouldn't have happened. We lost a good councilman, a young councilman, who was coming along and doing a good job for the city."*

"We have also lost a good fireman, a father and a husband." Ottley added.

Not too long after the service, I delivered an insurance check to Julie, Darrell's wife, and talked to her for a few moments. She was quite hurt and very depressed over the accident, but also appeared very strong. She was also very appreciative of receiving the life insurance check that the city provided all city employees at time of death while employed.

On Monday, July 11th during the first regular city council meeting of the month, I asked the council to observe a moment of silence in remembrance of Darrell Staley, who was serving his first term on the council representing Ward lll.

City Councilwoman Julie Lehman was quoted by the *Herald* stating that Staley was *"the epitome of the national son. He loved this commu-*

nity and its people. He was the most dedicated person in public service that I ever knew and when he wasn't doing things with the fire department he was involved in other community activities. The last couple of months I saw him grow and develop as a councilman. It's a waste of a human being."

At a later meeting in 1989 Councilman Tom Hutchinson requested that the city build a shrine in honor of Darrell Staley for his selfless dedication as an Evanston citizen. He agreed to act as chairman of the project and suggested that we use the entire side of the left wall, as you walk in, of the city council chambers as a shrine in Darrell's honor. The council totally agreed and the shrine was completed in a few weeks, with a dedication program conducted in his honor. That shrine is still in place to this day, thanks to former Councilman Tom Hutchinson.

The Downtown Improvement Committee requested that the city replace some of the sidewalks on downtown Main Street because some of them were crumbling, and replace some of the curbing that was causing seepage problems in front of some of the businesses along Main.

There was some concern about the city using city crews to do the work replacing the sidewalks and curb. A Letter to the Editor was printed in the July 8th issue of the *Uinta County Herald*, complaining that if the city crews were doing the job it meant that the monies were coming out of the budget and that wasn't legal for the city to use city employees and equipment for that kind of construction.

Printed by the editor of the *Herald* in the July 8th issue with a photo of Main Street was: *The City of Evanston is replacing curbs along Main Street in front of selected businesses which have had seepage problems in the past, according to Mayor Dennis Ottley. The work is being done by the city crews rather than being contracted out, Ottley said, because, "It's not a big job." In addition, the city will break up the sidewalks for those businesses who want it, but the cost of sidewalk replacement, Ottley said, is the responsibility of the business. The work will be completed within a couple of weeks,* the *Herald* concluded.

The *Uinta County Herald* of July 13th published: *Noting that to not re-place Darrell Staley on the City Council expediently "would cheat those people in Ward lll of their representation," said Mayor Dennis Ottley. He asked the council to prepare to make an appointment by the next meeting, July 25.*

The article continued: *the council voted in favor of taking names only until Tuesday, July 19 at 5 p.m. with interviews to follow the next week and a replacement named in time for the next meeting [July 25]. Anyone interested should call to submit their name with the Mayor's office at 890-9690.*

Staley was remembered Monday night [July 11] with a moment of silence before the meeting got underway. At the July 25 meeting, his widow Julie will be present to accept a token of appreciation from the council, the Herald article concluded.

Uinta County Herald

New Freedom Shrine dedicated

FREEDOM SHRINE DEDICATION — Was held July 5 at Evanston City Hall. The plaques were dedicated in the honor of Darrel Staley and the Evanston Volunteer Firemen. Those on hand were; left to right, Jon Lunsford, Dan Yates, Jerry Cazin, Julie Staley, Kim Staley, Glenn Bluemel and Tom Hutchinson.

The above Freedom Shrine was dedicated on July 5, 1989, a year almost to the day of Darrel Staley's tragedy.

Only three names were submitted for consideration for Staley's seat on the city council, all residing in Ward lll. Those submitted were Craig Nelson, Bill George and Roger Fife. All had previously served as a member of the Evanston City Council. This year of 1988 was election year for three members of the city council, and at that time, Nelson had already filed to be on the ballet running for the seat presently held by Tom Hutchinson, who was running for re-election, and Brian D. Welling had also filed for the seat.

Interviews were scheduled for the three applicants, to be conducted by the city council on Thursday, July 24th. At the regular meeting on Friday, July 25th the city council made their decision by selecting Craig Nelson, and I agreed, stating that *he had been a very dedicated member before and I'm sure he will be again.*

The Evanston Post issue of July 28th reported on the July 25th meeting that: *The council passed a resolution declaring the intention to annex Bear River State Park. The 280-acre parcel of land that borders the interstate on the east side of Evanston will be a great benefit to the city, according to Mayor Ottley. "It will be 'neat' to say it's in the city limits," he said. "We will have more of a hold on it and because of promotion and tourism I think it is a good idea to annex it."*

The resolution to annex the park was introduced by one of the council members and passed and adopted by motion and a second with all voting in favor.

It was also reported in *The Evanston Post*: *Evanston Mayor Dennis J. Ottley yesterday [July 20th] issued a memo declaring a water shortage in the city and designated personnel to enforce irrigation hours as set forth in the City's Ordinances.*

The mayor's memo said, "City Ordinance 23-52 stipulates that during any period of water shortage, no user of Utility Services shall use such water to irrigate for any purposes during the hours of ten (10) a.m. to six (6) p.m. daily.

"The Ordinance also stipulates that notwithstanding, it is unlawful for any user to irrigate between the hours of ten (10) p.m. to six (6) a.m. daily, unless otherwise authorized by the Directors of Public Works."

The *Post* article continued: *After the mayor's memo was issued, the Public Works Department issued a weekly water update which said, "We appreciate all who are helping to conserve on water usage. The Bear River is continuing to diminish in stream flow but so far, we have been able to supply daily Community needs by supplementing our river diversion with water from wells.*

The economy was getting worse with people leaving their homes in foreclosure, and going somewhere else where they could find work. There was getting to be more and more HUD (U.S. Department of Housing and Urban Development)-financed properties being fore-closed on, causing property values to consistently drop. Other lenders and loan guarantors were also feeling the foreclosure impact, such as FHA (Federal Housing Authority), W.C.D.A. (Wyoming Community Development Administration), V.A. (Veteran's Administration), and many banks and other financing firms.

Housing was doing badly in Evanston at the time and there was nothing changing to make it any better. Even Lair Petroleum, Inc., the new gas refinery constructed a few years ago, east of Evanston about ten miles, had shut down. The only things Evanston had going at this time, as far as private industry was concerned, were the Amoco/Chevron Business Building, the gas treatment plants and Union Tank Car Company, but even they were no longer hiring. It was an indication that Evanston may have overbuilt in housing, as some folks indicated we would.

Uinta Realty, Inc.'s business was slowing down more and more. It was getting to the point where I was considering putting in my letter of resignation as mayor, or selling U.R.I., or just shutting it down. But I wanted to stay on as mayor. I wanted to help the city get out of this slump.

My son Randy and his associates, Tim and Lisa Burridge, offered to buy me out. Their offer was quite a bit lower than I hoped for, but my wife and I did not have much choice. We thought it was a lot better than just shutting down the business.

But Sandy and her partner Peggy Harvey kept cleaning fore-closed-on houses, most of them very dirty and full of garbage. With Sandy cleaning the houses, it helped keep me in office, and I stayed with Uinta Realty, Inc. as an associate broker, but things were not looking good at that time for us.

After I sold U.R.I. to Randy and his associates, they bought into the ERA franchise and changed the name to ERA Uinta Realty, Inc., which they thought would be better for business. In a few months the owner of the old town hall was going to raise their rental rates, which pissed them off, causing them to move the U.R.I. realty agency south of Evanston on Highway 150, into office space in the South Valley Business Center.

During the month of August, Evanston and area were starting to have flooding problems caused from the hot summer and the fast thawing of the mountain snows. Just when we were winding up the completion of the Sulphur Creek Reservoir project, flooding was starting to give the contractor some trouble, but handled the problem with very little loss of time.

The flood came mostly from the overflow into Sulphur Creek itself from the fast and high waters that were coming into the reservoir, but the contractor was able to keep the flooding under control by diverting the creek into an old river channel on the Wes Myers property before it reached the reservoir.

It was reported in the *Uinta County Herald* of August 8th that the reservoir project was ahead of schedule. The article went on: *Ames Construction is putting the finishing touches on the Sulphur Creek Dam and Reservoir this week. Work was scheduled for completion in December.*

The total cost of the complete project, the dam and the pipelines, will be in the $20 million area rather than the $25 million originally estimated.

High Plains Construction has completed the Evanston pipeline which runs approximately 8 miles from the water treatment plant to the reservoir. This includes the valve, which is placed near the Broken Circle Cattle Company. This valve can regulate the water, determining if it comes to Evanston to be processed or goes back up the pipeline to the reservoir to be stored for later use.

The *Herald* article continued: *"At this time the valve at the reservoir is open and the Evanston pipeline is full of water. We are not using the water, but we could open the valve at the treatment plant and use reservoir water,"* Brian Honey, City Engineer, explained.

The Bear River portion of the pipeline is also about half completed and a finishing date of late September is expected.

As soon as the pipeline has been completed, even though the river intake isn't completed, the river water will be diverted into the line to fill the reservoir before winter sets in and the reservoir water freezes.

"All of the contractors have been good to work with," Honey said of the operation, the Herald article concluded.

An article in the Herald's August 12th edition stated: "The money is in good hands and will be treated as good as before," Mayor Dennis Ottley pledged, speaking about the funds to pay off the Sulphur Creek project.

The city's 25 percent of repayment will be approximately $5 million. However, payment on the state loan won't start until 5 years after completion of the Sulphur Creek project.

The project was near completion, and the contractors were all payed off immediately after completion upon a thorough inspection for acceptance. All contractors were previously required to be bonded for the benefit of the city in case of any malfunctioning of the project.

"With the 75-25 percent match on the Sulphur Creek Project it is possible that we may have the $5 million state loan paid off within 5 years," the article quoted me saying. I was talking about after the deferred time of 5 years was up, and I wasn't too far off, because that debt was paid off many years ago.

During the regular city council meeting on Monday August 8th it was announced that the public hearing on the annexation of the Bear River State Park into the city had been postponed from the August 22nd date to September 12th at 7:00 p.m. at City Hall. All interested citizens were urged to attend and voice their opinions.

"Wyoming's economy remains the number one concern among the people of Wyoming," according to the 1988 Wyoming Heritage Foundation's Attitudes and Issue Survey, The Uinta County Herald reported in their August 24th edition headlined: ECONOMY REMAINS TO BE CONCERN.

The article continued: The survey, which was conducted between August 1 and August 8, is the Foundation's ninth annual survey. It enjoys a 95 percent confidence rating.

"On balance, the 1988 Wyoming Heritage Foundation Poll shows an unmistakable sense of realism in our state," according to Heritage

Society Director Bill Schilling. "People remain concerned about the economy, believe that economic diversification efforts are important, think that economic development works best at the local level rather than through the state programs."

I also felt that way. That was why I always said that a community should never stop trying to build their economy. They should always continue to locate new industry to come and create good jobs. That is what builds a healthy community, and that was what I was trying to accomplish, and hopefully the members of the council felt the same way.

Evanston's First Annual Bear River Mountain Men Rendezvous was held at the Bear River State Park on August 26th. Booshway Ben Morphew invited me, as mayor, to attend and participate in some of their events. Morphew and Assistant Booshway Jack Underkoffer said that the heart of the rendezvous were the shooters so I was asked to participate in the *black powder rifle* contest. I hit the target.

One other event that I was required to participate in was the "raw egg" event. This was a shooting event where the target was a swinging raw egg. The rule was if I didn't hit the egg I had to eat it. Well, I knew it wasn't going to be easy hitting that swinging egg. I missed, so I was required to eat the damn thing. It was not particularly something I was looking forward to, but I wanted to be a good sport. So I did, very hesitantly, swallow the raw egg. It wasn't too bad but I swallowed it and I was glad I did, but never again. I also participated in other events such as the tomahawk and knife throwing contest. I didn't do so great, but I had a good time and was glad to have been invited (except for the egg swallowing event).

Morphew said that he felt they had a good turnout, and the event was very successful for the first year. They had approximately 30 lodges and 40 Indian dancers to entertain visitors. They also had what they called "Traders' Row": booths where visitors could buy mountain man souvenirs such as beads, knives, powder horns, furs, buckskins, walking sticks, hats and many other items.

He also said that the rendezvous event was a great opportunity for citizens to take a step back into history and see how our pioneer ancestors lived and survived. *We are hoping to make this an annual event here at the park,* he said, *and there is no admission to get into the rendezvous,* he stressed.

The *Uinta County Herald* announced in their August 24th edition that the *Herald* was to be sold. It stated in the article that owners Mel and Esta Baldwin had been with the paper since February 1, 1946 and was the only newspaper in Evanston until *The Evanston Post* began in the early 1980s.

The Baldwins said they were planning to retire and would be selling the *Herald* to Wyoming Newspapers, Inc. which should take place on November 1, 1988.

Mel and Esta had worked very hard, putting in long hours, to publish the *Herald* through all those years, keeping the Evanston folks abreast of all the local and national news.

The paper won't be quite the same without them. They will be missed, especially Mel's "Mel-o-tones and Discords" column which everyone enjoyed very much. I especially enjoyed reading his final remarks following his Mel-o-tones column, "Just a Rumor." The one I remember was one quoting *"The trouble with doing something right the first time is that nobody appreciates how difficult it was."* How right he was.

However, Mel and Esta would still be around and still quite active in the community, and they were very much appreciated by everyone.

The September 15th edition of *The Evanston Post* printed an article reporting on the Evanston City Council's Monday meeting of September 12th. The article read: *The Evanston City Council, meeting in regular session on Monday night, renewed 28 liquor licenses in the city, but denied renewal and change of location for the E & O Enterprises license.* The article continued: *E & O Enterprises, David Ottley and Doug Eastman obtained a retail liquor license two years ago [during Mayor Martin's administration] and had plans to open the Parlor Bar in the Old Town Hall. "It is not feasible for us to continue with our plans,"* Eastman told the council during the public hearing on the liquor license renewals. *"A person in Salt Lake bought the building and has raised the rent beyond our means at this time,"* Eastman said.

Mark Harris, attorney for E & O, told the council that he wanted to accomplish three things Monday night. "Mr. Robert Ottley will be added as a name on the license, the owners want to transfer the license to the Flying J truck stop, and they want to renew the license," Harris said.

The Post article continued: Harris said that the city council had granted the property a restaurant license in 1982. "Mr. Robert Ottley was not involved in the operation of the business at that time," Harris said. "Planning and Zoning has granted a conditional use permit for the applicants. The only opposition at that meeting was expressed by Dave Moon, and I don't think he is in attendance here tonight."

The idea was to add Robert Ottley, owner of Flying J to E & O's license and have it relocated at the truck stop, but there was a lot of opposition at the meeting.

During the public hearing, conducted by City Attorney Dennis Boal, the opposition to the transfer and renewal of the E & O license had the opportunity to speak first. Most of the folks in attendance were either people who resided close by or were other liquor dealers that were located in the same area.

The Post article continued: Mayor Dennis Ottley said that although he had no real conflict of interest, because he would not gain monetarily, but because a brother and a son were two of the applicants, that he would abstain from voting on the transfer and renewal.

But what the Post didn't say was that I also had a brother, Mack Lott, who owned a full liquor license at Lotty's Restaurant just across the street from the Flying J Truck Stop. And they didn't mention that, after the public hearing was over and the meeting was turned back to the council, I excused myself because I felt I had a real conflict. Just before the motion was made and seconded to honor the transfer and location request by E & O Enterprises I turned the meeting over to President of the Council, Jon Lunsford, and left the chambers until the motion was completed. The motion failed by a unanimous vote of 0 for, 6 against, denying the transfer of the added name and the location of the license.

The same article of the Post continued: Another liquor industry related resolution came before the council on Monday night and that was to set the *prices for the various classes of liquor licenses for the coming year. The Local Liquor Dealers Association had requested a $250 decrease in license fees except for private clubs licenses. [J. D.] Kindler, speaking for the liquor dealers, said, "The road construction and increased drinking age has really hurt business. The federal tax stamp went from $54 to $250 this year and with the reduction in license fees, more of us might stay open. It has been a trying year this past year," he added.*

But the council didn't accept that reasoning and kept the fees as they had been. Therefore, the resolution was adopted unanimously to keep the fees the same.

Uinta County Herald, August 31, 1988

Mayor Dennis Ottley takes aim at a swinging raw egg...

...he missed, in Mountainman tradition he's got to eat the egg...

...some things you just have to do and get it over with...

...but it helps to be praised by a pretty Indian maiden.

Mountain men enjoy first local rendezvous.

The highway construction on the west end of Evanston had been completed on schedule and with very few complaints. The state highway department and the contractors did everything they possibly could to keep the road open while under construction. Everything went quite smoothly and Harrison Drive (Highway U.S. 30 S) west of Lombard Street ended up much nicer, with sidewalks and curbing and a lot safer for everyone.

As reported in the *Uinta County Herald* of September 21st: *It had been a very dry season during the summer months when on Saturday, September 17th a grass fire broke out causing 2,500 acres to burn south of Evanston. We had a west wind causing the fire to move fast towards homes on the west side of Wyoming State Highway 150 South, plus homes in the Aspen Groves and the Brookhollow Subdivision areas.*

We not only had the entire voluntary firefighter crew from Evanston, but we also had 100s of private citizens helping fight the fire. We had a number of firefighters from Mountain View, Lyman and Fort Bridger coming over to help, and many local companies provided men and equipment, including Chevron USA, Amoco, Mountain States, Johnson Construction, Searle Brothers Construction, Searle Oil Field Consultants, and Lindley Construction, Evanston City Public Works, Uinta County Road and Bridge, Uinta County Sheriff's Department, Evanston City Police and the Wyoming Highway Department were also all involved in fighting the fire.

Smoke was so heavy firefighters could not see where the fire was. Chevron Geosciences provided a Rocky Mountain helicopter in which the Uinta County Fire Department's fire inspector, Rusty Megeath, kept track of the direction of the fast-moving blaze.

Seven motor graders and three bulldozers were used to make fire breaks that were 60 feet wide in some areas. One grader was damaged and there was minor damage to other equipment. One truck's paint got so hot it caught fire.

Fire Chief Jon Lunsford said, *We were lucky, we didn't have to make the decision as to whether to stop the fire or take care of houses. The valiant people who used their garden hoses to put water on the fire, helped make this unnecessary.*

Mayor Dennis Ottley and Michael Klein, city building inspector, show off the new city street signs which are being erected around town. The city officials also ask residents to make sure their house numbers are clearly visible on homes. Emergency services, such as ambulance and fire, are having problems finding addresses. The time lost hunting for a location could mean the loss of a life.

Uinta County Herald, September 14, 1988.

The fire call came into the station at 12:57 p.m. and appeared to have started at an east corner of the Ranch at Evanston subdivision off Yellow Creek Road and spread east towards State Highway 150.

When we arrived, we spotted two juveniles running towards Twin Ridge subdivision, Lunsford stated, speculating on the cause for the blaze.

I was called immediately by Superintendent of Public Works Allen Kennedy. He told me he was just off Highway 150 behind the old Mathson ranch home fighting the fire. When I spotted him he was manning one of the department's fire hoses trying to keep the fire from reaching the homes on the highway. Other firefighters were also in the area doing the same.

When I got to Allen he told me he had to go get some other equipment, so I grabbed the hose from him and told him to get going. There I was in my white shirt and tie, fighting with a fire hose, trying to help the other firefighters keep the blaze from spreading and reaching the houses and other buildings in the area.

By 5:00 p.m. the fire was pretty much under control, and folks who had evacuated their homes were returning. By 9:00 p.m. the firefighters were able to leave the area. I was a mess with my white shirt and tie all wet and black from the smoke, and my face was so black it was hard to tell who I was. When I approached Sandy, she backed off, not recognizing me until I yelled at her.

It moved (speaking of the fire) unbelievably fast in the hills. In my 19 years as a fireman it's the first time I've ever seen fire move like that, Lunsford marveled.

The same Herald issue reported that *The United States Postal service employees in Evanston hosted an open house and officially cut the ribbon to open their new post office that replaced the 80-year-old facility this year.*

Retired postal employees Robert Lowham, Emerson Hartzell, Roy Turner, James Smith and Ernest Perkins cut the ribbon provided by the Evanston Chamber of Commerce Red Carpet Committee.

The Herald quoted me saying that the new facility "has really helped the downtown area."

The Alexander "Ragtime", Publisher of *The Evanston Post* announced that the month of September would be their last editions, because they were closing down. I imagined the reason was the slow economy and that there wasn't enough interest among the folks in the area for two newspapers. *The Post* was a weekly newspaper published every Thursday, while the *Uinta County Herald* was semi-weekly, published on Wednesday and Friday of each week. I hated to see the *Post* quit because I felt they had become a very important part of Evanston, and a lot of folks looked forward to reading it, including me.

However, as the *Post* had quit, the Evanston City Council had to once again put the city's minutes and legal notices, that are required by law to be published, out for bid once again. The only bid was submitted by the *Uinta County Herald*. Therefore, the city council minutes and legal notices would, once again, be published in the *Herald* where they had been published for many, many years.

On Friday, October 7th, Evanston McDonald's celebrated their Founder's Day, marking the birthday of McDonald's late founder, Ray A. Kroc, and celebrating the basic principles of the organization – quality, service, cleanliness and value.

Owner/operator Rich Coleman invited me, as mayor, to work at McDonalds for a few hours that day. I was required to wear plastic gloves as all employees did while working with the food. I was amazed at how clean the fast food establishment was, especially in the kitchen and the serving area. I had no problems with frying French fries, putting hamburgers together, making salads or even serving the customers. My first customer was Sandra Sporn of Evanston.

All the employees called me "McRookie," I guess because I was a first time worker there, but I was there only for a few hours. I really enjoyed helping out during that day and had a lot of fun. I thanked Mr. Coleman for the opportunity to be able to see firsthand just how fast food operations worked.

Because of a mistake in the distribution of sales tax by the Wyoming Revenue Department, Evanston was told that they owed the state for an overpayment by them to the city in the amount of $40,000. This was because of a mistake in the population count of the latest census. This was thoroughly discussed in one of our meetings.

The question was, *just how are we going to convince the state that it was the fault of the state revenue department, and that they were completely wrong about the census?* Our budget was pretty tight already, and the city couldn't afford to make that kind of payment.

Thanks to Councilman Clarence Vranish for writing a letter to Governor Mike Sullivan and explaining to the governor what had happened and how we felt that the City of Evanston was not at fault. The governor received the letter and took it very seriously. He looked into the matter, and after talking to the attorney general, and finding out that what Vranish said in the letter was valid, he directed the revenue department to drop the matter immediately, and let $40,000 remain in Evanston's funds.

Sullivan replied with good news. *After review and consultation with the attorney general, I have directed the department to utilize the same federal census for refund purpose as was originally used to make the revenue distribution. This should result in an equitable dollar for dollar from each of the affected local entities.*

This matter was credited to Councilman Vranish's actions, and the council and I adhered to that. The city owed him a big thank you. The second annual Support Your Community Week was to be held from October 24th to October 30th. Once again, sponsored jointly by the City of Evanston and the Evanston Chamber of Commerce, we were trying to build the economy up by getting all ages involved in the community.

Support Your Community Week would be a full week of fun where those of all ages can participate. This year we would have an addition in the program: Governor Mike Sullivan's "Capital of the Day," which would be on October 28th. Governor Sullivan named Evanston the Capital of the Day, a program the state officials started to help bring Wyoming communities together and discuss city problems across the state. Those state officials to be in Evanston that day would be Governor Sullivan, Margie White, representing Secretary of State Kathy Karpan, who couldn't make the trip, and other representatives in place of the other elected state officials who couldn't make the trip.

Governor Sullivan would be here to sign documents and chat informally with any citizens who would like to ask questions or air gripes. The Evanston Exchange Club would be hosting a breakfast for the governor and his entourage Friday morning, October 28th.

We made a special point to invite the public to the regular Evanston City Council meeting Monday evening, October 24th, because I, as mayor, promised to come up with a controversial issue for those who attended to "get their teeth into." It turned out to be one of the largest attended meetings that we had ever had at a regular city council meeting.

In other programs for the week we had Evanston school students participate in an essay contest on *"Why I love Evanston"* or *"What Evanston Means to Me."* The winners would be announced at a special city council meeting held on Wednesday evening.

We also had the Mayor's Prayer Breakfast Tuesday morning with everyone invited, and the Senior Recognition Day Lunch on Thursday. To top off the week of activities we held the Second Annual Appreciation Dinner on Saturday evening, where we honored those senior citizens who were nominated by the public for their community involvement while living in Evanston. This year those honored for their lifetime achievements were Marie Hicks, Mel and Esta Baldwin, Jerry and Ethel Cazin and Percy Hudson. Percy had died during the year prior to this banquet, but he was still nominated by someone for his many years of service as City Clerk and Treasurer, and in many other capacities. Also nominated and honored were the Uinta County Volunteer Fire Fighters. This was a first for honoring a group, but they were well worthy of the honor.

October 24th was the meeting we invited the public to, because I had promised to bring up a topic that all citizens should be interested in. The topic concerned the fate of the old railroad roundhouse and turntable that the Union Pacific had deeded to the City of Evanston back in the early 1970s.

According to the October 26th edition of the *Uinta County Herald, Evanston's City Council was surprised Monday evening at the number of people who turned out to add input to the lease agreement to be joined into by the city and Union Tank Car for the old Union Pacific Roundhouse property.*

The proposed lease agreement would give Union Tank Car the use of the property for 30 years.

The rent would be $3,000 per month [and the tank car company would pay the property taxes and the insurance on all facilities as if they owned the property, as they always had] subject to downward adjustments—if the company's regular full time employees drop below 25, the rent will decrease by $50.00 per month.

However, the final lease had not been approved at that time and would have many changes after the city met with the tank car company officials.

The *Herald* article continued: *The people in the audience were more interested in making sure that the preservation of the roundhouse and turntable were assured, along with rights to inspect the property periodically.*

Maintenance and improvements for the buildings which are on the Federal Historic Register was a vital concern, the article read.

Jim Davis of Urban Renewal pointed out the roundhouse is the only one left in the state and the turntable is one of two left in the state. "We want to make sure they are not destroyed," he said.

"The whole site now is a disgrace to the community," he continued. "We're glad they're being used, but we want them to maintain the property so in another 25 years, they're not completely gone."

The *Herald* continued: *Councilman Jon Lunsford argued that it would "take a lot of bucks to fix" the old buildings and the "turntable was not in shape for large, heavy equipment."*

Councilwoman Julie Lehman agreed with the participants, saying she felt the history in the area could be in jeopardy.

"Once it's gone, it's gone; we're fighting to keep our heritage in Evanston. Once it's gone down the tube you can't get it back," John Bowers told the council.

Lunsford stressed he would like to see the buildings in good repair but "don't want to kill the golden goose," worrying that the company [Union Tank Car] may take its operation to Utah, the *Herald* article concluded.

Discussion on the Union Tank Car Company lease and the round-house and turntable would not stop at that point. It was a subject that would be brought up time and time again.

During the month of October, James Sherer, Regional Director of the Environmental Protection Agency (E.P.A.) and his co-worker, Dick Long, were in town to reward the Evanston Wastewater Treatment Plant crew for their operation and maintenance of the plant operation.

Mr. Sherer explained that eight state E.P.A. districts would be given five awards this year, and praised the work at the plant and the staff's efforts to be cost effective, having no declaration problems, having a communication program, providing additional training for staff, maintaining good records and the plant's sludge disposal.

Plant Superintendent Randy Roper, Frank Sheets, Kevin Dean, Paul Vozakis and "Stub" Julian were the employees that were recognized. The city council and I were very pleased with the honors and we made those employees well aware of our feelings, something to be very proud of.

The November election was over and Vice President George H. W. Bush, Republican, was elected President of the United States, beating out Mike Dukakis, Democrat, who was running against him.

In the city election Clarence Vranish got re-elected in Ward l, Jerry Wall was elected for the vacated seat of Julie Lehman in Ward ll, and Tom Hutchinson was re-elected to represent Ward lll once again.

Our council would now, as of the first meeting in January, be made up of Will Davis and Clarence Vranish for Ward l, Jon Lunsford and Jerry Wall for Ward ll, and Tom Hutchinson and Craig Nelson for Ward lll. As always I was looking forward to working with the new council because they had always seemed to be a very workable group, with a mind of their own.

In November a beautiful quilt was sewn together by sisters, Bessie and Evelyn Bell, and pieced together by Ann Pennington. The design, by Roma Perkins, was to commemorate the history of Evanston. It was designed with the logo of the Union Pacific Railroad, the original company that established the Town of Evanston; it honored the active part the Chinese played in helping to build the town; and the design also depicted the oil industry that helped the community to grow. Also, the quilt had been centered with a copy of the Wyoming cowboy sewed into it.

The quilt was beautiful and well put together, and was to be raffled off, but members of the city council and I were afraid that if it was raffled off, the quilt could end up out of town somewhere. So the council decided to buy it for $3,000 and donate it to the museum so that it would stay in Evanston where the folks could all have an opportunity to see it, because it was made by some of our most outstanding citizens. The money the city paid for it went to Evanston's Wyoming Centennial Committee.

The State of Wyoming would be celebrating their Statehood Centennial in 1990; therefore, we formed an Evanston Wyoming Centennial Committee, and I appointed Ann Widdop Bell to be chairman of the committee, which was confirmed by the council.

The State of Wyoming requested that each county and each community form a committee and come up with a project commemorating the history of the county or community. Ann Bell's committee, approved by the city, came up with the idea of building a replica of the original Chinese Joss House, which was built circa 1894, six years before the railroad depot was completed. The old Joss House, a place of worship for the Chinese people in Evanston, had burned down with the rest of old China Town. It was one of only three in the United States at the time it was built and played a very vital part in Evanston's history.

Ann Bell called the Joss House project Evanston's contribution to the centennial celebration's lasting legacy. *We feel the Joss House will be a value to the middle and high school students in Uinta County as that is the time they are taught Wyoming history, along with attracting tourism for Depot Square,* Bell said.

The city had given the committee $15,000 as seed money, and the committee was asking for more donations and volunteers to help build the replica of the Chinese Joss House.

The project was expected to be completed during next year of 1989, but wouldn't be dedicated until July 14, 1990, the date of Wyoming's Statehood.

The *Uinta County Herald* of November 25th published their Friday edition headlining it: INTERNAL INVESTIGATION ORDERED. The article reported: *An internal investigation has been ordered at the Evanston Police Department after last Monday, November 14th's high speed chase involving several Evanston officers in pursuit of Tom Gerrard, 19, of Evanston.*

The chase began on Front Street and ended beyond the Utah State line on Highway 150 South.

According to Police Chief R. Dennis Harvey, the internal investigation will center around the possible violation of the department's policy regarding vehicle pursuits.

The *Herald* continued: *The city manual reads: "Pursuit should not be carried to such an extent as to appreciably endanger the lives of innocent users of the highway or the lives of the officers. Pursuit should always be tempered with common sense and foresight of likely hazard to which one must expose himself and others will depend upon the hazard with which the violation threatened other persons or traffic."*

Harvey stated it was the department's policy to discontinue pursuit, but he felt it was a judgment call if the officer should pursue a suspected drunken driver.

Harvey also was asked about rumors regarding the suspect being "roughed up" by police. He stated he hadn't had any proof, the officers were being questioned, but at this time he did not know, the *Herald* added.

When I heard the news I was pretty upset, especially about the police pursuing a drunk driver in a high speed chase south on Highway 150, a two lane highway, and going out of the city limits and across the Utah State line (about twenty-five miles). Although it was late at night, there had been a lot of accidents on that highway over the past years, some involving livestock and wildlife, but also some rollovers that were fatal. But I was told by one of the officers that the police cars were, at times, even going side by side. On a two-lane highway?? That really pissed me off.

The *Herald* quoted me: *I'm upset about the chase. I can't justify the fact they went after him … He was identified before he went out of the city limits."*

"It was poor judgment. That's what we have radios for. There could have been a cow on the road, someone could have been hurt badly and we would have never heard the last of it," he pointed out.

"It also bothers me they would leave the city with only one officer on duty," Ottley continued.

"The officers involved are good officers, they have done a tremendous job in other areas; something set them off," he said. "The officers have to make good spur of the moment decisions, but this wasn't one of those times."

He stated that the high speed chase should be used for fleeing forceable felons when all other resources have failed.

He said the police commission is looking into disciplinary action under the advisement of City Attorney Dennis Boal and according to the present manual.

Ottley, too, had heard the rumor of abuse of the driver.

"We will be meeting with the police officers in the near future," he said, the *Herald* article concluded.

The chase ended when Gerrard, the driver of the suspect's car, rammed the police car barricade causing approximately $1,000 damage to the police cars.

I guess some of the officers were upset with me for making those statements to the newspaper, and I apologized, but I was still pretty angry. I just didn't feel it was right for city cops to go that far out of the city limits, chasing a local person who had already been identified. And going across the Utah state line, where we absolutely had no jurisdiction! I felt that they could have used their radio for assistance from the Uinta County Sheriff's Department once they were out of the city. And I thought their judgment put not only the entire town in jeopardy, but also the suspect and the officers making the pursuit in a very hazardous situation. They did arrest the suspect.

About the rumor concerning the driver of the car, Tom Gerrard, getting roughed up by the officers: There was some force used in the effort to get Gerrard out of the car; he would not do what he was told to do, but by no means was he unnecessarily beaten, and that part of the report was dropped.

After the investigation, if there was to be any disciplinary action for the four officers involved, it would be handled by the chief of police, who would give a statement publicly after he had a chance to discuss the case with the city attorney.

Evanston's grand celebration of the Christmas season began with the ceremonial lighting of the Christmas tree located now at Depot Square near the Beeman-Cashin Building. I was scheduled to flip the switch to light the tree at 6:00 p.m. on Friday, November 25th, following Thanksgiving. Everyone was invited to attend the annual ceremony and enjoy hot chocolate, holiday candy, cookies and listen to the carolers.

The *Uinta County Herald* reported: *At 9:00 a.m. Saturday, November 26th, the jolly old elf himself will be arriving in the area to take all those special orders from good little girls and boys. Santa will tour the city on a horse-drawn wagon starting at the Uinta County Library.*

The Christmas season was upon us, and normally the city workers would be feeling happy and jolly and appreciating what had been accomplished through the past year. This year was a little different as the annual Christmas shop party that the public works employees put on every year became a fiasco.

At the party on December 22nd, a big dispute between two employees ended up in a brutal fight in which one of them got his leg broken. The one employee involved had a little too much to drink, causing an argument that ended up in something much worse.

The employee with the broken leg was treated at a Salt Lake City hospital after the incident.

The city did not, at that time, have a policy regarding the off-duty consumption of alcohol on city property by employees, and the party was after hours, but I told the press that I believed that hard liquor should not have been allowed.

I plan to talk to the city shop personnel about my stand on the drinking of hard liquor at holiday work parties, but their supervisors will investigate the situation when they return from vacation, I told the press.

Both City Engineer Brian Honey and Superintendent of Public Works Allen Kennedy were on vacation for the holidays.

It had been a 20-year city tradition that members of the business community and the public expressed their appreciation to city public work employees by bringing them food and drink to celebrate the holidays. Some of the drinks they brought were hard liquor.

I don't know what started the fight and I don't know the details, I told the press. *It's hard to pinpoint who was at fault and I'm not looking for fault. All I want to do is prevent it from happening in the future,* I added.

The employee with the broken leg would not receive pay while he was recovering, but he was entitled to sick pay and his insurance would pay for medical bills. He had about 800 hours accumulated in sick leave.

I pointed out that Honey and Kennedy would return on January 3, 1989 from vacation and investigate the situation. They would prepare a report and make recommendations to the city on what action should be taken, if any, against the involved employees. But I assured everyone that there would be a policy drawn up preventing any type of hard liquor or beer, or the consumption of it, during any parties by employees on city property.

After Honey and Kennedy returned from their vacations they looked into the cause of the dispute by the two employees. Their investigation found that the employee who started the ruckus had developed a fighting mood and several people tried to calm him down. Apparently he had too much to drink.

A letter of reprimand was placed in his file stating that his actions had affected his chances for future promotions with the city, and that if it happened again it would be grounds for immediate dismissal.

Both employees were supervisors of their departments and both had good clean records, and their job performance had been excellent.

On December 30th the city council called for a special council meeting to act on the resolution to finalize the purchase of the ice ponds property (approximately 43 acres) from the Union Pacific Land Resources Corporation (Upland Industries) for the total amount of $185,000.

With only Councilmen Clarence Vranish, Tom Hutchinson, Will Davis and me present to vote on the resolution, motion was made and seconded to adopt the resolution to finalize the purchase. Motion was passed for adoption by a unanimous vote. Union Pacific retained the mineral rights to the property, but the city refused to relieve U.P. from liability associated with the property being used in the past as a dumping ground.

In the past some of the property had been used as an informal dumping ground and the city did not want to be responsible for cleanup costs if any toxic materials were found to have been placed there. The corporation would have liked a release from the possible repercussions of a cleanup if a problem was found.

But the city did agree to fence the railway right-of-way in order to protect the public. The fence was needed before the property could be opened for public use.

In addition to the 43 acres, an additional piece of property was given to the city by the U.P. Corporation. It was a "cloverleaf" shaped piece which would clean up the company's holdings in the area. The property would be turned over to the Bear River Project Committee for further development after the property had been surveyed and the city secured a corrected and proper title deed.

Other than some of the mishaps, such Staley's death, the year of 1988 actually turned out to be very successful, but the economy was still looking quite bleak. However, I would be looking forward to the next year for better days. As they say, *"the only easy day was yesterday."* I don't look forward to any easy day, and only look back at what mistakes may have been made and hopefully, learn from them.

ACKNOWLEDGEMENTS

This book would never have been written if it hadn't been for a number of people who had assisted me in remembering some of the events and occurrences mentioned in the book, and making minutes of meetings and other materials available to me. In showing my appreciation I wish to name those folks.

First of all, I would like to thank my wife Sandy for all her support and encouragement she gave me to help me through this book. There were many times when I was ready to quit, but with her encouragement and her editing, I was able to get it finished.

I also wish to thank Maryl Thompson, Receptionist and Administrative Assistant of my real estate agency, Uinta Realty, Inc., for all the assistance she gave me in using my computer. When I had a computer problem, she was always on hand to help me through it, as did Tonya Dennis, Associate Broker in the office, who also assisted me on the computer when necessary.

Also, I want to thank the Executive Assistant to the Mayor of Evanston and Deputy City Clerk Nancy Stevenson for her time and hard work in providing me with 16 years of copies of the minutes of all the official meetings of the Evanston City Council during my tenure as Mayor of Evanston, 1979-1983 and 1987-1995, plus the term of Mayor Gene Martin, 1983-1987.

Other folks I wish to thank and show appreciation to are Shelly and Deann Horne of Creative Ink Images for their assistance in preparing the book cover; and Former City Engineer Brian Honey for information he provided me concerning the Sulphur Creek Dam Project and many other projects that were constructed during my term as Mayor. Brian was City Engineer under me for my last eight years in office. Thanks are also due to City Attorney Dennis Boal for straightening me out on a few matters. Dennis was my City Attorney also during my final eight years of my term as mayor. Thanks also to retired Urban Renewal Agency Director Jim Davis for providing me with information for my book; and former City Councilmember Tom Hutchinson for the information and input that he provided me. Other city employees that I wish to thank are Paul Knopf, former city planner, Public Works Superintendent Allan "Oop" Hansen and Engineering Tech Bob Liechty for their input to my story.

I also want to thank the Uinta County Library in Evanston for the use of their equipment, the Uinta County Museum in Evanston and the Evanston Chamber of Commerce for materials provided me to be used in my book; and the *Uinta County Herald* for giving me the opportunity to look through many of their old newspapers.

I appreciate all those named above for the completion of this book *"Evanston, Wyoming…Boom-Bust-Politics".*

However, I want to let you, the reader, know that almost all of the material used in this story was from my personal collection of photos, newspaper clippings, letters, etc., and from the actual minutes of the Evanston meetings during the period from 1967 to 1995. But some material is also from my own memory and from talking to some of those folks I mentioned above.

Thank You…
April 25, 2018

ABOUT THE AUTHOR

Born January 28, 1932 in Salt Lake City, Utah, Dennis ended up in Evanston, Wyoming. He quit high school and joined the 141st Tank Battalion of the Wyoming National Guard.

When the Korean War started in 1950, his unit was called to active duty in September, but he and his wife, Sandy got married on July 26, 1950 before he left for active duty, and to serve time in Korea.

Dennis and Sandy settled in Evanston, where he served three 4-year terms as a member of the Evanston city council and three 4-year terms as mayor. Dennis retired at the age of 81 from his real estate agency, and after raising four sons and over 68 years of marriage, he and his wife Sandy still reside in Evanston.

**Be sure to look for
Volume 4 of Evanston Wyoming**

www.ingramcontent.com/pod-product-compliance
Lightning Source LLC
Chambersburg PA
CBHW030410100426
42812CB00028B/2901/J